NEGATIONS

NEGATIONS

ESSAYS IN

CRITICAL THEORY

By HERBERT MARCUSE

With Translations from the German
by Jeremy J. Shapiro

BEACON PRESS : BOSTON

ALSO BY HERBERT MARCUSE

Reason and Revolution: Hegel and the Rise of Social Theory

Eros and Civilization: A Philosophical Inquiry into Freud

Soviet Marxism: A Critical Analysis

One-Dimensional Man: Studies in the Ideology of Advanced Industrial Society

A Critique of Pure Tolerance (with Robert Paul Wolff and Barrington Moore, Jr.)

CONTENTS

My translation of the foreword and the first five essays in this volume are from the German text in *Kultur und Gesellschaft* (2 volumes, 1965). The translation of "Industrialization and Capitalism in the Work of Max Weber" is principally the work of Professor Kurt Wolff of Brandeis University, who had translated an earlier version of the German text. He has graciously allowed me to use his translation, which I have modified in accordance with the revised German text published in *Kultur und Gesellschaft*. Professor Wolff has inspected the changes and made improvements.

I should like to thank Shierry Weber for giving generously of her time and energy in providing what proved to be indispensable assistance at every stage of the translation. I am grateful also to Rusty Simonds and Sharon Herson for several useful suggestions and to Roberta Fitzsimmons for negentropy.

J.J.S.

MANY of the essays collected here were written in the years from 1934 to 1938. They developed out of my work at the Institute for Social Research in New York and were formulated in discussion with my friend Max Horkheimer, at that time director of the Institute, and his coworkers. I have let them be republished unchanged. No revision could bridge the chasm that separates the period in which they were written from the present one. At that time, it was not yet clear that the powers that had defeated fascism by virtue of their technical and economic superiority would strengthen and streamline the social structure which had produced fascism. The question remained open, whether this conquest would not be superseded by more progressive and general historical forces. Capitalist society had not yet revealed all its strength and all its rationality, and the fate of the labor movement was still "uncertain." The first of these essays closes with that uncertainty, which is common to all of them, as is the hope, that fascism might perhaps be vanquished by forces (or rather, that its destruction would set free forces) that would make possible a more human and more rational society. For if there was one matter about which the author of these es-

xi

says and his friends were *not* uncertain, it was the understanding that the fascist state was fascist society, and that totalitarian violence and totalitarian reason came from the structure of existing society, which was in the act of overcoming its liberal past and incorporating its historical negation. This presented the critical theory of society with the task of identifying the tendencies that linked the liberal past with its totalitarian abolition. This abolition was not restricted at all to the totalitarian states and since then has become reality in many democracies (and especially in the most developed ones). The present did not appear to be in immediate opposition to the past: it was necessary to exhibit the mediation by means of which bourgeois freedom could become unfreedom. But it was also necessary to indicate the elements that opposed this transformation. Thus the theme of the first essay is common to all of them.

The focal point is the interpretation of some of the leading ideas of intellectual culture — of ideology. In political economy, Marxian theory had traced to their origins the tendencies that linked the liberal past with its totalitarian liquidation. What I attempted was to detect and trace these tendencies in culture, more specifically in its representative philosophy. For it was mind, reason, consciousness, "pure" thought that in the traditional culture was supposed to constitute the autonomy of the subject, the essential freedom of man. Here was the sphere of negation, of contradiction to the established order, of protest, of dissociation, of criticism. Protestantism and the bourgeois revolutions proclaimed the freedom of thought and of conscience. They were the sanctioned forms of contradiction — often the only ones — and the most precious refuge of hope. Only rarely and in exceptional cases did bourgeois society dare to infringe on this refuge. Soul and mind were (at least officially) considered holy and awesome. Spiritually and mentally, man was supposed to be as autonomous as possible. This was his inner freedom, which was his authentic and essential freedom; the other liberties were taken care of by the economy and the state. Normally it was not necessary for society to intervene in this sphere; a total coordination and subordination of individuals was not required. The productive forces had not yet reached that stage of development at which the sale of the products of social labor demanded the systematic organization of needs and wants,[1] including intellectual ones. The market regulated for better or worse the operation and output of a labor apparatus not yet dependent upon uninterrupted mass consumption. At a low level of productive forces, bourgeois society did not yet have the means to administer soul and mind without discrediting this administration through terroristic violence. Today total administration is necessary, and the means are at hand; mass gratification, market research, industrial psychology, computer mathematics, and the so-called science of human relations. These take care of the nonterroristic, democratic, spontaneous-automatic harmonization of individual and socially necessary needs and wants, of autonomy and heteronomy. They assure the free election of individuals and policies necessary for this system to continue to exist and grow. The democratic abolition of thought, which the "common man" undergoes automatically and which he himself carries out (in labor and in the use and enjoyment of the apparatus of production and consumption), is brought about in the "higher learning" by those positivistic and positive trends of philosophy, sociology, and psychology that make the established system into an insuperable framework for conceptual thought.

But the rapidity with which it was possible to achieve the social organization and administration of the mind suggests the question whether the mind did not itself bear part of the responsibility for such a development. In other words, did intellectual culture prepare its own liquidation? Were its autonomy, inwardness, purity, and the happiness and fulfillment that it promised already permeated with unfreedom, adjustment, unhappiness, and renunciation? Did this culture have an affirmative character even where it was the negation of the status quo? In regard to these questions I investigated several concepts of idealism and materialism. Ideas such as essence, happiness, or theory bore evidence of inner disunity. In an authentic way they revealed the genuine potentialities of man and of nature as being in contradiction to the given reality of man and of nature; thus they were eminently critical concepts. At the same time, however, they invalidated this contradiction by giving it ontological stability. This was the specific situation of idealism that culminated in Hegelian philosophy; contradiction becomes the very form of truth and movement, only to be enclosed in a system and internalized. But by adhering to reason as the power of the negative, idealism made good the claim of thought to be a condition of freedom. The classical connection between German idealism and the Marxian labor movement was valid, and not merely as a fact of the history of ideas.

It was in this perspective that the essays dealt with the legacy of idealism, with the element of truth in its repressive philosophy. But the legacy and truth of materialism, and not only historical materialism, were of equal import. In the insistence of thought upon the abolition of misery and of need, upon happiness and pleasure as contents of human freedom, the tabooed tasks of revolution were preserved: tasks which even in socialist theory and practice had already been long suppressed or postponed. The more "materialistic" society became in the advanced industrial countries, i.e. the higher the standard of living rose for broad strata of the population, the clearer became the extent to which this progress stabilized misery and unhappiness. Productivity bore destruction within it and turned technology from an instrument of liberation into one of new enslavement. Faced with a society in which affluence is accompanied by intensified exploitation, militant materialism remains negative and revolutionary (even where exploitation becomes more comfortable and does not penetrate into consciousness). Its idea of happiness and of gratification can be realized only through political practice that has qualitatively new modes of human existence as its goal.

That most of this was written before Auschwitz deeply separates it from the present. What was correct in it has since become, perhaps not false, but a thing of the past. To be sure, the concern with philosophy expressed in these essays was already, in the thirties, a concern with the past: remembrance of something that at some point had lost its reality and had to be taken up again. Precisely at that time, beaten or betrayed, the social forces in which freedom and revolution were joined were delivered over to the existing powers. The last time that freedom, solidarity, and humanity were the goals of a revolutionary struggle was on the battlefields of the Spanish civil war.[2] Even today the songs sung for and in that struggle are, for the young generation, the only persisting reflection of a possible revolution. The end of a historical period and the horror of the one to come were announced in the simultaneity of the civil war in Spain and the trials in Moscow.

The new period saw the suppression, crippling, and neutralization of the classes and forces that, due to their real interests, embodied hope for the end of inhumanity. In the advanced industrial countries, the subordination and coordination of the suppressed is effected through the total administration of the productive forces and the growing satisfaction of needs, which insulate society against its necessary transformation. Productivity and prosperity in league with a technology in the service of monopolistic politics seem to immunize advancing industrial society in its established structure.

Is this concept of immunity still dialectical? To be sure, for critical theory it implies the sorrow of concern with something that has disappeared (this was the tenor of the essay "Philosophy and Critical Theory"). But does it also offer hope that the social tendencies comprehended through this concept promise something other than what they are? Perhaps the very break with the past exhibited in the neutralization and liquidation of the opposition is an indication. In the essay just mentioned, I wrote: "Critical theory must concern itself to a hitherto unknown extent with the past — precisely insofar as it is concerned with the future." Has social development perhaps attained a stage when the remembrance and constructive abolition of the past demands more radical concepts than those which were formed in the pretotalitarian period? Today critical theory is essentially more abstract than it was at that time; it can hardly think of "taking hold of the masses." But may not the abstract, "unrealistic" character of the theory at that time have lain in its having been attached too strongly to the society that it comprehended, so that in its concept of negation it did not go far enough in surpassing that society? In other words, did not its concept of a free and rational society promise, not too much, but rather *too little?* In view of the capacity and productivity of organized capitalism, should not the "first phase" of socialism be more and qualitatively other than it was projected to be in Marxian theory? Is not this the context in which belongs socialism's affinity for and successes in preindustrial and weakly industrialized societies? The Marxian concepts of capitalism and of socialism

xvi

were decisively determined by the function of human labor, physical labor in social reproduction. Marx's image of the realm of necessity does not correspond to today's highly developed industrial nations. And in view of the frantic expansion of totalitarian mass democracy, the Marxian image of the realm of freedom beyond the realm of necessity must appear "romantic." For it stipulates an individual subject of labor, an autonomy of creative activity and leisure, and a dimension of unspoiled nature that have long since been liquidated in the progress of domination[3] and industrialization.

Does this progress perhaps show that the contradiction and negation were not radical enough, that they rejected too little and held too little to be possible, that they underestimated the qualitative difference between the really possible and the status quo? Has not late industrial society already surpassed, in a bad form, the idea of socialism — as in bad planning, bad expansion of the productive forces, bad organization of the working class, and bad development of needs and of gratification? Of course, all the wealth, the technology, and the productivity of this society cannot match the ideas of real freedom and of real justice which are at the center of socialist theory. Nevertheless, these ideas appear in forms worked out substantially as the potentiality[4] and negation of a capitalism that was not yet fully developed. Developed industrial society has already won for itself much of the ground on which the new freedom was to have flourished. This society has appropriated dimensions of consciousness and nature that formerly were relatively unspoiled. It has formed historical alternatives in its own image and flattened out contradiction, which it can thus tolerate. Through this totalitarian-democratic conquest of man and of nature, the subjective and objective space for the realm of freedom has also been conquered.

In return, forces of total transformation are at work in the realm of necessity itself. The same mathematization and automation of labor and the same calculated, public administration of existence that tend to make society and the nature that it appropriates into one single apparatus, into an object of experimentation and control in the hands of the rulers, create an apparatus from which men can more easily withdraw, the more calculable and automatic it becomes. Here appears the chance of the transformation of quantity into quality, the leap into a qualitatively different stage. Marx described this transformation as an explosive tendency in the final transmutation of the capitalist labor process. Capital

> diminishes labor time . . . in the form of necessary labor in order to augment it in the form of surplus labor. It therewith in increasing measure sets the surplus as a condition — question de vie et de mort — of the necessary. On the one hand it calls to life all the forces of science and of nature as well as of social combination and of social intercourse, in order to make the creation of wealth (relatively) independent of the labor time expended on it. On the other hand it wants to measure against labor time the gigantic social forces that have been created, and to confine them within the limits required in order to preserve as value the value already created.[5]

The growing automation of the labor process and the time that it sets free transform the subject himself, and man then enters as a different subject

> into the immediate process of production. Considered in relation to developing man, the process of production is discipline. At the same time, in relation to developed man, in whose head exists the accumulated knowledge of society, it is practice, experimental science, and materially creative, self-objectifying knowledge.[6]

xviii

It can be seen that precisely the most exaggerated, "eschato-logical" conceptions of Marxian theory most adequately anticipate social tendencies: for instance, the idea of the abolition of labor, which Marx himself later rejected. Behind all the inhuman aspects of automation as it is organized under capitalism, its real possibilities appear: the genesis of a technological world in which man can finally withdraw from, evacuate, and oversee the apparatus of his labor — in order to experiment freely with it. Irresponsible as it may seem, in view of existing poverty and existing need, to summon up the image of such freedom, it is just as irresponsible to conceal the extent to which existing poverty and existing need are perpetuated only by the interests that rule the status quo. Despite all planning and organization, however, the fundamental tendencies of the system realize themselves against the will and the intentions of individuals — as blind forces even where they are scientifically mastered and calculated and obey the requirements of the apparatus. The apparatus becomes in a literal sense the subject; this is practically the definition of an automaton. And to the extent to which the apparatus itself becomes the subject, it casts off man as a serving and working being and sets him free as a thinking, knowing, experimenting, and playing being. Freedom from the need for the intervention of human service and servitude — that is the law of technological rationality. Today the latter is enmeshed in the apparatus of domination, which perpetuates the necessity whose abolition it makes possible. To experiment and play with the apparatus is at present the monopoly of those who work for the preservation and expansion of the status quo. Perhaps this monopoly can be broken only by catastrophe. Catastrophe, however, appears not only in the constant menace of atomic war, in play with annihilation, but also in the social logic of technology, in play with ever-growing productivity, which falls into ever-clearer contradiction to the system in which it is caught. Nothing justifies the assumption that the new form of the classic contradiction can be manipulated permanently. It is just as unjustifiable, nevertheless, to assume that it cannot lead once more to new forms of oppression. More than before, breaking through the administered consciousness is a precondition of liberation. Thought in contradiction must be capable of comprehending and expressing the new potentialities of a qualitatively different existence. It must be capable of surpassing the force of technological repression and of incorporating into its concepts the elements of gratification that are suppressed and perverted in this repression. In other words, thought in contradiction must become more negative and more utopian in opposition to the status quo. This seems to me to be the imperative of the current situation in relation to my theoretical essays of the thirties.

In totalitarian technological society, freedom remains thinkable only as autonomy over the entirety of the apparatus. This includes the freedom to reduce it or to reconstruct it in its entirety with regard to the pacification of the struggle for existence and to the rediscovery of quiet and of happiness. The abolition of material poverty is a possibility within the status quo; peace, joy, and the abolition of labor are not. And yet only in and through them can the established order be overcome. Totalitarian society brings the realm of freedom beyond the realm of necessity under its administration and fashions it after its own image. In complete contradiction to this future, autonomy over the technological apparatus is freedom *in* the realm of necessity. This means, however, that freedom is only possible as the realization of what today is called utopia.

Herbert Marcuse

NEGATIONS

I. THE STRUGGLE AGAINST LIBERALISM
IN THE TOTALITARIAN VIEW OF THE STATE

THE establishment of the total-authoritarian state was accompanied by the annunciation of a new political weltanschauung: "heroic-folkish[1] realism" became the governing theory.

> Blood rises up against formal understanding, race against the rational pursuit of ends, honor against profit, bonds against the caprice that is called "freedom," organic totality against individualistic dissolution, valor against bourgeois security, politics against the primacy of the economy, state against society, folk against the individual and the mass.[2]

The new worldview[3] is a great reservoir for all the currents that have been deluging "liberalist" political and social theory since World War I. The struggle first began far from the political arena as a philosophical controversy with the rationalism, individualism, and materialism of the nineteenth century. A united front emerged which, with the intensification of economic and social conflict after the war, soon revealed its political and social function; compared with the latter, the

3

struggle against liberalism (as we shall show in what follows) became no more than peripheral. Let us first briefly survey the most important sources of the current theory —

The Heroizing of Man

Long before World War I, the celebration of a new type of man became prevalent, finding its adepts in almost all branches of the social sciences and humanities, from economics to philosophy. Right down the line, an attack was launched against the hypertrophic rationalization and technification of life, against the "bourgeois" of the nineteenth century with his petty joys and petty aims, against the shopkeeper and merchant spirit and the destructive "anemia" of existence. A new image of man was held up to this paltry predecessor, composed of traits from the age of the Vikings, German mysticism, the Renaissance, and the Prussian military: the heroic man, bound to the forces of blood and soil — the man who travels through heaven and hell, who does not reason why, but goes into action to do and die, sacrificing himself not for any purpose but in humble obedience to the dark forces that nourish him. This image expanded to the vision of the charismatic leader[4] whose leadership does not need to be justified on the basis of his aims, but whose mere appearance is already his "proof," to be accepted as an undeserved gift of grace. With many modifications, but always in the forefront of the fight against bourgeois and intellectualistic existence, this archetype of man can be found among the ideas of the Stefan George circle, of Möller van den Bruck, Sombart, Scheler, Hielscher, Jünger, and others. Its philosophical justification has been sought in a so-called —

4

Philosophy of Life

"Life" as such is a "primal given" beyond which the mind cannot penetrate, which is withdrawn from any rational foundation, justification, or evaluation. Life, when understood in this way, becomes an inexhaustible reservoir for all irrational powers. Through it the "psychic underworld" can be conjured up, which is "as little evil as [is] the cosmic . . . , but is rather the womb and refuge for all productive and generative forces, all forces that, though formless, serve every form as content, all fateful movements."[5] When this life "beyond good and evil" is seen as the force that actually "makes history," an antirational and antimaterialist view of history is created whose sociological fertility is demonstrated in political existentialism and its theory of the total state.

This philosophy of life resembles Dilthey's *Lebensphilosophie* in name only and took from Nietzsche only odds and ends and pathos. Its social functions come to light most clearly in the works of Spengler,[6] where they become the substructure of an imperialist economic theory.

The tendency common to both of these currents, namely "liberating" life from the compulsion of a "universally" obligatory reason that stands above specific ruling interests (and the mandate, derived from this reason, to create a rational human society) and delivering up existence to pregiven "inviolable" powers, leads to —

Irrationalistic Naturalism

The interpretation of the historical and social process as a natural-organic process goes behind the real (economic and social) motive forces of history into the sphere of eternal and immutable nature. Nature is interpreted as a dimension of

5

mythical originality (well characterized in the phrase "blood and soil"), present in all things as a prehistorical dimension. Human history truly begins only when this dimension is overcome by being transformed. In the new weltanschauung, mythical, prehistorical nature has the function of serving as the real adversary of responsible, autonomous, rational practice. As something justified through its mere existence, this nature stands opposed to that which requires rational justification; as what must be absolutely acknowledged, against all that is first to be known critically; as the essentially dark, against all that derives its substance from the clarity of light; as the indestructible, against everything subject to historical change. Naturalism is based on an equation that is constitutive of the new worldview: nature, as original, is simultaneously the natural, genuine, healthy, valuable, and sacred. That which is beneath reason elevates itself, by means of its function "beyond good and evil," to what is beyond reason.

But the keystone of the entire edifice is still missing. The hymn to the natural-organic order contrasts too crassly with the factual, established order. There is a screaming contradiction between the relations of production on the one hand and the attained level of productive forces and the satisfaction of needs it makes possible on the other. Nature is confronted with an economy and society that are "unnatural," an order perpetuated by means of the violence of a gigantic apparatus that can represent the whole against the individual because it wholly oppresses him, a "totality" that subsists only through the total domination of all. The theoretical transfiguration of this totality results in —

Universalism

We shall not discuss here those elements of a genuine contribution to philosophical and scientific knowledge (e.g. Ge-

6

stalt theory) present in universalism. In the present context, what is significant is that in the area of social theory universalism quickly took over the function of a doctrine of political justification. Compared with individuals, the social totality as self-subsistent and primary reality becomes, by virtue of its pure total character, a self-subsistent and primary value: the totality is, as totality, the true and the genuine. Universalism does not ask whether every totality does not first have to prove itself before the tribunal of individuals, to show that their potentialities and needs are realized in it. When the totality is no longer the conclusion but the axiom, the path of theoretical and practical social criticism leading to this totality is blocked off. Totality is programmatically mystified. It can "never be grasped by hands, nor seen with outer eyes. Composure and depth of spirit are necessary in order to behold it with the inner eye."[7] In political theory this totality is represented by the folk (*Volk*), as an essentially "natural-organic" unity and totality that is prior to all social differentiation into classes, interest groups, etc. With this thesis universalism rejoins naturalism.

Here we interrupt our sketch of the currents that come together in heroic-folkish realism; later we shall deal both with their unification in a total political theory and their social function. Before interpreting their interconnection it is necessary to define the historical locus of their unification. It becomes visible from its antipode. Heroic-folkish realism indiscriminately brings together everything against which it fights under the title of *liberalism*. "Liberalism is the destruction of the nations"; these words stand at the head of that chapter of his book which Möller van den Bruck devoted to the mortal enemy.[8] It was as a counter to liberalism that the theory of the total-authoritarian state became a "weltanschauung." Only in this combat position did it attain its political sharpness (and even Marxism always appears to it in the train of liberalism[9] as its heir or partner). We must initially ask, therefore: What does this theory mean by liberalism, which it damns with a virtually eschatological pathos, and what brought this damnation upon it?

If we ask the spokesmen of the new weltanschauung what they are fighting in their attack on liberalism, we hear in reply of the "ideas of 1789," of wishy-washy humanism and pacifism, Western intellectualism, egotistical individualism, sacrifice of the nation and state to conflicts of interest between particular social groups, abstract, conformist egalitarianism, the party system, the hypertrophy of the economy, and destructive technicism and materialism. These are the most concrete utterances[10] — for the concept "liberal" often serves only for purposes of defamation, and political opponents are "liberal" no matter where they stand, and are as such the simply "evil."[11]

Most surprising in this catalogue of sins is their abstract generality and ahistorical quality. Scarcely one of them is characteristic of historical liberalism. The ideas of 1789 have by no means always been on the banner of liberalism and have even been sharply attacked by it. Liberalism has been one of the strongest supports of the demand for a powerful nation. Pacifism and internationalism were not always causes it adopted, and it has often enough accepted considerable intervention of the state in the economy. What remains is a vague "weltanschauung" whose historical association with liberalism is not at all clear, although its qualification as an object for the attacks of the totalitarian theory of the state will, we hope, become clear later. But supplanting the real content of liberalism with a weltanschauung is in itself decisive in what it conceals and leaves unsaid. The concealment points to the true battlefront: it avoids the economic and social structure of liberalism. It is necessary to reconstruct (however summarily) this structure in order to know the historical and social terrain which makes the struggle of the "weltanschauungen" understandable.

Liberalism was the social and economic theory of European industrial capitalism in the period when the actual economic bearer of capitalism was the "individual capitalist," the private entrepreneur in the literal sense. Despite structural variations in liberalism and its bearers from one country or period to another, a uniform foundation remains: the individual economic subject's free ownership and control of private property and the politically and legally guaranteed security of these rights. Around this one stable center, all specific economic and social demands of liberalism can be modified — modified to the point of self-abolition. Thus, during the rule of liberalism, powerful intervention in economic life by state authority frequently occurred, whenever the threatened freedom and security of private property required it, especially if the threat came from the proletariat. The idea of dictatorship and of authoritarian direction of the state is (as we shall see shortly) not at all foreign to liberalism. And, often enough, national wars were fought in the period of pacifistic-humanitarian liberalism. Those basic political demands of liberalism, resulting from its economic views, that are so hated today (such as freedom of speech and of the press, complete publicity of political life, the representative system and parliamentarianism, the separation or balance of powers) were never, in fact, completely realized. Depending on the social situation, they were curbed or dropped.[12]

In order to get behind the usual camouflage and distortion and arrive at a true image of the liberalist economic and social system, it suffices to turn to Von Mises' portrayal of liberalism:

9

The program of liberalism . . . , summed up in a single word, should read "Property," that is, private property in the means of production. . . . All other demands of liberalism derive from this basic demand.

In the free, private initiative of the entrepreneur he sees the surest guarantee of economic and social progress. That is why liberalism considers "capitalism the only possible order of social relations," and why it has only one enemy: Marxian socialism. On the other hand, liberalism maintains that

fascism and all similar attempts at dictatorship . . . have momentarily saved European culture. The merit that fascism has thereby acquired will live on eternally in history.

We can already discern the reason why the total authoritarian state diverts its struggle against liberalism into a struggle of "weltanschauungen," why it bypasses the social structure basic to liberalism: it is itself largely in accord with this basic structure. The latter was characterized as the organization of society through private enterprise on the basis of the recognition of private property and the private initiative of the entrepreneur. And this very organization remains fundamental to the total-authoritarian state; it is explicitly sanctioned in a multitude of programmatic declarations.[13] The considerable modifications and restrictions of this organization that are put into effect everywhere correspond to the monopoly-capitalist requirements of economic development itself. They leave untouched the principle of the organization of production relations.

There is a classic document illustrating the inner relationship between liberalist social theory and the (apparently so antiliberal) totalitarian theory of the state: a letter addressed to Mussolini by Gentile at the time when the latter joined the Fascist party. There he writes:

As a liberal by deepest conviction, I could not help being convinced, in the months in which I had the honor to collaborate in the work of your government and to observe at close quarters the development of the principles that determine your policies, that liberalism as I understand it, the liberalism of freedom through law and therefore through a strong state, through the state as ethical reality, is represented in Italy today not by the liberals, who are more or less openly your opponents, but to the contrary by you yourself. Hence I have satisfied myself that in the choice between the liberalism of today and the Fascists, who understand the faith of your Fascism, a genuine liberal, who despises equivocation and wants to stand to his post, must enroll in the legions of your followers.[14]

No documents are needed to show that, quite apart from this positive connection, liberalism is entirely at one with the new worldview in its fight against Marxian socialism. To be sure, we often encounter in heroic-folkish realism vehement invective against the monstrosity of capitalism, against its bourgeois (*Bürger*) and his "greed for profit" and so on. But since the foundations of the economic order, the sole source of the possibility of this bourgeois, remain intact, such invectives are always directed against only a specific type of bourgeois (that of the small and petty "merchant breed" [*Händlertum*] and against a specific form of capitalism (represented by the model of the free competition of independent and individual capitalists). They never attack the economic functions of the bourgeois in the capitalist production process. The forms of the bourgeois and of capitalism that are attacked here are those which have already been displaced by the course of economic development; nevertheless the bourgeois capitalist remains as the subject of the capitalist economy. The new weltanschauung reviles the "merchant" and cele-

the folk-nation (and nations) as a natural given and product of historical becoming."[21]

Granted, liberalist naturalism is part of an essentially rationalist system of thought, antiliberalist naturalism part of an irrationalist one. The distinction must be maintained in order not to obliterate artificially the boundaries of both theories and not to misunderstand the change in their social function. But liberalist rationalism already contains, preformed, those tendencies that later, with the change from industrial to monopoly capitalism, take on an irrationalist character.

The position which critical analysis leads a scientific theory of society to take with regard to the antithesis rationalism-irrationalism has been presented elsewhere.[22] In what follows we have only worked out the fundamental irrationalist tendency of the social theory that we have taken as our theme. "Irrationalism" is a counterconcept; in order to understand an essentially irrationalist worldview, it is necessary to construct an "ideal-type" of a rationalist view of society.

A theory of society is *rationalist* when the practice it enjoins is subject to the idea of autonomous reason, i.e. to the human faculty of comprehending, through conceptual thought, the true, the good, and the right. Within society, every action and every determination of goals as well as the social organization as a whole has to legitimate itself before the decisive judgment of reason and everything, in order to subsist as a fact or goal, stands in need of rational justification. The principle of sufficient reason,[23] the authentic and basic principle of rationalism, puts forward a claim to the connection of "things" or "facts" as a "rational" connection: the reason, or cause, posits that which it causes as *eo ipso* also in accordance with reason.[24] The necessity of acknowledging a fact or goal never follows from its pure existence; rather, acknowledgment oc-

14

curs only when knowledge has freely determined that the fact or goal is in accordance with reason. The rationalist theory of society is therefore essentially *critical;* it subjects society to the idea of a theoretical and practical, positive and negative critique. This critique has two guidelines: first, the given situation of man as a rational organism, i.e. one that has the potentiality of freely determining and shaping his own existence, directed by the process of knowledge and with regard to his worldly happiness; second, the given level of development of the productive forces and the (corresponding or conflicting) relations of production as the criterion for those potentialities that can be realized at any given time in men's rational structuring of society.[25] The rationalist theory is well aware of the limits of human knowledge and of rational social action, but it avoids fixing these limits too hurriedly and, above all, making capital out of them for the purpose of uncritically sanctioning established hierarchies.

The *irrationalist* theory of society finds it unnecessary to deny radically the reality of critical reason: between binding reason to pregiven "natural-organic" facts and enslaving it to the "beast of prey within man," there is sufficiently wide latitude for all sorts of derivative reason. Decisive here is that irrational givens ("nature," "blood and soil," "folkhood," "existential facts," "totality," and so forth) are placed prior to the autonomy of reason as its limit *in principle* (not merely in fact), and reason is and remains causally, functionally, or organically dependent on them. Against all attempts to fight shy of this conclusion, it cannot be emphasized often enough that such functionalization of reason or of man as a rational organism annihilates the force and effectiveness of reason at its roots, for it leads to a reinterpretation of the irrational pregivens as *normative* ones, which place reason under the heteronomy of the irrational. In the theory of contemporary

15

society, playing up natural-organic facts against "rootless" reason means justifying by irrational powers a society that can no longer be rationally justified and submerging in the hidden darkness of "blood" or the "soul" contradictions recognized by the light of conceptual knowledge. This is intended to truncate comprehension and criticism. "Reality does not admit of knowledge, only of acknowledgement":[26] in this "classical" formulation irrationalist theory arrives at the extreme antipode to all rational thought and at the same time reveals its deepest intentions. Today the irrationalist theory of society is as essentially uncritical as the rationalist theory is critical; it is essentially antimaterialist, for it must defame the worldly happiness of man that can be brought about only through a rational organization of society and replace it with other, less "palpable" values. What it offers as an alternative to materialism is a heroic pauperism: an ethical transfiguration of poverty, sacrifice, and service, and a "folkish realism" whose social meaning we shall come to later. Compared with heroic-folkish realism, liberalism is a rationalist theory. Its vital element is optimistic faith in the ultimate victory of reason, which will realize itself above all conflicts of interest and opinion in the harmony of the whole. In keeping with its economic views, liberalism links this victory of reason (and here begins the typical liberalist conception of rationalism) to the possibility of a free and open rivalry of divergent views and elements of knowledge, which is to result in rational truth and rightness.[27]

As the economic organization of society is built upon the free competition of private economic subjects, in other words, on the unity of opposites and the unification of the dissimilar, so the search for truth is founded on open self-expression, free dialogue, and convincing and being convinced through argument — at root, that is, on contradicting and criticizing one's opponent. All the tendencies from which the political demands of liberalism derive their theoretical validity (such as freedom of speech and of the press, publicity, tolerance, parliamentary government) are elements of a true rationalism.

There is another source that furnishes liberalist society with a rationalist underpinning. The third fundamental right proclaimed in the Declaration of the Rights of Man is *sûreté*. This security means very definitely a guarantee of freedom in economic conduct — not only the state's guarantee of disposal over private property, but also the private entrepreneur's assurance of obtaining the greatest possible profitability and stability. This has two primary corollaries: a maximum of legal security for all private contracts and a maximum of exact calculability of profit and loss, supply and demand. In the liberalist epoch of capitalism, the rationalization of law and the rationalization of the enterprise (the elements demonstrated by Max Weber to be decisive for the spirit of Western capitalism) are realized to a previously unknown extent. But at this very point, liberalist rationalism comes up against barriers that it can no longer surmount of itself. Irrationalist elements seep into it and explode its basic theoretical conception.

The liberalist rationalization of economic life (as of social organization in general) is essentially *private*. It is tied to the rational practice of the individual economic subject or of a multiplicity of individual economic subjects. In the end, of course, the rationality of liberalist practice is supposed to demonstrate itself in the whole and characterize the whole, but this whole itself is outside the sphere of rationalization.[28] The harmony of general and private interests is supposed to result *of itself* from the undisturbed course of private practice. On principle it is not subject to criticism, nor does it fall within the bounds of rational projects for practice.

17

Through this *privatization of reason*, the construction of society in accordance with reason is deprived of the end which is supposed to provide its goal (just as in irrationalism it is deprived of its beginning through the functionalization of reason). Thus, precisely the rational determination and condition of that "generality" in which the "happiness" of the individual is supposed to be realized is missing. To this extent (and only to this extent) the reproach that liberalism's talk of general interest or humanity remains caught in pure abstractions is correct. The structure and order of the whole are ultimately left to irrational forces: an accidental "harmony," a "natural balance." The plausibility of liberalist rationalism thus ceases immediately when, with the intensification of social conflict and economic crises, general "harmony" becomes increasingly improbable. At this point liberalist theory must grasp at irrational justifications. Rational critique gives up; it is all too readily prepared to acknowledge "natural" privileges and favors. The idea of the charismatic, authoritarian leader is already preformed in the liberalist celebration of the gifted economic leader, the "born" executive.

This rough sketch of liberalist social theory has shown how many elements of the totalitarian view of the state are already present in it. Taking the economic structure as a point of reference, we see an almost unbroken continuity in the development of the social theory. We shall here assume some prior knowledge of the economic foundations of this development from liberalist to totalitarian theory:[29] they are all essentially part of the transformation of capitalist society from mercantile and industrial capitalism, based on the free competition of independent individual entrepreneurs, to monopoly capitalism, in which the changed relations of production (and especially the large "units" such as cartels and trusts) require a strong state mobilizing all means of power. Economic theory declares openly and clearly the reason *why* liberalism now becomes the mortal enemy of social theory:

> Imperialism has . . . put the expedient of a strong state at the disposal of capitalism. . . . The liberal ideas of free-floating competition between individual economic enterprises have proved themselves unsuited to capitalism. . . .[30]

The turn from the liberalist to the total-authoritarian state occurs within the framework of a single social order. With regard to the unity of this economic base, we can say it is liberalism that "produces" the total-authoritarian state out of itself, as its own consummation at a more advanced stage of development. The total-authoritarian state brings with it the organization and theory of society that correspond to the monopolistic stage of capitalism.

This organization and its theory, it is true, also contain "new" elements that go beyond the old liberal social order and its mere negation: elements in which a clear dialectical reaction against liberalism is perceptible, but which presuppose for their realization the abolition of the economic and social foundations preserved by the total-authoritarian state. The new political and social theory must not, therefore, be interpreted simply as a process of ideological adaptation. In order to contribute to comprehension of its real social function, we shall interpret its basic features by analyzing its three constitutive components: universalism, naturalism (organicism), and existentialism.

Universalism

The priority and primacy of the whole over its "members" (parts) is a basic thesis of heroic-folkish realism. The whole is

19

understood not only as a sum or abstract totality, but as the unity that unifies the parts, a unity which is the precondition for the fulfillment and completion of each part. The demand for the realization of such a totality occupies the first place in the programmatic proclamations of the total-authoritarian state. In the organic order of life

> the whole is primally given in its organic segmentation: the members serve the whole, which is superordinate to them, but they serve it according to the unique character that appertains to them as members . . . , and, at the same time, it is in this uniqueness that their personal destiny and the meaning of their personality are fulfilled to the extent that they participate in the whole.[31]

As a historical entity this whole is supposed to encompass the entirety of historical occurrences and relationships: within it are "enclosed both the national and the social idea."[32]

We have seen that the exclusion of the whole from the process of rational action was a serious omission on the part of liberalist theory. Those demands of liberalism that go beyond safeguarding and exploiting private property in really intending a rational plan for human practice require for their realization precisely the rational planning of the *whole* of the relations of production within which individuals have to live. The primacy of the whole over individuals is real, insofar as the forms of the production and reproduction of life, which are "general," are pregiven to the individuals and insofar as the appropriate organization of these forms is the precondition of the individual happiness of men. But released from its economic and social content, the concept of the whole has absolutely no concrete meaning in social theory. We shall see that its organicist version, i.e. the interpretation of the relation of totality to members as an organic-natural relationship, is not able to provide this meaning. Even the "folk" becomes a real totality only by virtue of its economic and social unity, not vice versa.

The strong universalist tendency does not, indeed, arise as a philosophical speculation; economic development actually requires it. One of the most important characteristics of monopoly capitalism is that it brings about, in fact, a quite definite "unification" within society. It creates a new "system of dependencies of the most diverse kinds," such as that of small- and middle-sized enterprises on cartels and trusts or of landed property and large-scale industry on finance capital.[33]

Here, in the economic structure of monopoly capitalist society, are located the factual bases of universalism. But in the theory they are totally reinterpreted. The whole that it presents is not the unification achieved by the domination of *one* class within the framework of class society, but rather a unity that combines *all* classes, that is supposed to overcome the reality of class struggle and thus of classes themselves: the "establishment of a real folk community, which elevates itself above the interests and conflicts of status groups and classes."[34] A classless society, in other words, is the goal, but a classless society on the basis of and within the framework of — the existing class society. For in the totalitarian theory of the state the foundations of this society, i.e. the economic order based on private property in the means of production, are not attacked. Instead, they are only modified to the degree demanded by the monopolistic stage of this very economic order. In consequence, all contradictions that inhere in such an order and make a real totality impossible are carried over into the new stage and its theory. Realizing the desired unifying totality would be in truth primarily an *economic* task:

21

elimination of the economic order that is the source of classes and class struggles. But it is just this task that universalism cannot and will not take on; indeed, it cannot even recognize it as an *economic* one: "It is not economic conditions that determine social relations but, to the contrary, it is moral views that determine economic relations."[35] Universalism must divert both consciousness and action from the only possible way to realize the "whole" and from the only possible form of that whole into another, less dangerous direction: it substitutes the "primal given" of the *folk, of folkhood.*

We shall not go into the various attempts that have been made to define the concept "folk." What is decisive is that it aims at a "primal given" that, as a "natural" one, is prior to the "artificial" system of society. It is the "social structure of the organic level of occurrence"[36] and as such represents an "ultimate," "germinated" unity. "The folk is not a structure that has originated through any human power";[37] it is a "divinely willed" groundwork of human society. In this way the new social theory arrives at the equation through which it is led to the premises of irrationalist "organicism": as a natural-organic whole, the first and last totality, the foundation and limit of all ties and obligations, is the genuine, divinely willed, eternal reality in contrast with the inorganic, "derived" reality of society. As such, owing to its origins, it is largely withdrawn from the range of all human planning and decision. Hence all attempts are "a priori" discredited that would overcome the present anarchically conflicting strivings and needs of individuals and raise them to a true totality by means of a planned transformation of the social relations of production. The path is cleared for "heroic-folkish" organicism, which provides the basis necessary for totalitarian political theory to fulfill its social function.

22

Naturalism

In ever new formulations, heroic-folkish realism emphasizes the natural properties of the totality represented by the
folk. The folk is "subject to blood," it arises from the "soil,"
it furnishes the homeland with indestructible force and
permanence, it is united by characteristics of "race," the
preservation of whose purity is the condition of the folk's
"health." In the train of this naturalism follows a glorification of the peasantry[38] as the only estate still "bound to
nature." It is celebrated as the "creative, original source," as
the eternal pillar of society. The mythical glorification of the
renewal of agriculture has its counterpart in the fight against
the metropolis and its "unnatural" spirit. This fight expands
into an attack on the rule of reason in general and sets loose
all irrational powers—a movement that ends with the total
functionalization of the mind. "Nature" is the first in the
series of restricting conditions to which reason is subordinated. The unconditioned authority of the state seems to
be the last. "Nature" as celebrated by organicism, however,
does not appear as a factor of production in the context of actual relations of production, nor as a condition of production,
nor as the basis, itself historical, of human history. Instead it
becomes a *myth,* and as myth it hides the organicist depravation and forcible displacement of historical and social processes. Nature becomes the great antagonist of history.

The naturalistic myth begins by apostrophizing the natural
as "eternal" and "divinely willed." This holds especially for
the totality of the folk, whose naturalness is one of the myth's
primary claims. The particular destinies of individuals, their
strivings and needs, their misery and their happiness — all this

is void and perishable, for only the folk is permanent. The folk is nature itself as the substructure of history, as eternal substance, the eternally constant in the continual flux of economic and social relations. In contrast with the folk, the latter are accidental, ephemeral, and "insignificant."

These formulations announce a characteristic tendency of heroic-folkish realism: its *depravation* of *history* to a merely temporal occurrence in which all structures are subjected to time and are therefore "inferior." This dehistoricization marks all aspects of organicist theory: the devaluation of time in favor of space, the elevation of the static over the dynamic and the conservative over the revolutionary, the rejection of all dialectic, the glorification of tradition for its own sake.[39] Never has history been taken less seriously than now, when it is primarily adjusted to the preservation and service of a national heritage, when revolutions are held to be "background noise" or "disturbances" of natural laws, and when the determination of human happiness and dignity is delivered over to natural forces of "blood" and "soil." In this dehistoricization of the historical, naturalist theory gives itself away; it expresses an interest in stabilizing a particular form of the conditions of life, one that can no longer be justified in its present historical situation. If history were really taken seriously, it could all too easily remind men that this form is in crisis and that possibilities for changing it can be derived from the history of its origins. In short, it could remind men that the established social order is transitory, that "the hour of its birth . . . is the hour of its death" (Hegel). It is ideologically perpetuated when it is claimed to be the "natural order of life."

Nonetheless, the new doctrine of history and society resists speaking of race, folkhood, blood, and soil in terms of a naturalistic biologism. It stresses that it conceives of these natural-organic data as simultaneously and essentially "historical-spiritual" facts out of which grows a historical "community of destiny." But if the word "destiny" is supposed to do more than stop short of knowledge of the real motive forces and factors of history, then it cancels the organicist myth of the "natural community" and thus the theoretical basis of the very philosophy of history from which it derives. Certainly every nation or people (folk) has its own destiny (insofar as it is an economic, geopolitical, and cultural unity), but it is precisely this destiny that cleaves the nation's unity into social antagonisms. Common destinies affect the different groups within the nation in different ways, and each reacts to them differently. A war, which undoubtedly affects the entire nation, can throw the masses into terrible poverty while particular ruling strata derive nothing but advantages from it. In a general crisis the economically powerful have much more ample opportunities for resistance and for avoiding dire consequences than does the economically weaker majority. The community of destiny almost always operates at the expense of the large majority of the people: it thus cancels itself out as a community. In previous human history, this cleavage of national or communal unity into social antagonisms is not merely secondary, nor is it the fault or responsibility of individuals. Rather, it comprises history's real content, which cannot be changed through adaptation to any sort of natural order. In history there are no longer any natural patterns that could serve as models and ideas for historical movement. Through the process in which men in society contend with nature and with their own historical reality (whose state at any given time is indicated by the various conditions and relations of life), "nature" has long been historicized, i.e. to an increasing degree denuded of its naturalness and subjected to rational human planning and technology. Natural orders and data occur structured as economic and social relations (so that, for example, the peasant's land is less a clod in the homeland than a holding in the mortgage section of the land register).[40]

This real structure, it is true, remains hidden from the consciousness of most people.

> The form of the social process of life, that is, the material process of production, strips off its nebulous, mystical veil as soon as it is under the conscious, planned control of freely associated men as their product.[41]

Until then it will be in the interest of those groups whose economic situation contradicts the attainment of this goal to represent specific social relations as perpetual and thus "natural" in order to preserve the established order and guard against the disturbance created by criticism.

The path that organicist theory takes in following this interest leads beyond naturalizing the economy as such to the naturalization of the monopoly capitalist economy as such and of the mass poverty it brings about; all of these phenomena are sanctioned as "natural." At the end of this path (of which we shall suggest only the most important stages) comes the point where ideology's function of creating illusions turns into one of disillusionment: transfiguration and camouflage are replaced by open brutality.

The economy is viewed as a "living organism" that one cannot transform "in one blow." It is constructed according to "primitive laws" rooted in human "nature." That is the first stage.

The step from the economy in general to the current economy is quickly taken. The current crisis is "nature's revenge" on the "intellectual attempt to violate its laws. . . . But nature always wins in the end. . . ." The transfiguration of economic and social relations to natural archetypes must inevitably and repeatedly come up against the so completely "unnatural" facticity of the current forms of life. In order to paper over this contradiction, a radical devaluation of the material sphere of existence, of the "external riches" of life, is necessary. They are "overcome" in the "heroism" of poverty and "service," of sacrifice and discipline. For heroic-folkish realism, the fight against materialism is necessary in both theory and practice. It must disavow, in favor of "ideal" values (honor, morality, duty, heroism), the worldly happiness of men that the social order it upholds can never bring about. This tendency toward "idealism," however, is countered by another very strong trend. For monopoly capitalism and its political situation demand from men the utmost exertion and permanent tension in the provision of the "worldly" goods that are to be produced. It follows from this that all of life is comprehended under the categories of service and work — a pure "inner-worldly" asceticism. Another factor that discredits idealism is that classical idealism was essentially rationalist, an idealism of the "mind," of reason. To the extent that it always contains, in some form, the autonomy of reason and places human practice under the idea of knowledge engaged in active comprehension, it necessarily brings down upon itself the enmity of the total-authoritarian state. The latter has every cause to consider reason's critique dangerous and hence to bind it to preordained states of fact. "German Idealism must therefore be overcome in form and content if we want to become a political, an active people."[42]

A fundamental ambiguity thus runs through antiliberalist theory. While on the one hand it advocates a constant, hard, almost cynical realism, on the other it extols "ideal" values as the first and last meaning of life and cries out for the salvation of the "spirit." We find two sets of pronouncements juxtaposed. The first attacks the weak "idealist," alienated from the world, to the advantage of the new type, the heroic man: "He lives not from the mind, but from blood and earth. He lives not from culture, but from action."[43] The second consists of passages such as this:

> The banner of the spirit waves over mankind as its distinctive mark. Although from time to time we may be carried away by glorious and impulsive urges of the will, the spirit always re-establishes its rights."[44]

All sorts of "metaphysical certainties" are conjured up, but they have probably never been as carelessly proffered and elevated to an official weltanschauung as today, when the final victory over the metaphysics of humanist idealism is announced while the big stick of imperialism is being brandished overhead:

> We no longer live in the age of education, of culture, of humanitarianism, and of the pure spirit, but rather under the necessity of struggle, of shaping political reality, of soldiery, of folkish discipline, of folkish honor and of the future of the folk. What is required of the men of this era, consequently, is not the idealist but the heroic attitude as both task and necessity of life.[45]

Never, moreover, has that anti-idealist "shaping of reality" been seen and interpreted in a bleaker and poorer manner: "Service that never ends because service and life coincide."[46] In fact, it takes a heroism that cannot possibly be rationally justified to make the sacrifice required for the preservation of the established order. In view of the everyday poverty of the masses and the danger of new and terrible wars and crises, appealing to the "naturalness" of this order is of no avail. It is not "nature" but capitalism in its true form that has the last word. We are now at the last stage, where this theory lets fall its veil of transfiguration and discloses the true face of the social order: "We hold . . . the lowering of the standard of

28

living to be inevitable and deem the most urgent consideration to be the way we are to view this occurrence and react to
it." Thus theory's efforts are not directed toward the elimination of mass poverty. To the contrary, it regards the growth of
this poverty as its inevitable presupposition. Nowhere has the
new "realism" come closer to the truth, which it faithfully
pursues as follows: "What is first necessary is that everyone
realize that poverty, restriction, and especially the renunciation of 'cultural goods' are required of all." Very likely, not
everyone will concede this necessity: people "at the present
time still resist [it] with biological individual instincts." The
main business of theory will thus be "to bring [these instincts]
to heel." The theoretician's acumen lets him know that this
cannot be accomplished by the "faculty of reason" alone, but
only "when poverty again acquires the stamp of an ethical
virtue, when poverty is no longer a shame or misfortune but
rather a dignified attitude taken as a matter of course with
regard to a grave and universal destiny." And the theorist
reveals to us the function of this and similar "ethics": it is the
"pedestal needed by the politician . . . in order to make
policy decisions with certainty."[47]

Heroism, the ethic of poverty as the "pedestal" of politics:
here the struggle against the materialist worldview reveals
itself in its final meaning, that of "bringing to heel" instincts
that rebel against the falling standard of living. A functional
change in ideology, characteristic of certain stages of social
development, has taken place. This ideology exhibits the status
quo, but with a radical transvaluation of values: unhappiness
is turned into grace, misery into blessing, poverty to destiny.
Vice versa, striving for happiness and material improvement
becomes sin and injustice.

The performance of duty, the sacrifice, and the devotion
that "heroic realism" requires of men are brought into the

service of a social order that perpetuates the misery and un-happiness of individuals. Although these sacrifices are made at the "brink of meaninglessness," they have nonetheless a concealed, very "rational" purpose: factually and ideologi-cally stabilizing the current system of producing and repro-ducing life.[48] Heroic realism offends against the great ideas of duty, sacrifice, and devotion by programmatically incorporat-ing into the apparatus of a system of domination what can only occur as the free gift of free men.

As we have seen, the model of man projected by today's heroic realism is of one whose existence is fulfilled in unques-tioning sacrifices and unconditional acts of devotion, whose ethic is poverty and all of whose worldly goods have been melted down into service and discipline. This image stands in sharp opposition to all the ideals acquired by Western man in the last centuries. How justify such an existence? Since man's material well-being is not its goal, it cannot be justified on the basis of his natural needs and instincts. But neither can its goal be his spiritual welfare, or salvation, since there is no room for justification by faith. And in the universal struggle against reason, justification by knowledge can no longer count as a justification.

To the extent that totalitarian theory moves within the bounds of scientific discussion, it becomes aware of this prob-lem. Thinking of the "emergency" in which sacrificing one's own life and killing other men are demanded, Carl Schmitt inquires into the reason for such sacrifice: "There is no ra-tional end, no norm however correct, no program however exemplary, no social ideal however beautiful, and no legiti-macy or legality that could justify men's killing one an-other."[49] What, then, remains as a possible justification? Only this: that there is a state of affairs that through its very ex-istence and presence is *exempt* from all justification, i.e. an

30

"existential," "ontological" state of affairs — justification by mere existence. "Existentialism" in its political form becomes the theory of the (negative) justification of what can no longer be justified.

Existentialism

We shall be dealing here not with the philosophical form of existentialism but with its political form, i.e. that in which it has become a decisive element of totalitarian political theory.

It must be stressed right from the start that in political existentialism there is not even an attempt to define the "existential" conceptually. The only thing we have to go on in elucidating the intended meaning of the existential is the passage by Carl Schmitt cited above. There the existential appears essentially as a contrast to the "normative," i.e. as something that cannot be placed under any norm lying outside it. From this it follows that one absolutely cannot think, judge, or decide about an existential condition as a "nonpartisan third [party]." "The possibility of correct knowledge and understanding and therewith also the competence to participate in speaking and to judge is given here only by existential partaking and participation."[50] There is no fundamental or general criterion in existentialism for determining which facts and conditions are to be considered existential. That remains left in principle to the decision of the existential theoretician. But once he claims a state of fact as existential, all those who do not "participate and partake" in its reality are to keep silent. Predominantly *political* conditions and relations are sanctioned here as existential, and within the political dimension it is the relation to the enemy,[51] or war, that counts as the simply and absolutely existential relationship ("the folk and folk membership" have been added as a second, equally existential, relationship).

Given this lack of any exact conceptual character, it is necessary to turn briefly from political to philosophical existentialism. The meaning of philosophical existentialism lay in regaining the full concretion of the historical subject in opposition to the abstract "logical" subject of rational idealism, i.e. eliminating the domination, unshaken from Descartes to Husserl, of the *ego cogito*. Heidegger's position before his *Sein und Zeit* was philosophy's furthest advance in this direction. Then came the reaction. With good reason, philosophy avoided looking more carefully at the historical situation, with regard to its material facticity, of the subject to which it addressed itself. At this point concretion stopped, and philosophy remained content to talk of the nation's "link with destiny," of the "heritage" that each individual has to adopt, and of the community of the "generation," while the other dimensions of facticity were treated under such categories as "they" (*das Man*), or "idle talk" (*das Gerede*), and relegated in this way to "inauthentic" existence. Philosophy did not go on to ask about the nature of this heritage, about the people's mode of being, and about the real powers and forces that *are* history. It thus renounced every possibility of comprehending the facticity of historical situations and distinguishing between them.

Instead, something like a new anthropology gradually began to crystallize, absorbing in an ever more superficial way the fertile discoveries of existential analysis. This anthropology then took on the job of furnishing a philosophical foundation for the ideal of man projected by heroic realism.

The theoretical man to whom the value concepts currently in circulation refer is a fiction. . . . Man is essentially a political creature, i.e. . . . , he is not a creature whose being is determined by his participation in a higher "spiritual world" . . . , but he is rather an originally acting creature.[52]

A total activation, concretization, and politicization of all dimensions of existence is demanded. The autonomy of thought and the objectivity and neutrality of science are repudiated as heresy or even as a political falsification on the part of liberalism. "We are active, enterprising beings and incur guilt if we deny this our essence: guilt by neutrality and tolerance."[53] The proclamation includes the affirmation that "all science is life-conditioned, reality-oriented, historically conditioned, and situationally bound."[54] Many of these theses have long been part of the conceptual makeup of scientific social theory. The conditions at their root have already been identified by historical materialism. That knowledge originally developed to *fight* the established order is now applied in its *service* shows how the dialectic realizes itself in the realm of theory: the stabilization of the current social structure is only possible in a way that at the same time sets free progressive forces of development. Politically, these forces are coerced into a form that obstructs their original movement and makes their liberating effect illusory. This change in function is simultaneously expressed in the attempt to ground them in theory. The concrete social meaning of positing man as a primarily historical, political, and politically acting being is revealed only when we ask: What manner of "historicity" is meant, what form of political action and of practice is intended? What kind of action is it, then, that the new anthropology enjoins as the "authentic" practice of man?

Action does not mean "deciding in favor of" . . . , for that presupposes that one knows in favor of what one is deciding; rather, action means "setting off in a direction," "taking

33

sides," by virtue of a mandate of destiny, by virtue of "one's own right." . . . It is really secondary to decide in favor of something that I have come to know.[55]

This typical formulation sheds light on the sorry picture that "existential" anthropology paints of active man. He acts — but he knows not what for. He acts — but he has not even decided for himself in favor of what he acts. He simply "takes sides" or "goes into action" — "It is really secondary to decide in favor of something I have come to know." This anthropology derives its pathos from a radical devaluation of Logos as knowledge that reveals and decides. It was Aristotle's view that it is precisely Logos that distinguishes man from animal: the capacity "to set forth the expedient and the inexpedient, and therefore likewise the just and the unjust."[56] Existential anthropology believes that knowing the reason for one's decision, the goal which gives all human action meaning and value, is secondary. It is essential only *that* a path be taken, *that* one take sides. "The horrifying differences of standpoint do not reside in the sphere of pure material objectivity" but rather "in the synthetic force of existentially rooted ways of looking at things."[57] Only when existential anthropology attains this irrational tone does it become capable of fulfilling its social function in the service of a system of domination to which nothing can be less opportune than a "material, objective" justification of the action it requires.

Seen in this perspective, the strong emphasis on the historicity of existence reveals itself as empty, for it is possible only on the basis of the above-mentioned depravation of history. Genuine historicity presupposes a cognitive relation of existence to the forces of history and, derived from it, the theoretical and practical *critique* of these forces. But in existential anthropology the corresponding relation is limited to one of accepting a "mandate" issued to existence by the "folk." It is considered self-evident that it is the "folk" — and not any particular interest group — which issues the mandate and for which it is exercised. A secularized theological image of history emerges. Every folk receives its historical mandate as a "mission" that is the first and last, the unrestricted obligation of existence. In a *salto mortale* (the speed of which cannot obscure that in it the entire tradition of philosophical and scientific knowledge is thrown by the board) the "will to knowledge" is subjected to the alleged mandate of one's own folk. And the folk is considered a unity and totality underlying the socio-economic sphere. Existentialism, too, sees in "earthy and bloody forces" the real forces of history.[58] Thus the existentialist currents, too, are nourished from the great naturalistic reservoir.

On this point political existentialism is more sensitive than its philosophical counterpart. It knows that even the "earthy and bloody forces" of a folk become historical only in particular political forms, that is, if a real structure of domination, *the state,* has been erected over the folk. Existentialism, too, needs an explicit political theory: *the doctrine of the total state.* We shall not provide here an express critique of this theory and shall stress only what is decisive in our context.

Political relationships and conditions are interpreted as existential ones, as in accordance with Being. This view would be self-evident if it meant nothing more than that man, with respect to his nature, φύσει (*physei*), is a political organism. But it does mean more. We saw that the existential as such is exempt from any rational standard or norm lying beyond it; it is itself the absolute norm and is inaccessible to any and all rational criticism and justification. Accordingly, political conditions and relationships are now posited as the most emphatically significant factors "deciding" existence.

35

And within the political sphere all relationships are oriented in turn toward the most extreme "crisis," toward the decision about the "state of emergency," of war and peace. The true possessor of political power is defined as beyond all legality and legitimacy: "Sovereign is he who decides on the state of emergency."[59] Sovereignty is founded on the factual power to make this decision (decisionism). The basic political relationship is the "friend-enemy relationship." Its crisis is war, which proceeds until the enemy has been physically annihilated. There is no social relationship that does not in a crisis turn into a political relationship. Behind all economic, social, religious, and cultural relations stands total politicization. There is no sphere of private or public life, no legal or rational court of appeal that could oppose it.

At this point occurs the release of progressive forces to which we have already referred. Total activation and politicization do away with the inhibiting neutrality of broad strata of the population and create, along a front never before matched in length and breadth, new forms of political struggle and new methods of political organization. The separation of state and society, which liberalism had attempted to carry out in the nineteenth century, is abolished: the state takes over the political integration of society. And, in the process of the existentialization and totalization of the political sphere, the state also becomes the bearer of the authentic potentialities of existence itself. It is not the state that is responsible to man but man who is responsible to the state; he is delivered over to it. At the level on which political existentialism moves, there can be absolutely no question whether the state in its "total" form is right in making such demands, whether the system of domination that it defends with all available means guarantees anything like the possibility of more than illusory fulfillment for most men. The existentiality of the political structure is removed from such "rationalistic" questions; even asking them is a crime: "All these attempts to dispute the state's newly gained effective right signify sabotage . . . . Relentlessly to exterminate this sort of thought is the noblest duty of the state today."[60]

No longer founded on the pluralism of social interests and their parties, and exempt from all formal legality and legitimacy, this state's form of domination is that of the authoritarian leader and his "following."

> In conscious opposition to the liberal and civil [bürgerlich] constitutional state, the national constitutional state, in its politics and constitutional law, has the form of the authoritarian leader-state [Führerstaat]. The authoritarian leader-state sees in state authority the most essential feature of the state.[61]

Essentially, authoritarian leadership draws its political qualifications from two sources, which are themselves linked: an irrational, "metaphysical" power, and a "non-social" power. The idea of "justification" still disquiets the theory: "An authoritarian government needs a justification that goes beyond the personal." There is no material or rational justification. Thus the "justification must be metaphysical . . . . As a principle of state order, the distinction between leaders and led can be made only metaphysically."[62] The political and social meaning of the concept "metaphysical" gives itself away: "A government that governs only because it has a mandate from the folk is not an authoritarian government. Authority is possible only if it comes from transcendence . . . ."[63] The word "transcendence" ought to be taken seriously here. The foundation of authority lies beyond all social facticity, so that it does not depend on it for validation. Above all, it surpasses the "folk's" factual situation and power of comprehension: "Authority presupposes a status that is valid over against the folk because the folk does not confer it but acknowledges it."[64] Acknowledgment is the foundation of authority: a truly "existential" proof!

Let us now briefly consider the "dialectical" fate of existentialist theory in the total state. This dialectic is "passive," for it passes over the theory without the latter being able to incorporate it and develop it further. With the realization of the total-authoritarian state, existentialism abolishes itself — rather, it undergoes abolition.

> The total state must be a state of total responsibility. This means that the state becomes the only source and object of every individual's duties. Being in this state of duty abolishes the private character of individual existence.[65]

Existentialism, however, was originally based on the "private" character of individual existence, its irremovable, personal "always-being-my-own" (*Jemeinigkeit*). The total state takes over total responsibility for the individual existence; existentialism had claimed the inalienable self-responsibility of existence. The total state decides existence in all its dimensions; existentialism had put forth as the fundamental category of existence that "decidedness" (*Entschlossenheit*) which can be the project only of each individual existence. The total state demands total duty without even allowing inquiry into the truth of such obligation; existentialism (here in agreement with Kant) had celebrated the autonomous self-giving of duty as the real dignity of man. The total state has "overcome [individual freedom] as a postulate of human thought . . .";[66] existentialism (again in accord with Kant) had placed "the essence of human freedom," as the autonomy of the person[67] at the origin of philosophizing, and made freedom the condition of truth.[68] This freedom was seen as man's "self-authorization" for his existence and to the realm of beings as such; conversely man is now "authorized to freedom by the authoritatively led community of the folk."[69]

There would appear yet one escape from this hopeless heteronomism. One can screen the abolition of human freedom with the pretext that only the bad liberalist concept of freedom is being abolished and then define the "true" concept of freedom somewhat as follows: "The essence of freedom lies precisely in obligation to the folk and the state."[70] Now even the most convinced liberal never denied that freedom does not exclude obligation but rather demands it. And since Aristotle, in the last book of the *Nichomachean Ethics,* inseparably linked the question of man's "happiness" to the question of the "best state," essentially grounding "politics" and "ethics" in each other (with the former as the fulfillment of the latter), we know that *freedom is an eminently political concept.* Real freedom for individual existence (and not merely in the liberalist sense) is possible only in a specifically structured polis, a "rationally" organized society. In consciously politicizing the concept of existence, and deprivatizing and deinternalizing (*Ent-Innerlichung*) the liberalist, idealist conception of man, the totalitarian view of the state represents progress — progress that leads beyond the basis of the totalitarian state, propelling the theory beyond the social order that it affirms. As long as it remains within the latter's bounds, the progress operates regressively: the process of politicizing and deprivatizing annihilates individual existence instead of truly raising it to "universality."[71] This becomes clear in the antiliberalist concept of freedom.

The political identification of freedom and obligation is more than an empty phrase only if the community to which the free individual is a priori obligated secures him the possibility of a fulfilled existence worthy of man, or if the community can be directed toward such a possibility. The question that the identity of freedom and political obligation (an identity which as such deserves to be recognized) impels one to ask, rather than dispenses one from asking, is this: What is this community like, to which I am to obligate myself? Can it sustain human happiness and dignity? The "natural" affiliations of "blood" and "soil" alone can never justify the total surrender of the individual to the community. Man is more than nature, more than an animal, "and we can never leave off thinking. For man is a thinking being, that is how he distinguishes himself from animals."[72] Nor can totally delivering over the individual to the state that factually exists at a given moment be demanded merely on the grounds that man is "ontologically" a political being or that political relationships are "existential." Unless it is to annihilate human freedom rather than to fulfill it, the political obligation of freedom can be only the free practice of the individual himself. This practice begins with critique and ends with the free self-realization of the individual in a rationally organized society. This organization of society and this practice are the mortal enemies that political existentialism combats with all available means.

Existentialism collapses the moment its political theory is realized. The total-authoritarian state for which it longed gives the lie to all its truths. Existentialism accompanies its debacle with a self-abasement unique in the history of ideas, bringing its own history to end as a satyr play. In philosophy, existentialism begins as the antagonist in a great debate with Western rationalism and idealism, intending to save their conceptual content by injecting it into the historical concretion of individual existence. It ends by radically denying its own origin; the struggle against reason drives it blindly into the arms of the powers that be. In their service and with their protection, it turns traitor to the great philosophy that it formerly celebrated as the culmination of Western thought. The abyss between them is now unbridgeable. Kant was convinced that there are "inalienable" human rights, which "man cannot surrender even if he so wills."

> Human right must be kept sacred, no matter how great the sacrifice it costs the ruling powers. One cannot go only halfway and contrive a pragmatically conditioned right. . . . All politics, rather, must bend the knee before sacred human right. . . .[73]

Kant had obligated man to self-given duty, to free self-determination as the only fundamental law; existentialism annuls this law and obligates man "to the leader and the following that is immediately pledged to him."[74] Hegel could still believe that

> what is true, great, and divine in life is so through the Idea. . . . All that holds human life together and that has merit and validity is of a mental and spiritual [*geistig*] nature and this realm of the mind and spirit exists only through the consciousness of truth and right, through the comprehension of Ideas.[75]

Today existentialism knows better: "Let not doctrines and 'Ideas' be the rules of your being. Today and in the future, only the *Führer* himself is German reality and its law."[76]

The question of philosophy's "standpoint" arose in the period of rationalist idealism as it does today. As Kant wrote,

> Here we see philosophy now accorded, in fact, a precarious standpoint, which is supposed to be stable in spite of not being supported by or attached to anything either in heaven or on earth. Here it is to prove its integrity as keeper of its own laws, not as the herald of those insinuated to it by some

41

inveterate disposition or by who knows what tutelary nature. . . .[77]

Today philosophy is accorded just the opposite standpoint:

What should philosophy do in this hour? Perhaps there is left for it today only the business of justifying, through employment of its profound knowledge of man, those who want not to know but to act.[78]

With relentless consistency, this philosophy has followed through to the end the road from critical idealism to "existential" opportunism.

Existentialism, which at one time understood itself to be the heir of German Idealism, has given up the greatest intellectual heritage of German history. It was not with Hegel's death but only now that the Fall of the Titans of German philosophy occurs.[79] At that time, in the nineteenth century, its decisive achievements were preserved in a new form in scientific social theory and the critique of political economy. Today the fate of the labor movement, in which the heritage of this philosophy was preserved, is clouded with uncertainty.

Originally published in German in Zeitschrift für Sozialforschung, *vol. III (1934).*

II. THE CONCEPT OF ESSENCE

In philosophy, there are fundamental concepts whose meta-physical character sets them far apart from the sociohistorical roots of thought. That their content remains the same in the most diverse philosophical theories would appear the sound-est justification for the idea of a *"philosophia perennis."* Yet even these loftiest conceptions of philosophy are subject to historical development. It is not so much their content as it is their position and function within philosophical systems which changes. Once this is seen, it becomes clear that these very concepts provide a clearer indication of the historical transformation of philosophy than those whose contents are far closer to facticity. Their metaphysical character betrays more than it conceals. For so much of men's real struggles and desires went into the metaphysical quest for an ultimate unity, truth, and universality of Being[1] that they could not have failed to find expression in the derived forms of the philosophical tradition.

The concept of essence belongs to these categories. Its manifold forms have as their common content the abstraction and isolation of the one true Being from the constantly changing multiplicity of appearances. Under the name of "essence" this Being is made into the object of "authentic," certain, and secure knowledge. The way in which modern philosophy has understood and established knowledge of essence contrasts with that of ancient and medieval philosophy. The historical situation of the bourgeoisie, the bearer of modern philosophy, comes out in modern interpretations of the relation of essence and appearance. According to the view characteristic of the dawning bourgeois era, the critical autonomy of rational subjectivity is to establish and justify the ultimate essential truths on which all theoretical and practical truth depends. The essence of man and of things is contained in the freedom of the thinking individual, the *ego cogito*. At the close of this era, knowledge of essence has primarily the function of binding the critical freedom of the individual to pregiven, unconditionally valid necessities. It is no longer the spontaneity of the concept but the receptivity of intuition that serves as the organon of the doctrine of essence. Cognition culminates in recognition, where it remains fixated. Husserl's phenomenology can be considered a delayed attempt to reinvigorate bourgeois theory with the basic forces and concepts of German Idealism (in which the doctrine of essence had found its classical form). Although eliminating their critical (Kantian) orientation, Husserl's philosophy thus still belongs to the liberalist period. The material eidetics (Scheler) that came in Husserl's train, however, represents the transition to a new stage: the preparation of thought for the ideology of authoritarian forms of domination. The intuition of essence is misused to establish orders of value in which the relations of hierarchy and subordination required by the established order are derived from the "essence" of man, of nationality, and of race. From Descartes to modern eidetics, the concept of essence has followed a course leading from autonomy to heteronomy, from the proclamation of the

44

free, rational individual to his surrender to the powers of the authoritarian state.

The current form of the doctrine of essence no longer preserves the comprehension that led to the separation of essence and appearance; neither does the abstract cancellation of this separation demanded by positivism. A theory that wants to eradicate from science the concept of essence succumbs to helpless relativism, thus promoting the very powers whose reactionary thought it wants to combat. Positivism cannot provide an effective critique of the idealist doctrine of essence. Doing so devolves upon the materialist dialectic. Before this task is attempted, we shall analyze some typical forms of the idealist doctrine of essence.

*　　*　　*

In Plato's theory of Ideas, where the concept of essence was first clearly formulated, it was an outcome of the quest for the unity and universality of Being in view of the multiplicity and changeability of beings. That things, even though each of them is "individual," are nevertheless similar and dissimilar, like and unlike; that in the endless multiplicity of their attributes they are comprehended as one and the same; that quite diverse phenomena accord in being considered good, beautiful, just, unjust, and so forth; in short, that the world of beings is divided into species and genera, subsumed under the highest categories, and known by means of universal concepts is the philosophical substratum of the problem of essence. This problem was not one of epistemology alone. For when the unity in multiplicity, the universal, is conceived as what truly exists, critical and ethical elements enter into the concept of essence. The isolation of the one universal Being is connected to that of authentic Being from inauthentic, of what should and can be from what is. The Being of things is not

45

exhausted in what they immediately are; they do not appear as they could be. The form of their immediate existence is imperfect when measured against their potentialities, which comprehension reveals as the image of their essence. Their *eidos*, or Idea, becomes the criterion by means of which the distance between existence and what it could be, its essence, is measured in each case.

Accordingly, the attributes of this concept of essence do not have a primarily logical or epistemological basis. Seeking the unity, universality, and permanence of Being and "remembering" the essence are motivated by the critical consciousness of "bad" facticity, of unrealized potentialities. The essence as potentiality becomes a force within existence. Beginning with the late version of the theory of Ideas in the *Sophist* and the *Philebus,* the Idea as *dynamis* enters into the process in which "true Being" originates as the result of becoming. This is the first form in which the critical and dynamic character of the concept of essence is fully realized. The Idea means fundamentally the *agathon,* or what exists as it can be according to its own measure; existence is in motion toward this *agathon.*[2] The dynamic of this relation also governs Aristotelian ontology. The concepts of essence *ousia* and *ti en einai* attempt to grasp the manner in which beings constitute and preserve themselves as identical in the various phases of their movement. From Plato on the ancient theory of essence was impelled by the unrest of the unresolved tension between essence and existence.

The Christian philosophy of the Middle Ages pacified the critical consciousness of this antithesis in an onto-theological principle, which it eternalized as a structural law of the created world. For Thomas Aquinas the essence, as *essentia* of existence, is that according to, through, and in which existence is what it is. The *essentia* is, in other words, the inner

46

structure of existence, in which it operates as the principle of form for each kind of being. The essence has always already been realized in whatever is the case; yet — and this is the crucial point — this reality is never that of the essence itself. In all finite being, essence and existence are ontologically separated. The latter supervenes to the former "from outside," and, in relation to existence, the essence as such has the ontological character of pure potentiality, *potentia transcendentalis.* It is eternal, unchanging, and necessary: the "Idea" as the original model of existence in the divine intellect. The essence conceived in this way can become real only through a principle that is "exterior" to it. In its material concreteness, the form of its real existence remains an irrevocable contingency.[3] Human beings are thus exonerated from concern with the "ontic" difference between essence and existence in the realm of finite being.[4]

No matter how much it mitigated the critical tensions implied in the concept of essence, Thomistic philosophy persevered in conceiving the difference between essence and existence as indicative of a characteristic of beings themselves, as they are given to man in spatio-temporal reality. In this way, the reduction of the problem of essence to one of logic and epistemology was impeded. This reduction occurred only in the development of modern thought that began with Descartes and ended with Husserl. The concept of essence enters the sphere of the self-certain *ego cogito,* or transcendental subjectivity. Liberated from the bonds and obligations of the medieval order and empowered to shape his own world, the autonomous individual saw his reason presented with the task that had been metaphysically hypostatized in the doctrine of essence: realizing the authentic potentialities of beings on the basis of the discovery that nature can be controlled. Essence became the object of theoretical and practical reason. The

47

transcendental, subjective form of the concept of essence is typical of bourgeois theory and was first fully worked out by Descartes.

In his attempt to provide philosophy with a new foundation, Descartes sought an instance of absolutely certain, necessary, and universally valid knowledge. He found it in the individual's consciousness, in the *ego cogitans*. To a considerable extent, the concept of theory guiding Descartes was patterned on mathematically formulated natural science, but this does not adequately account for the significance of his approach. At the same time, science was making its pioneering discoveries, and the ideal of "objectively" ascertained knowledge, fulfilled in a nature subjected to calculation and domination, seemed attainable as never before. Why then did Descartes have recourse to the "subjective" certainty of the *ego cogito?* Why is his anchoring of theory in the consciousness of subjectivity to be found right alongside his mechanistic philosophy, his analytical geometry, and his treatise on machines?

The difficulty of circumscribing the significance of Descartes' approach derives from its thoroughly contradictory nature: simultaneous liberation and impotence, representing the simultaneous affirmation and flight or protest with which the individual, released from medieval hierarchy, reacted to the law of bourgeois society. Universal doubt, the demand that the proof of all judgments be appealed to the sovereign reason of the individual, and the incorporation of mathematics and mechanics into philosophy expressed the new, self-possessed individuality that appeared with demands for the free shaping of the conditions of life and for the subjection of nature and its newly discovered wealth. Intense activism is manifest in the programmatic connection, emphasized by Descartes, between theory and practice: theory, absolutely certain of its knowledge, is to serve as a sure organon of practice. "It suffices to judge well in order to do well, and to judge as well as one can in order to do one's best, that is to say, to acquire . . . all the other goods that one can acquire."[5] Descartes believed in a *philosophie pratique* instead of the ancient *philosophie spéculative,* a practical philosophy

> by means of which, knowing the force and the actions of fire, water, air, the stars, the heavens, and all the other bodies that surround us . . . we should be able to utilize them in like manner for all the uses to which they are suited and thus render ourselves masters and possessors of nature.[6]

But in the contemporary form of social organization, the domination of nature through rational methods of production as envisioned by Descartes was neither joined to nor directed by the sovereign reason of the associated individuals. The fate of bourgeois society announces itself in its philosophy. When the liberated individual as the subject of practice actually sets himself to shaping the conditions of his life, he sees himself subjected to the laws of the commodity market, which operate as blind economic laws behind his back. At most, his first step, the beginning of his career, can appear free, as though dictated by his own reason. All subsequent ones are prescribed him by the conditions of a commodity-producing society, and he must observe them if he does not want to go under.

The transparent relations of dependence characteristic of the medieval order were replaced by a system in which relations of dependence could no longer be grasped as such by the individual. The conditions of labor become autonomous; subjected to their mechanism, the individual's fate in such a society appears to him as a mere contingency. Spatio-temporal reality becomes a merely "external" world that is not rationally connected with man's authentic potential, his "substance" or "essence." This external reality is not organized by the activity of human freedom, although modern science shows such organization to be possible and modern philosophy requires it as a task. In practice, the fulfillment of this task comes up against an obstacle whose removal would lead beyond this society's limits. As long as philosophy does not adopt the idea of a real transformation, the critique of reason stops at the status quo and becomes a critique of pure thought. The uncertainty and unfreedom of the external world is countered by the certainty and freedom of thought as the individual's only remaining power base. He must recognize that he must conquer himself rather than fortune, his wants rather than the "order of the world," and "that there is nothing aside from our thoughts which is completely within our power, so that, after we have done our best with regard to things outside us, all wherein we fail to succeed is absolutely impossible on our part."[7] If the individual is to be salvaged and human freedom to be preserved, then the "essence" of man must be located in thought. Here is where his authentic potentialities and the ontological certainty of his existence must be found: "I conclude with assurance that my essence consists exclusively in my being a thing that thinks, or a substance whose entire essence or nature is only to think."[8]

It is often asserted today that Descartes, by beginning with the *ego cogito,* committed the original sin of modern philosophy, that he placed a completely abstract concept of the individual at the basis of theory. But his abstract concept of the individual is animated by concern with human freedom: measuring the truth of all conditions of life against the standard of rational thought. Hegel said of Descartes: "It is the interest of freedom that is fundamental here. What is known to be true is to have the function of preserving our freedom through our thinking."[9] That this freedom is freedom "only" of thought, that only the "abstract" individual is free, that concern with human freedom becomes concern with the absolute certainty of thought, demonstrate the historical veracity of Cartesian philosophy. As the counterpart to his factual unfreedom, the individual, aiming at the greatest truth and certainty possible within bourgeois practice, is left only with the freedom of thought. The "reason" of this epoch is necessarily "abstract"; in order to remain true to itself and avoid falling into irrationality, reason must disregard not only the given form of spatio-temporal existence, but even the concrete content of thought at any time, and retain only thought as such, the pure form of all *cogitationes*. Reason cannot unfold itself in the rational domination and shaping of objects by free individuals. Rather, objectivity becomes a postulate of pure knowledge and is thus released from the "interest of freedom":

> The impulse to freedom is in fact basic, but predominating, at least in consciousness, is the goal of arriving at something solid and objective — the element of objectivity, not the moment of subjectivity (i.e. that it is posited, known, and verified by me).[10]

After Descartes defined the essence of man as "thinking" and thought as *fundamentum inconcussum* (unshakable foundation), the problem of essence moved into the sphere of cognitive subjectivity. The question of essence — of the truth, unity, and authenticity of Being — became the question of the truth, unity, and authenticity of knowledge. Post-Cartesian idealism retains this fundamental philosophical idea of the bourgeois period, the idea that the "organization" of existing things in accordance with their comprehended potentialities is a function of the free, critical reason of the individual. In

51

the reified world in which work relations are no longer "essentially" related to men's potentialities and appear rather as an effect of over-powering conditions of production, the idea that an organization of existing things in terms of their "essential" relationships could be the result of a future change disappears; organization becomes a matter of pure cognition. In transcendental philosophy the notion of a critical, rational organization of existing things underwent the decisive reduction to a formal a priori that has always already preceded any factual experience. To be sure, the relation of the a priori syntheses to experience is in the mode of absolute simultaneity; but in that the syntheses, which are eternally valid, precede every possible future experience and cannot be surpassed by any future experience, the essence of man as cognitive subject and of the objects of cognition is cut off from the future and oriented toward the past. This is the dominant motif of the transcendental method, the method specific to bourgeois philosophy.

With Kant the characteristics of essence — such as unity, universality, permanence — reappear in the context of pure theoretical reason, where they are incorporated partly in the pure concepts of the understanding or in their transcendental apperception, partly in the transcendental Ideas of reason. Thus they appear on the one hand as the categorical forms of conceptual synthesis, which are prior to all future experience, and on the other as Ideas or pure concepts of reason which "extend beyond the limit of all experience," in which "no object can ever appear that would be adequate to the transcendental Idea."[11] In the first case, the critical and dynamic opposition of essence to experience is eliminated by being completely absorbed into the timeless history of cognition. In the second it is more immediately and explicitly clear that the problem of essence has been taken up into "reason" — and not only because Kant consciously associated himself with the Platonic doctrine of essence by calling the concepts of reason "Ideas." Reason is the locus of the final unity, totality, and universality of knowledge: "the faculty that unifies the rules of the understanding under principles."[12] As a pure concept of reason, the Idea is directed toward the "totality of the conditions for a given conditioned thing"; it is the "concept of the unconditioned."[13] Now, Kant says that these Ideas "perhaps make possible a transition from natural concepts to practical ones."[14] The age-old philosophical question of realizing the essence in existence becomes here the problem of the transition from the concepts of theoretical to those of practical reason. Kant emphasized that reason's interest in these Ideas was "a practical interest": in the Ideas the "foundation stones of morality and religion"[15] were at stake. And precisely here that thought whose structure Kant is unfolding becomes tangled in paralogisms and antinomies, in a "natural and unavoidable illusion," which "is still deceptive even when one is no longer at its mercy."[16]

It is characteristic of the historical situation of idealist thought that the "Ideas" as concepts of reason become part of the dialectic of transcendental illusion and that when the dialectic first reappears in idealism it is one of illusion: of necessary illusion. The essence of man is still seen as lying in reason, "which alone is called upon to do away with all errors"; Kant still insists that this reason "knows no other judge than universal human reason, in which each man has a voice; and since it is from reason that every improvement of which our condition is capable must spring," freedom is its original right "and may not be restricted."[17] But it is not accidental that two different concepts of reason are intertwined in Kant's work: reason as the unifying totality of man's cognitive faculty (as which it is the subject of the "critiques" of pure and practical reason), and reason in a narrower sense, as a single faculty that rises "above" the understanding, as the faculty of those "Ideas" that can never be adequately represented in experience and have a merely regulative function. It is reason in this second, more narrow sense through which, for Kant, the transition to practical concepts occurs. It occurs under the aegis of the concept of freedom: the "Idea" is transformed into a "postulate" and the "postulate" into a "fact" of practical reason. In this way reason's freedom undergoes still another limitation. Through the stipulation that man's free reason be united with the empirical world of necessity, freedom is hypostatized as a timeless occurrence: it can exercise its causality on the empirical world only insofar as the world has no effect whatsoever on it. Free reason is limited in function to furnishing the determining ground of actions, to "beginning" them. Once begun, actions enter the unbreakable causal nexus of natural necessity, and they proceeed in accordance with its laws forever after.

Thus this doctrine mirrors the fate of a world in which rational human freedom always can take only the initial step freely, only to encounter afterward an uncontrolled necessity which remains contingent with respect to reason. The causality of reason, operating in one direction only, cuts off the possibility of the empirical world affecting the intelligible essence of man. It thus imprisons this essence in a past without future:

> The intelligible essence of every thing, and especially of man, stands, according to this [idealism] outside of every causal connection, as it stands outside of or above all time. Thus it can never be determined by anything that has gone before it, in that it rather is prior, not so much temporally as logically, to everything else that is or becomes within it.[18]

*   *   *

54

In the development of transcendental philosophy after Kant, this stabilization of the concept of essence was broken down and a dynamic theory of essence achieved. Hegel's dialectic, in which this dynamic theory of essence was developed, received no further elaboration in idealist philosophy: its development forms part of a different trend of thought and will be discussed later. When Husserl undertook to found anew the theory of essence, he based it on the theory of transcendental subjectivity as it was worked out from Descartes to Kant.

Phenomenology did not, to be sure, start out as transcendental philosophy. The pathos of purely descriptive, scientific objectivity which characterizes the *Logische Untersuchungen* ("Logical Investigations") is indicative of an inner connection with positivism, even where Husserl attacks it. Husserl himself pointed to Hume as the first to "make serious use of Descartes' pure inward focus."[19] But where the theory of essence becomes central in Husserl's philosophy, its elaboration forces phenomenology to base itself ever more radically on transcendental apriorism. For this reason the stage represented by the *Logische Untersuchungen* does not need to be considered here.

Husserl defines essence in opposition to the individual, spatio-temporally existing real thing, the "fact," object of all empirical sciences:

> the significance of this contingency, which is called facticity,
> is limited by its correlation to a *necessity* that does not stand
> for the mere factual existence of a valid rule for the co-ordi-
> nation of spatio-temporal facts; rather, it has the character
> of *essential necessity* and is thus related to *essential univer-
> sality.*

Part of the "meaning of everything contingent . . . is to have an essence and thus an *eidos* that is to be grasped in its purity. This *eidos* is a component of essential truths of various levels of generality."[20] At first glance, these attributes do not differ at all from those of the traditional conception of essence as *quidditas* and *essentia,* as it was formulated by the Scholastics and incorporated into philosophy. But the context in which phenomenology deals with the concept of essence is completely different: the sphere of transcendental consciousness, "purged" of all acts intending spatio-temporal existence. For Husserl, the concept of essence is relevant only within the dimension of pure subjectivity that remains as a residuum after the phenomenological "annihilation of the world" and that "precedes the being of the world as constituting in itself the meaning of that being" — a "completely self-contained reality," "something existing absolutely."[21] The essential truths that make their appearance in this dimension "do not contain the slightest assertion about facts, and thus from them alone not even the most meager factual truth can be derived."[22]

After his *Ideen* ("Ideas"), Husserl programmatically defined his philosophical work in relation to Descartes. The relationship of Husserl to Descartes is not only one within the history of philosophy: it is the *relationship of advanced bourgeois thought to its beginnings.* Transcendental phenomenology itself represents, in its own content, an endpoint. Its attempt at a new foundation of philosophy as rigorous science presents itself as the end, no longer to be surpassed, of the line of thought that tried to anchor the absolute certainty, necessity, and universal validity of knowledge in the *ego cogito.* Once again the fundamental characteristics of bourgeois theory are at stake, and in the struggle for them resignation and the transition to a new stage are already in evidence. Only in this context does the significance of phenomenology's restitution of the concept of essence become clear.

In his *Formale und transzendentale Logik* ("Formal and Transcendental Logic") Husserl gives an account of his relation to Descartes and to transcendental philosophy. He sees Descartes as the originator of transcendental philosophy and accepts this origin as valid for himself as well, for "all objective knowledge must be founded on the single apodictic givenness . . . of the *ego cogito*."[23] But he calls it a great error that Descartes saw in this ego a "primary, indubitably existing particle of the world" and deduced the rest of the world from it. This "realism" on Descartes' part, according to Husserl, is a naïve prejudice with which phenomenology cannot concur.[24] On the other hand, the Kantian critique of reason "erred" in directing itself toward the constitution of the given spatio-temporal world rather than toward "all possible worlds."[25] Thus, for Husserl, Kant's critical thought remained caught in "mundane" realism. Phenomenology insisted on distinguishing itself from the start from this critical thought: "Phenomenology cannot distance itself from critical thought, because it was never at one with it."[26]

Now, it is precisely this point — where the *ego cogito* is construed as an "indubitably existing particle of the world" and at the same time serves as the only springboard into the world — that links Cartesian philosophy with the progressive tendencies of the bourgeoisie. Only when the ego as something really existing in the world becomes the first certainty in the realm of beings can its reason provide the critical standard of real knowledge and serve as the organon for the ordering of life. And only as long as reason is constitutively directed toward empirically given "material" can its spontaneity be more than mere imagination. Once this connection between rational thought and spatio-temporal reality is severed, the "interest of freedom" disappears completely from philosophy.

But this severance belongs from the start to the program of

the phenomenological reductions. Spatio-temporal facts in their spatio-temporal relevance are excluded from the field of genuine phenomenological study. What remains after the first reduction are the facts of consciousness, a world whose factual quality and richness are "the same" as the "natural" world's — with one very decisive difference: the phenomenological index modifies the meaning of reality in such a way as to make all facts, as facts of intentional consciousness, of equal validity;[27] they are "exemplary" in principle. Thus

> the whole spatio-temporal world, to which man and the human ego ascribe themselves as subordinate individual realities, acquires the meaning of merely intentional being, that is, being that has the merely secondary and relative meaning of being for a consciousness. It is a being posited by consciousness in its experiences, a being which in principle can be intuited and determined only as that which is identical in the motivated manifolds of appearances but which aside from that is nothing.[28]

The full import of this reduction of facts to "exemplars" is revealed in the phenomenological definition of the relation of essence and fact in the prehension[29] of essence (*Wesenserfassung*). In a second reduction, the essential content and essential organization of the facts of consciousness are distinguished from their factual being. Thus all contents of consciousness function equally as "exemplary": the elucidation of essence (*Wesenserklärung*) can take place on the basis of a perception or any other kind of representation — moreover and significantly, "free fantasies acquire a preferential position with respect to perceptions."[30] Essence results as the invariant within the infinitely manifold variations which representational acts undertake with regard to their object. Variation resulting in essence is generated

58

in the freedom of pure fantasy and in the pure consciousness of arbitrariness — of "pure at-all-ness" . . . thereby simultaneously entering a horizon of openly and endlessly manifold free possibilities for ever new variants. This variation is thus fully free, unbound from all a priori facts. It comprises all variants of the openly endless horizon, including the "example" itself, freed of all facticity, as something "arbitrary." . . . In this variation, they are in a continuous, pervasive synthesis of "coinciding opposites." But in this very coincidence appears the *invariant*, that which is necessarily constant in the free and continuously reformed variation, that which is indivisibly the same in that which is other and recurrently other — in short, universal *essence* — to which all "thinkable" modifications of the example remain tied.[31]

This text, which leads deep into the inner mechanism of the phenomenological prehension of essence, also provides the best insight into the changed function of the theory of essence. All the decisive concepts which played a role in the theory of essence since its beginnings reappear here, and all in a characteristically changed form. Freedom has become a mark of pure fantasy, as the free arbitrariness of ideational possibilities of variation. The constant, identical, and necessary is no longer sought as the Being of beings but as what is invariant in the infinite manifold of representational modifications of "exemplars." Possibility is no longer a force straining toward reality; rather, in its open endlessness it belongs to mere imagination.[32]

As the *ego cogito* and the essence which appear to it become the object of phenomenology, there is no longer a critical tension between them and factual existence. Phenomenology is therewith in principle a *descriptive* philosophy: it always aims only at describing what is as it is and as it presents itself, not, for instance, at showing what could and should be. The theoretical radicalness which seemed audible in the call, "To the things themselves!" reveals its quietistic, indeed *positivistic,* character as phenomenology progresses. The "things" become so for phenomenology only after they have been stripped of their actual materially objective character and have entered the "levelling" sphere of transcendental subjectivity for which everything is equi-valent (in-different) as a fact of conscious-ness. In this dimension, speaking of essence no longer means setting reality against its potentiality and what exists against what could be; essence has a purely descriptive and epistemo-logical character. A philosophy that considers "all pre-given beings with their exact evidence" equally "prejudgments"[33] no longer has any basis for distinguishing critically among these beings. Universal freedom from presuppositions here becomes equivalent to universal acknowledgment. Phenome-nology's concept of essence is so far removed from any critical significance that it regards both the essential and the inessen-tial, the object of phantasy as well as that of perception, as "facts." The epistemological antipositivism of this doctrine ill conceals its positivistic orientation.

The abatement of the dynamic movement contained in the concept of essence can also be seen in the few remnants of a position on Husserl's part with regard to knowledge of (spatio-temporal) facticity. The formal epistemological version of the concept of essence lets facticity subsist as a self-contained realm "alongside" the realm of essence. To know it does not involve changing or abolishing any aspect of it, but "only understanding." "Through my phenomenological reflection, the transcendent world . . . is neither abolished, devalued, nor changed, but only understood. . . ."[34] The phenomeno-logical *epoché,* which was intended to be so much more radi-cal than Descartes' methodical doubt, contains a quietistic indifference, which regresses behind Descartes, with regard to the established order. With Husserl, concern with the present has become concern with eternity: the eternity of pure science, whose timeless and absolute truth is supposed to provide the present with security. He considers the "spiritual distress" of our time the "most radical distress of life" and declares:

> We must not sacrifice eternity for the sake of alleviating our distress in the present. We must not bequeath to our descendants an accumulation of distress such that it becomes an ultimately indestructible evil.[35]

Positivistic indifference, however, is only one way in which the altered function of transcendental philosophy is expressed in phenomenology. Phenomenology appeared on the scene with the radical claim of beginning anew. That phenomenology explicitly speaks once more of "essence" in opposition to "fact" and makes essence the object of an independent "intuition" is a significant novelty that cannot be explained exclusively as a development of the transcendental method. The pathos of the evidence of universal, necessary, and objective truths, the demand of arriving at "the things themselves," and the renaissance of metaphysics in the wake of phenomenology belong to a new historical trend. While retaining the transcendental approach philosophy professes to be truly concrete and to take concrete objects as its point of departure. A sign of material "objectivity" and diversity can be seen in the renewed consideration of essence as the object of an independent, originally "giving" intuition. It is significant that phenomenology claims that the verification, "meaning," and truth of cognitive judgments no longer reside on the "side of the subject," of the *ego cogito,* but on the "side of the object." It is the object itself which appears there and whose essence prescribes, as it were, the cognitive acts directed toward it. The phenomenological doctrine of essence binds the transcendental freedom of the *ego cogito* to objectively pregiven essences and essential objects. This is the point where, within phenomenology, the new situation of thought imposes itself: the introduction of material eidetics, in which the entire perspective is changed. The philosophy of the bourgeois era was founded by Descartes as a subjective and idealist one, and this resulted from an inner necessity. Every attempt to ground philosophy in objectivity, in the sphere of material reality, without attacking the real presuppositions of its conceptual character, i.e. without integrating into the theory a practice aimed at transformation, necessarily surrenders its rationally critical character and becomes heteronomous. This fate befell the material doctrine of essence; it led, just as with positivism, to the subjection of theory to the "given" powers and hierarchies. With regard to knowledge, the basic meaning of the intuition of essence is that it "lets itself be given" its object, that it passively accepts it and binds itself to it as "something absolutely given."[36] That which gives itself in evident "congruent unity" (*Deckungseinheit*) is "at the same time absolute Being, and the object that is now the object of such Being, such pure essence, is to an ideal degree adequately given."[37] The intuition of essence is (despite the "freedom" of ideational variations) receptive. At the apex of philosophy, the receptivity of the intuition of essence replaces the spontaneity of the comprehending understanding that is inseparable from the idea of critical reason.

The sacrifice of the idea of critical reason paved the way to resignation for the doctrine of essence, to its gradual transition to a new ideology. Bourgeois philosophy lost the Archimedian point where it had anchored the freedom of the knowing individual, and without it, it has no basis from which the weapon of critique can be employed against the claims of specific facts and hierarchies to be "essential." The material doctrine of essence began with the elaboration of a new ethics, which was outlined in opposition to Kant's ethics. The law-like character of ethical valuation no longer resides in the obedience of the autonomous individual to a freely self-given, absolutely obligatory, "norm," but follows, to the contrary, "from the effectiveness of personally structured prototypes and antitypes."[38]

> I assert, in other words, that value systems, and especially the systems of norms and laws that depend on them and which man obeys or disobeys, are in the last analysis always to be reduced to *personal prototypes,* to value patterns in the form of a person. We do not choose them, for they possess us and attract us before we can choose.[39]

Material value-ethics (*Wertethik*) becomes the ethics of personal prototypes, where the norms of action are no longer given by individual or universal reason, but are instead *received;* here, too, the autonomy of freedom is replaced by receptive heteronomy. This is part of the annunciation of the ideology of the monopoly-capitalist period, in which domination by the most powerful economic groups is effected by means of the delegation of power to prototypical leader personalities and in which the interests of these groups are concealed by means of the image of an essentially personal order of values (leadership and following, status order, racial elite, and so forth). The intuition of essence helps to set up "essential" hierarchies in which the material and vital values of human life occupy the lowest rank, while the types of the saint, the genius, and the hero take first place. Renunciation, sacrifice, and humility are considered "essential" as the central values of the individual, while "blood and soil" are supposed to constitute the "essence" of the nation (*Volkstum*). We shall not delineate here the further development of these

theories. It was our intention only to indicate their conceptual links to the material doctrine of essence.[40]

The function of the intuition of essence in material eidetics
leads to the abdication of the critical freedom of reason, to the
cancellation of its autonomy. From Descartes on, the idea of
the autonomy of reason was linked to the progressive tendencies of the bourgeoisie. Its restriction to abstract cognitive
reason characterized the retreat of these tendencies. In the
epoch of monopoly capitalism, reason is replaced by the ac-
quiescent acknowledgment of "essential" givens, in whose
verification reason initially plays only a derivative role, and
subsequently none at all.

It is material eidetics against which the positivist attack on
the concept of essence was directed. The *positivist opposition*
to the "metaphysics" of the doctrine of essence conceived itself primarily as an epistemological critique: our experience
of reality (reality by no means being identified with the immediately given) does not at all justify the assumption of two
ontologically different "worlds," an assumption presupposed
by the opposition of thing and appearance, essence and fact.

> There is no fact that compels or even justifies us in mak-
> ing such a contrast between two irreducible realities. . . .
> We arrive at a satisfactory picture of the world only when
> we accord *everything* real, the contents of consciousness as
> well as all Being outside of consciousness, the same sort and
> the same degree of reality, without any distinction. All things
> are in the same sense self-subsistent, yet all are in the same
> sense interdependent.[41]

With this contention, positivism takes a decisive step beyond
epistemological empiricism. For with its concept of fact, the
facticity of an object of knowledge establishes not only its
"reality" but simultaneously its cognitive equi-valence to

every other reality. With respect to knowledge, all facts are as such equi-valent. The world of facts is, so to speak, one-dimensional. The real is "absolutely (*schlechthin*) real" and as such precludes any metaphysical or critical transcendence toward essence.

> There is only *one* reality, which is always *essence* and cannot be decomposed into essence and appearance. There are, to be sure, many sorts of real objects, perhaps even infinitely many, but there is only one sort of reality, and all of them partake of it equally.[42]

Here the thesis of the essentiality of the facts is associated with absolute acknowledgment of reality, "which is always essence." Cognition, freed from the tension between facts and essence, becomes recognition. The very theory that intended to eliminate from science the concept of essence makes the same sacrifice of critical reason performed by phenomenological eidetics in liberating essence from all opposition to spatio-temporal facts and arriving at an equi-valence of all facts for transcendental consciousness. When all facts are indiscriminately held to be essential, and when each fact is indiscriminately held to be an essence, philosophy's attitude toward reality is fundamentally identical. To be sure, positivism comprehended the critical and moral motivation of the theory of essence: "One kind of Being is considered higher, more genuine, more noble, and more important than the other, i.e. an evaluative conception has been introduced."[43] But for it this is only a confusion of the "evaluative viewpoint with the logical viewpoint," the *proton pseudos* or false premise of a scientific theory. Positivism adheres to the bourgeois ideal of presuppositionless, pure theory, in which the absence of "ethical neutrality" or the commitment of taking a position signifies delinquency in rigor. Compared with the ideology which material eidetics became, in which the language of the essential priority of specific values concealed their establishment by regressive social interests, positivism retains a certain critical tendency. But the world of "absolutely real" facts is dominated by powers concerned with the preservation of this form of reality, in the interest of small and powerful economic groups, against the already real possibility of another form of reality; and the tension between essence and appearance determines the historical image of reality in the shape of universal social contradiction. Under these conditions a theory for which reality is "always essence" can only be one of resignation. As with phenomenological eidetics, the positivist annulment of the opposition of essence and fact is not a new beginning, but an end.

*   *   *

The theme of the philosophical theories of the last decades has been the reconsideration of bourgeois thought's traditional preoccupation with absolutely certain, unconditioned, universally valid knowledge. Concern for the self-certain critical freedom of the individual was transformed into this epistemological ideal. The various forms of transcendental reduction reflect the stages of the historical development of this thought up to its adaptation to the anti-individualistic and antirationalistic ideology of the present. From it both the "interest of freedom" and interest in the true happiness of the individual have disappeared. The social groups which during their rise to power developed and supported these interests oppose them under present forms of domination. The critical impulses in the theory of essence, abandoned by eidetics as well as positivism, have been incorporated into materialist theory. Here, however, the concept of essence takes on a new form. This theory conceived concern with the essence of man

66

as the task of a rational organization of society, to be achieved through practice that alters its present form. Materialist theory thus transcends the given state of fact and moves toward a different potentiality, proceeding from immediate appearance to the essence that appears in it. But here appearance and essence become members of a real antithesis arising from the particular historical structure of the social process of life. The essence of man and of things appears within that structure; what men and things could genuinely be appears in "bad," "perverted" form. At the same time, however, appears the possibility of negating this perversion and realizing in history that which could be. This antagonistic character of the historical process as it is today turns the opposition of essence and appearance into a dialectical relationship and this relationship into an object of the *dialectic*. Materialist theory takes up the concept of essence where philosophy last treated it as a dialectical concept — in Hegel's *Logic*.

For Hegel appearance and essence are two modes of being which stand in reciprocal relation to one another, so that the existence of appearance presupposes the suppression of merely self-subsistent essence. Essence is essence only through appearing, that is, through emerging from its mere self-subsistence: "Essence must appear." And appearance, as the appearance of what is in itself, becomes "what the thing in itself is, or its truth."[44] "By this token essence is neither in back of nor beyond appearance; rather, existence is appearance because it is essence that exists."[45] Hegel conceives of essence as a process in which "mediated being" is posited through the overcoming of unmediated being; essence has a *history*. And the critical theme of the theory of essence is reactivated in the meaning of this history, in this movement from unmediated "Being" through "essence" to mediated "existence." "When, further, it is said that all things have an essence, what is being ex-

67

pressed is that they are not in reality what they show themselves to be," "that their immediate existence does not correspond to what they are in themselves."[46] The movement of essence has the task of doing away with this bad immediacy and positing the sphere of beings (*das Seiende*) as that which it is in itself: "Now the process of reality is itself of this sort. Reality is not simply something which *is* immediately, but rather, as essential Being, it is the overcoming of its own immediacy and therefore mediates itself with itself."[47]

Essence is conceived as something which "has become," as a "result" that itself must reappear as a result and that enters into relation with the dynamic categories of the inessential, illusion, and appearance. In this way, it is conceived as part of a process which takes place between unmediated Being, its overcoming and preservation in essence (as its being-in-itself) and the realization of this essence. But with Hegel the process remains ontological; it is the Being of beings which undergoes it and is its subject. It thereby proves itself to be Logos, "reason." The movement through which unmediated Being is "recollected"[48] to essence as to its being-in-itself, "reflection," in which immediacy is overcome and posited again as mediated existence, is a determination of Being itself, of Being as essence. "Essence as such is one with its reflection and not distinguished from the latter's own movement."[49] It is not man who recollects essence, who grasps the world of beings which confronts him, overcomes its bad immediacy and posits it anew through the knowledge of essence; rather, for Hegel all this occurs within rational Being itself. Man participates in this process only as the subject of cognition, insofar as he himself is rational Being.

Hegel's conception of essence already contains all the elements of a dynamic historical theory of essence, but in a dimension where they cannot be effective. Essence is for

Hegel a movement, but a movement in which there is no longer any actual change, a movement which takes place within itself. "Essence is the absolute unity of being-in-itself and being-for-itself; the process of its determination thus remains within this unity and is neither a becoming nor a transition to something else"; it is "the movement of becoming and of transition which remains within itself."[50] Hegel transposes the tension between what could be and what exists, between being-in-itself (essence) and appearance, into the very structure of Being; as such it is always prior to all states of fact. Hegel's theory of essence remains transcendental.

*   *   *

When the materialist dialectic as social theory confronts the opposition of essence and appearance, the concern for man which governs it gives the critical motif in the theory of essence a new sharpness. The tension between potentiality and actuality, between what men and things could be and what they are in fact, is one of the dynamic focal points of this theory of society. It sees therein not a transcendental structure of Being and an immutable ontological difference but a historical relationship which can be transformed in this life by real men; the incongruity of potentiality and actuality incites knowledge to become part of the practice of transformation. That appearance does not immediately coincide with essence, that self-subsistent potentialities are not realized, that the particular stands in conflict with the general, that chance on the one hand and blind necessity on the other rule the world — these conditions represent tasks set for men's rational practice. For the theory associated with this practice, the statement that all science would be superfluous when "the form of appearance and the essence of things immediately coincided"[51] has a new meaning. What is the significance here of

69

the divergence of essence and appearance, and of what sort is the process of transcendence from appearance to essence?

To the interest governing the materialist dialectic, its object, the totality of the process of social evolution, appears as an inherently multidimensional, organized structure. It is by no means the case that all of its data are equally relevant or "factual." Some phenomena lie close to the surface, others form part of the central mechanism. From this distinction results a first and still completely formal concretion of essence as what is essential: in a very general sense, essence is the totality of the social process as it is organized in a particular historical epoch. In relation to this process every individual factor, considered as an isolated unit, is "inessential," insofar as its "essence," i.e. the concept of the real content of an appearance, can be grasped only in the light of its relation to the totality of the process. Now the latter is structured in a second way; even though they interact, the various levels of social reality nevertheless are grounded in one fundamental level. The manner in which this occurs determines the whole of life. In the current historical period, the economy as the fundamental level has become "essential" in such a way that all other levels have become its "manifestations" (*Erscheinungsform*).

In materialist theory the difference between appearance (manifestation) and essence takes on a third significance, one which permits a further concretion of its object. Basic to the present form of social organization, the antagonisms of the capitalist production process, is the fact that the central phenomena connected with this process do not immediately appear to men as what they are "in reality," but in masked, "perverted" form. In the cases of work relations, the divisions of the social and political hierarchy, the institutions of justice, education, and science, the form in which they appear conceals their origin and their true function in the total social process. To the extent that individuals and groups base their actions and thoughts on immediate appearances, the latter are, of course, not "mere" appearances but themselves factors essential to the functioning of the process and to the maintenance of its organization. Nevertheless, in the course of the process a stage is reached where it is possible to comprehend the essence *in* the manifestation and to understand that the difference between essence and appearance is a historical constellation of social relationships. The nature of this difference and the necessarily dichotomous character it gives to materialist theory will be discussed below.

The three meanings which we have indicated here of the difference between essence and appearance in materialist theory permit an initial understanding of those characteristics fundamental to the dialectical concept of essence. The transcendence leading from facts to essence is historical. Through it, given facts are understood as appearances whose essence can be comprehended only in the context of particular historical tendencies aiming at a different form of reality. The theory's historical interest enters constitutively into its conceptual scheme and makes the transcendence of "facts" toward their essence critical and polemical. Measured against their real potentialities, the facts reveal themselves to be the "bad" manifestations of a content which must be realized by doing away with these manifestations in opposition to the interests and powers connected with them. Thus, even in the first form in which we encounter it, the dialectical concept of essence is distinguishable from phenomenology's conception of neutral essences as well as from positivism's neutral leveling of essence. In place of a static epistemological relationship of essence to fact emerges a critical and dynamic relationship of essence to appearance as parts of a historical process.

Connecting at its roots the problem of essence to social practice restructures the concept of essence in its relation to all other concepts by orienting it toward the essence of *man*. Concern with man moves to the center of theory; man must be freed from real need and real misery to achieve the liberation of becoming himself. When the essence of man becomes the object of inquiry in this way, the relation of essence and appearance is posited as a historical disproportion (*Miss-Verhältnis*). At the stage of development that man has presently reached, real potentialities for the fulfillment of human life are at hand in all areas, potentialities which are not realized in the present social structure. Here the concept of what could be, of inherent possibilities, acquires a precise meaning. What man can be in a given historical situation is determinable with regard to the following factors: the measure of control of natural and social productive forces, the level of the organization of labor, the development of needs in relation to possibilities for their fulfillment (especially the relation of what is necessary for the reproduction of life to the "free" needs for gratification and happiness, for the "good and the beautiful"), the availability, as material to be appropriated, of a wealth of cultural values in all areas of life. This definition of essence already implies the whole theory of history that deduces the totality of the conditions of life from the mode of social organization and that at the same time provides the methodological and conceptual tools making possible knowledge of the historical tendencies effective at a particular time. On the basis of this theory the essence of man is understood in connection with those tendencies which have as their goal a new form of social life as the "Idea" of that which practice must realize. Considered this way, the image of man represents not only what can already be made of man today, what "in itself" can already be today, but also — and this is the polemical demand theory raises by means of this concept of essence — the real fulfillment of everything that man desires to be when he understands himself in terms of his potentialities.

In making this demand of the essence of man, theory points the way from the bad current state of humanity to a mankind that disposes of the goods available to it in such a way that they are distributed in accordance with the true needs of the community. Here men would themselves take on the planning and shaping of the social process of life and not leave it to the arbitrariness of competition and the blind necessity of reified economic relations. The power of the conditions of labor over life, along with the separation of the immediate producers from the means of labor, would be abolished. Instead of life being placed in the service of labor, labor would become a means of life. Instead of degrading cultural values to the rank of privilege and object of "leisure," men would really make them part of the common existence. These determinations of essence are distinguished from utopia in that theory can demonstrate the concrete roads to their realization and can adduce as evidence those attempts at realization which are already under way. Of course these insights cannot be arrived at through a contemplative attitude; in order to justify them knowledge can have recourse neither to evidence afforded by mere perception nor to a universal system of values in which they are anchored. The truth of this model of essence is preserved better in human misery and suffering and the struggle to overcome them than in the forms and concepts of pure thought. This truth is "indeterminate" and remains necessarily so as long as it is measured against the idea of unconditionally certain knowledge. For it is fulfilled only through historical action, and its concretion can thus result only *post festum*.

73

When orientation toward historical practice replaces orientation toward the absolute certainty and universal validity of knowledge that prevailed in the traditional doctrine of essence, then the concept of essence ceases to be one of pure theory. Consequently it can no longer be fulfilled in pure thought and pure intuition. This does not mean that it gives up its claim to truth or that it contents itself with a "truth" valid only for particular individuals and groups.[52] But its verification occurs only within the total structure of the theory in which it has its place and where it is corroborated by all the other concepts. One criterion for the objective validity of dialectical theory's separation of essence and appearance is the suitability of its concept for service as the organizing principle in the explanation of a given group of appearances (e.g. constellations of political power among states of a specific era, their alliances, and conflicts). If the historical structure (e.g. "imperialism") postulated as "essential" for the explanation of such a grouping makes it possible to comprehend causally the situation both in its individual phases as well as in terms of the tendencies effective within it, then it is really the essential in that manifold of appearances. This determination of essence is true; it has held good within the theory. Yet the theory of which it is a part is itself at the same time a factor in the historical struggles that it aims to comprehend: only in them can the essential theoretical truths be ultimately verified.[53] And from this very historicity of dialectical concepts grows a new kind of "universal validity" and objectivity.

The materialist concept of essence is a historical concept. Essence is conceivable only as the essence of a particular "appearance," whose factual form is viewed with regard to what it is in itself and what it could be (but is not in fact). This relation, however, originates in history and changes in history. To every attempt to "historicize" the concept of essence, the

74

traditional doctrine of essence has objected that viewing the factually given appearance with regard to what it is in itself presupposes "having" this being-in-itself. In other words, according to this view, "measuring" the appearance against its essence, indeed, merely referring to a being as an "appearance" that does not immediately coincide with what it is in itself, presupposes prior acquaintance with the essence through intuition. Since Plato's theory of Ideas, this has been a principal motive for establishing the concept of essence as an a priori one. In truth, an a priori element is at work here, but one confirming the historicity of the concept of essence. It leads back into history rather than out of it. The immemorially acquired image of essence was formed in mankind's historical experience, which is preserved in the present form of reality so that it can be "remembered" and "refined" to the status of essence. All historical struggles for a better organization of the impoverished conditions of existence, as well as all of suffering mankind's religious and ethical ideal conceptions of a more just order of things, are preserved in the dialectical concept of the essence of man, where they have become elements of the historical practice linked to dialectical theory. There can also be experience of potentialities that have never been realized. They can be derived from reality as forces and tendencies. The a priori nature of the concept of essence has by no means always been comprehended transcendentally and suprahistorically. And the traces of the past within the concept of essence can be understood as an allusion to a historical condition,[54] as in Aristotle's notion of essence as "that which Being was" and Hegel's notion of the "recollection" of Being to essence.[55] Hegel speaks of essence as of "timelessly past" Being. Past, because it is an image of being-in-itself that no longer corresponds to immediate existence; timeless, because recollection has preserved it and kept it from disappearing

75

into the past. In idealist philosophy the timeless past dominates the concept of essence. But when theory associates itself with the progressive forces of history, the recollection of what can authentically be becomes a power that shapes the future. The demonstration and preservation of essence become the motive idea of practice aimed at transformation.

Here the thorough difference of the materialist concept of essence from that of idealist philosophy becomes clear for the first time. Just as the content of the materialist notion is historical and oriented toward practice, the way in which it is arrived at is also determined by historical and practical presuppositions. It is not an object of the contemplative receptivity of perception, nor is it a synthesis performed by the spontaneity of pure understanding. Rather, it is determined within the framework set by the historical goals with which materialist theory is linked. Not only do the interests resulting from these goals play a role in establishing what is essential, they enter into the content of the concept of essence. And yet the theory's particular interests are fulfilled in a real "universality," that of the general interest, whose material objectivity (in contrast to the formal "universal validity" of the idealist concept of essence) allows essence to validate itself as essence. Even positivism has acknowledged that theory is determined by interests: "Trends in scientific research are . . . never socially neutral, even though they are not always at the center of social conflict"; the sort of "propositional systems" set up depends on the "social situation" of "the group that promotes or tolerates this research."[56] But positivism concludes from this only that systems of hypotheses may be set up in more than one way and that all types can satisfy the requirements of internal consistency and accordance with "protocol sentences." It either holds the theories' different interests (like the "facts") to be indifferent with respect to knowledge

76

or, to compensate for the indeterminacy factor, incorporates them into the propositional system as "personal" evaluations made by the scientist. In contrast to all other theories, materialist theory, precisely by virtue of its guiding interest, advances a claim to truth for which value-free positivism affords absolutely no basis. Of the many social interests, it represents one and only one, which claims verifiability as "general" and "objective." Its claim differs completely from those put forth by all other philosophical theories, for it rejects the adequacy of a priori logical or epistemological validation. To be sure, it can be negatively delimited from all antirationalistic theories in that all its propositions must justify themselves before men's critical reason, and the "interest of freedom," originally the foundation of the philosophy of reason, is thus preserved in materialist theory. The source of materialist theory's substantial difference is that its particular interests aim at an organization of life in which the individual's fate depends no longer on chance and the blind necessity of uncontrolled economic relationships but rather on planned shaping of social potentialities. In such a society particular interests can be integrated into a universality which is thus concrete as a community and no longer abstract as a "universal." For the material conditions of life, previously unmastered, can now be incorporated into a general plan. They can be organized through and by individuals' social freedom; that is, they can be linked to the "essence" of the individual. At the end of the process, when former social antagonisms have been overcome in such a community, the "subjectivity" of materialist theory becomes objectivity — in the form of an existence where the interests of individuals are truly preserved in the community.

But this material universality of theory presupposes a complete change in its subject, which is no longer the isolated, abstract individual at the basis of idealist philosophy. Con-

77

sciousness no longer stands at the beginning of thought as the *fundamentum inconcussum* of truth, and it no longer stands at the end as the bearer of the freedom of pure will and pure knowledge. Theory has moved to another subject; its concepts are generated by the consciousness of specific groups and individuals who are part of the fight for a more rational organization of society.

Only when it has changed its historical standpoint in this way can theory meet the desideratum for which philosophy has struggled in vain in the last few decades. Dilthey's lifework can be regarded as an attempt to replace the abstract epistemological subject, who has been the starting point for philosophy since Descartes and in whose veins runs "not real blood but the diluted lymph of reason as mere mental activity," with concrete historical man in his "real life process."[57] Since Dilthey, the various trends of *Lebensphilosophie* (philosophy of life) and existentialism have concerned themselves with the concrete "historicity" of theory; phenomenology, too, as was mentioned above, was conceived as the philosophy of concrete material objectivity (*Sachlichkeit*). All such efforts had to fail, because they were linked (at first unconsciously, later consciously) to the very interests and aims whose theory they opposed. They did not attack the presupposition of bourgeois philosophy's abstractness: the actual unfreedom and powerlessness of the individual in an anarchic production process. Consequently, the place of abstract reason was taken by an equally abstract "historicity," which amounted at best to a relativism addressed indifferently to all social groups and structures.

Materialist theory moves beyond historical relativism in linking itself with those social forces which the historical situation reveals to be progressive and truly "universal." It under-

78

stands all theory as an element of the social process of life, borne by particular historical interests. Hitherto these interests have governed theory primarily "behind its back," unconsciously. As long as the production process operates unconsciously and by chance, so to speak, it reproduces life only in a bad form. It changes its content entirely when the reproduction of life is qualitatively (as well as quantitatively) improved by becoming a task for conscious planning. Similarly, the conceptual content of theory changes when its interest is consciously directed toward this task, for it then represents in its true form what formerly functioned as an unconscious motivation. The relationship of the historical concept of essence to traditional general concepts of essence is of this type. Behind the traditional concepts, too, lie concrete historical aims, but in the course of tradition they were watered down to general formal structural concepts and lost their dynamism. Once understood again as historical concepts, the original critical tension between them and reality is restored. What is true in them is preserved in the materialist notion of essence and expressed in accordance with the changed historical situation. Aristotle's doctrine of the essence of man is not comprehensible simply through his general "definition" of man as ζῷον λόγον ἔχον; ζῷον πολιτικόν (zoon logon echon; zoon politikon), for it presupposes his metaphysics as well as his ethics, politics, rhetoric, and psychology, from which come the notions logos, politikon, zoon. It presupposes no less his postulation of domination and servitude as modes of Being and his view of the role of material labor in the totality of the areas of life. In translating logos as ratio and defining man as "rational" late antiquity and the Middle Ages integrated man's being into Christian theology's worldview. The meaning of the Aristotelian definition was thereby completely transformed,

79

even though the definitions are literally the same. In a later period, the appeal to reason as that which is essential in man served to proclaim the freedom of the autonomous individual in bourgeois society. But at the same time, when man is conceived to be free only as a rational being, whole dimensions of existence become "inessential," of no bearing on man's essence. For Kant, "being master or servant" is one of the "inessential (*ausserwesentlich*) characteristics" of man,[58] designating only an accidental and "external relation of man." The connection, essential to Aristotle, between being master or servant and the particular mode of possessing *logos*,[59] reason, is completely dissolved. That relationships which were originally held to be essential should become inessential indicates a total change in the content of the concept of essence, even though reason is maintained as a dimension of the concept. That domination and servitude now appear contingent and inessential ensues from the form of human social organization which the new concept of essence reflects. With respect to the essence of man, the contingency of the master-servant relationship results from the blind necessity which the power of reified conditions of labor over the producers appears to be. Contingency is recognized as such, but its cause is not yet understood. Since "external relations" are not organized in accordance with man's needs and potentialities, with his "essence," they remain as a contingency outside the philosophical determination of essence as well.

This determination of the essence of man, which does not include "external relations" such as domination and servitude or the place of the individual in the material process of production in man's "essential characteristics," is true insofar as it comprehends man as he actually exists in the bourgeois epoch. Beyond that, it has no validity. When the associated individuals themselves have taken over the direction of the life process and have made the totality of social relations the work of their reason and their freedom, what man is in himself will be related to his existence in a new way. The formerly contingent and "inessential" will now represent the fulfillment of the most authentic potentialities. Man will then have to be "defined" not as a free rational being in opposition to contingent conditions of life but as the free and rational creator of his conditions of life, as the creator of a better and happier life.

So far we have attempted to show the significance of the problem of essence for materialist theory chiefly in terms of the concept of the essence of man. This has been by no means an arbitrary example. According to the theory's governing concern for real, concretely existing men, the questions raised by this concept are really essential to knowledge, and the theory must be linked to them at every point: not in the abstract form in which they have been presented here but as objective circumstances of a given state of the whole society, which in each case is concretized and transformed in historical practice. In this context, the way some other concepts of the theory of essence develop and take on new meaning will be outlined in what follows.

The essence that the theory attempts to conceptualize appeared first in the form of man's *potentiality* within a particular historical situation, in conflict with his immediate existence. The connection of the concept of essence with that of potentiality is as old as the problem of essence itself; it received its first explicit philosophical interpretation in Aristotle's notion of δύναμις (*dynamis*). In the postmedieval philosophical tradition the "potential" nature of essence increasingly lost its connection with the notions of force, striving, and tendency and became a matter of (formal and transcendental) logic. Hegel reinstated the notion of "real possibility" (potentiality) in his theory of essence:

> Formal possibility is reflection-into-itself (*Reflexion-in-sich*) only as abstract identity, the fact that something is not self-contradictory. But to the extent that one goes into the attributes, the circumstances, and the conditions of a thing in order to know its possibility, one is no longer restricting oneself to formal possibility but considering its real possibility. This real possibility is itself immediate existence.[60]

Real possibility exists. Therefore it can be known as such by theory, and as known it can be taken up by the practice for which theory is the guide and be transformed into reality. For Hegel the existence of a thing's real possibility consists in the "existing manifold of circumstances which relate to it."[61] The idealist dialectic considers this manifold "indifferent"; in the materialist dialectic, in keeping with the latter's historical interests, it is accentuated and operates as a tendency in men's actions and in the course of things. The basis for its determination has already been indicated. Reality, where man's essence is determined, is the totality of the relations of production. It is no mere "existing manifold of circumstances," but rather a structure whose organization can be analyzed, and within which it is possible to distinguish between form and content, essence and appearance, the concealed and the obvious. Its content is the maintenance and reproduction of society as a whole — the actual process of production and reproduction, based on a given level of the productive forces and of technology. Its form is the turnover of the production process as the realization of capital. Form and content can be separated, for the former is only a particular historical pattern in which the latter is realized; there are tendencies toward the abolition of the form at work in the content. When considered with regard to them, distinguished from its given form, and seen with a view to a different form, in which it would no longer function as the realization of capital, the content enters the mode of real possibility. In doing so it loses none of its reality, while preserving all its wealth, the full range of the productive forces it has acquired, and the power and amplitude of the work techniques it has developed. All this is, in fact, a condition for the transition to the new form. The content is reality in a "bad" form; it is possibility in that its emancipation from this form and its realization in a new form are still to be accomplished through men's social practice — but, given the conditions at hand, this transformation *can* be accomplished. This is what makes the possibility real.

Thus the dialectical relationship between reality and possibility is fulfilled: "When real possibility overcomes itself, something double is overcome, for it is itself double in being both reality and possibility."[62] Reality is overcome by being comprehended as the mere possibility of another reality; possibility is overcome by being realized (in this different reality). The relationships of possibility and reality and of form and content typify a trait of all the ways in which the opposition of essence and appearance appears in the materialist dialectic: both members of the relationship are real in the emphatic sense. The form, for instance, is no less real than the content; it does not exist only "subjectively" or "ideally." All such distinctions take place and change within the framework of the totality of society. This framework itself is never transcended, not even in concepts such as essence and potentiality. But its historical appearance is always shaped by particular interests and forces and is transcended under the direction of new ones. Essence and appearance belong to different spheres of interests and forces, as do potentiality and actuality, content and form. Nevertheless, the distinctions are not on that account indifferent or arbitrary; they apply not only to those who formulate them but also to their opponents. For these distinctions conceive the social totality from the standpoint of a set of goals toward which the particular goals of individuals can be transcended by being preserved in the real universality of a community.

The conceptual scheme of materialist theory in its present form exhibits a dialectical dichotomy grounded in the structure of its object. It derives from the antagonistic character of the social life process as the identity of the processes of production on the one hand and the realization of capital on the other. From this basis the antagonism permeates all areas of life. It brings about the differentiation of true and false consciousness (the former represented by correct theory, which transcends the form of the production process in the direction of its content, the latter by consciousness that remains on this side of such transcendence and considers the historical form of the production process to be eternally valid). Correspondingly, there are two different modes in which phenomena appear to and for consciousness. The concealment and distortion of decisive social matters in the consciousness of the subjects of the production process are caused by the independence from the subject attained by the conditions and relations of work, a process that necessarily follows from the capitalist form of production. This is why it is necessary to distinguish between essence and appearance in all their various forms. To the consciousness of men dominated by reified social relations, the latter appear in a distorted form which does not correspond to their true content — their origin and their actual function in this process. But they are not by that token in any way "unreal." It is precisely in their distorted form and as motives and "foci" in the calculating consciousness of those groups who control the process of production that they are very real factors which at first confront the immediate producers, degraded to mere objects, as independent, blindly necessary powers. Theory, which aims at overcoming this distortion, has the task of moving beyond appearance to essence and explicating its content as it appears to true consciousness.

At this level the tension between essence and appearance, between authentic potentiality and immediate existence, is reflected anew in the concrete notions with which theory attempts to grasp the social process of life in its antagonistic character. These concepts belong to two levels; some deal with phenomena in their reified form, as they appear immediately, and others aim at their real content, as it presents itself to theory once its phenomenal form has been transcended. Thus Marxian economics works with two different sets of concepts, corresponding to these levels. One set describes the economic process in its immediate appearance as production and reproduction, that is, it abstracts from its character as a process of capital realization. To this group belong concepts such as entrepreneurial profit and wages, employer and employee. The relations they designate are "real," even though they are only the forms in which things appear; they determine the thought and action of men insofar as they are the subjects and objects of the production process. The second set comprehends the same process in its antagonistic unity of production process and process of capital realization and relates every individual factor to this totality. The relations represented in the first set by such concepts as wages and entrepreneur, are here grasped by means of categories in which the class character of this method of production is expressed (for instance, surplus value). Both groups of concepts are equally necessary to the understanding of the antagonistic reality; nevertheless, they are not on the same level. In terms of dialectical theory, the second group of concepts, which has been derived from the totality of the social dynamic, is intended to grasp the essence and the true content of the manifestations which the first group describes as they appear.

The dialectical concepts transcend the given social reality in the direction of another historical structure which is present as a tendency in the given reality. The positive concept of essence, culminating in the concept of the essence of man, which sustains all critical and polemical distinctions between essence and appearance as their guiding principle and model, is rooted in this potential structure. In terms of the positive concept of essence, all categories that describe the given form of existence as historically mutable become "ironic": they contain their own negation. In economic theory this irony finds its expression in the relationship of the two sets of concepts. If, for instance, it is said that concepts such as wages, the value of labor, and entrepreneurial profit are only categories of manifestations behind which are hidden the "essential relations" of the second set of concepts, it is also true that these essential relations represent the truth of the manifestations only insofar as the concepts which comprehend them already contain their own negation and transcendence — the image of a social organization without surplus value. All materialist concepts contain an accusation and an imperative.

When the imperative has been fulfilled, when practice has created men's new social organization, the new essence of man appears in reality. Then the *current* historical form of the antithesis of essence and appearance, which expresses primarily the externality, lack of planning, and blind necessity of the present material conditions of life in the face of the individuals' true needs and potentialities, will have disappeared. But this does not mean that all grounds for the distinction between essence and appearance, potentiality and immediate

86

existence would cease. Nature remains a realm of necessity; the overcoming of need (*Not*), and the satisfaction of human wants will remain a struggle — a struggle, to be sure, which it will only then be possible to conduct in a manner worthy of man and without historically obsolete forms of social conflict. Into it will go the theoretical energy which has hitherto spent itself in the concern with absolutely certain and universally valid knowledge. The characteristics of essence no longer need to be stabilized in timeless eternal forms. The truth according to which the particular interests are preserved in the universal, the resulting objective "validity" of the universal, and the transparent rationality of the life process, will all have to prove themselves in the practice of the associated individuals and no longer in an absolute consciousness divorced from practice.

Originally published in German in Zeitschrift für Sozialforschung, *vol. V (1936).*

THE doctrine that all human knowledge is oriented toward practice belonged to the nucleus of ancient philosophy. It was Aristotle's view that the truths arrived at through knowledge should direct practice in daily life as in the arts and sciences. In their struggle for existence, men need the effort of knowledge, the search for truth, because what is good, beneficial, and right for them is not immediately evident. Artisan and merchant, captain and physician, general and statesman — each must have correct knowledge in his field in order to be capable of acting as the changing situation demands.

While Aristotle maintained the practical character of every instance of knowledge, he made a significant distinction between forms of knowledge. He ordered them, as it were, in a hierarchy of value whose nadir is functional acquaintance with the necessities of everyday life and whose zenith is philosophical knowledge. The latter has no purpose outside itself. Rather, it occurs only for its own sake and to afford men felicity. Within this hierarchy there is a fundamental break between the necessary and useful on the one hand and the "beautiful" on the other. "The whole of life is further divided into two parts, business and leisure, war and peace, and

88

of actions some aim at what is necessary and useful, and some at what is beautiful [τὰ καλά]."[2] Since this division is not itself questioned, and since, together with other regions of the "beautiful," "pure" theory congeals into an independent activity alongside and above other activities, philosophy's original demand disintegrates: the demand that practice be guided by known truths. Separating the useful and necessary from the beautiful and from enjoyment initiated a development that abandons the field to the materialism of bourgeois practice on the one hand and to the appeasement of happiness and the mind within the preserve of "culture" on the other.

One theme continually recurs in the reasons given for the relegation of the highest form of knowledge and of pleasure to pure, purposeless theory: the world of necessity, of everyday provision for life, is inconstant, insecure, unfree — not merely in fact, but in essence. Disposal over material goods is never entirely the work of human industry and wisdom, for it is subject to the rule of contingency. The individual who places his highest goal, happiness, in these goods makes himself the slave of men and things. He surrenders his freedom. Wealth and well-being do not come or persist due to his autonomous decision but rather through the changeable fortune of opaque circumstances. Man thus subjects his existence to a purpose situated outside him. Of itself, such an external purpose can vitiate and enslave men only if the material conditions of life are poorly ordered, that is, if their reproduction is regulated through the anarchy of opposing social interests. In this order the preservation of the common existence is incompatible with individual happiness and freedom. Insofar as philosophy is concerned with man's happiness — and the theory of classical antiquity held it to be the highest good — it cannot find it in the established material organization of life. That is why it must transcend this order's facticity.

89

Along with metaphysics, epistemology, and ethics, this transcendence also affects psychology. Like the extrapsychic[3] world, the human soul is divided into a lower and a higher region. The history of the soul transpires between the poles of sensuality[4] and reason. The devaluation of sensuality results from the same motives as that of the material world: because sensuality is a realm of anarchy, of inconstancy, and of unfreedom. Sensual pleasure is not in itself bad. It is bad because, like man's lower activities, it is fulfilled in a bad order. The "lower parts of the soul" drive man to covet gain and possessions, purchase and sale. He is led to "admire and value nothing but wealth and its possessors."[5] Accordingly the "appetitive" part of the soul, which is oriented toward sensual pleasure, is also termed by Plato the "money-loving" part, "because money is the principal means of satisfying desires of this kind."[6]

All the ontological classifications of ancient idealism express the badness of a social reality in which knowledge of the truth about human existence is no longer incorporated into practice. The world of the true, the good, and the beautiful is in fact an "ideal" world insofar as it lies beyond the existing conditions of life, beyond a form of existence in which the majority of men either work as slaves or spend their life in commerce, with only a small group having the opportunity of being concerned with anything more than the provision and preservation of the necessary. When the reproduction of material life takes place under the rule of the commodity form and continually renews the poverty of class society, then the good, beautiful, and true are transcendent to this life. And if everything requisite to preserving and securing material life is produced in this form, then whatever lies beyond it is certainly "superfluous." What is of authentic import to man, the highest truths, the highest goods, and the highest joys, is separated in significance from the necessary by an abyss. They are a "luxury." Aristotle did not conceal this state of affairs. "First philosophy," which includes the highest good and the highest pleasure, is a function of the leisure of the few, for whom all necessities of life are already adequately taken care of. "Pure theory" is appropriated as the profession of an elite and cordoned off with iron chains from the majority of mankind. Aristotle did not assert that the good, the beautiful, and the true are universally valid and obligatory values which should also permeate and transfigure "from above" the realm of necessity, of the material provision for life. Only when this claim is raised are we in the presence of the concept of culture that became central to bourgeois practice and its corresponding weltanschauung. The ancient theory of the higher value of truths above the realm of necessity includes as well the "higher" level of society. For these truths are supposed to have their abode in the ruling social strata, whose dominant status is in turn confirmed by the theory insofar as concern with the highest truths is supposed to be their profession.

In Aristotelian philosophy, ancient theory is precisely at the point where idealism retreats in the face of social contradictions and expresses them as ontological conditions. Platonic philosophy still contended with the social order of commercial Athens. Plato's idealism is interlaced with motifs of social criticism. What appears as facticity from the standpoint of the Ideas is the material world in which men and things encounter one another as commodities. The just order of the soul is destroyed by

the passion for wealth which leaves a man not a moment of leisure to attend to anything beyond his personal fortunes. So long as a citizen's whole soul is wrapped up in these, he cannot give a thought to anything but the day's takings.[7]

91

And the authentic, basic demand of idealism is that this material world be transformed and improved in accordance with the truths yielded by knowledge of the Ideas. Plato's answer to this demand is his program for a reorganization of society. This program reveals what Plato sees as the root of evil. He demands, for the ruling strata, the abolition of private property (even in women and children) and the prohibition of trade. This same program, however, tries to root the contradictions of class society in the depths of human nature, thereby perpetuating them. While the majority of the members of the state are engaged for their entire lives in the cheerless business of providing for the necessities of life, enjoyment of the true, the good, and the beautiful is reserved for a small elite. Although Aristotle still lets ethics terminate in politics, for him the reorganization of society no longer occupies a central role in philosophy. To the extent to which he is more "realistic" than Plato, his idealism is more resigned in the face of the historical tasks of mankind. The true philosopher is for him no longer essentially the true statesman. The distance between facticity and Idea has increased precisely because they are conceived of as in closer relationship. The purport of idealism, viz. the realization of the Idea, dissipates. The history of idealism is also the history of its coming to terms with the established order.

Behind the ontological and epistemological separation of the realm of the senses and the realm of Ideas, of sensuousness and reason, of necessity and beauty, stands not only the rejection of a bad historical form of existence, but also its exoneration. The material world (i.e. the manifold forms of the respective "lower" member of this relation) is in itself mere matter, mere potentiality, akin more to Non-Being than to Being. It becomes real only insofar as it partakes of the "higher" world. In all these forms the material world remains bare matter or stuff for something outside it which alone gives it value. All and any truth, goodness, and beauty can accrue to it only "from above" by the grace of the Idea. All activity relating to the material provision of life remains in its essence untrue, bad, and ugly. Even with these characteristics, however, such activity is as necessary as matter is for the Idea. The misery of slave labor, the degradation of men and things to commodities, the joylessness and lowliness in which the totality of the material conditions of existence continuously reproduces itself, all these do not fall within the sphere of interest of idealist philosophy, for they are not yet the actual reality that constitutes the object of this philosophy. Due to its irrevocably material quality, material practice is exonerated from responsibility for the true, good, and beautiful, which is instead taken care of by the pursuit of theory. The ontological cleavage of ideal from material values tranquillizes idealism in all that regards the material processes of life. In idealism, a specific historical form of the division of labor and of social stratification takes on the eternal, metaphysical form of the relationship of necessity and beauty, of matter and Idea.

In the bourgeois epoch the theory of the relationship between necessity and beauty, labor and enjoyment, underwent decisive changes. First, the view that concern with the highest values is appropriated as a profession by particular social strata disappears. In its place emerges the thesis of the universality and universal validity of "culture." With good conscience, the theory of antiquity had expressed the fact that most men had to spend their lives providing for necessities while a small number devoted themselves to enjoyment and truth. Although the fact has not changed, the good conscience has disappeared. Free competition places individuals in the relation of buyers and sellers of labor power. The pure abstractness to which men are reduced in their social relations extends as well to intercourse with ideas. It is no longer supposed to be the case that some are born to and suited to labor and others to leisure, some to necessity and others to beauty. Just as each individual's relation to the market is immediate (without his personal qualities and needs being relevant except as commodities), so his relations to God, to beauty, to goodness, and to truth are relations of immediacy. As abstract beings, all men are supposed to participate equally in these values. As in material practice the product separates itself from the producers and becomes independent as the universal reified form of the "commodity," so in cultural practice a work and its content congeal into universally valid "values." By their very nature the truth of a philosophical judgment, the goodness of a moral action, and the beauty of a work of art should appeal to everyone, relate to everyone, be binding upon everyone. Without distinction of sex or birth, regardless of their position in the process of production, individuals must subordinate themselves to cultural values. They must absorb them into their lives and let their existence be permeated and transfigured by them. "Civilization" is animated and inspired by "culture."

This is not the place to discuss the various attempts to define culture. There is a concept of culture that can serve as an important instrument of social research because it expresses the implication of the mind in the historical process of society. It signifies the totality of social life in a given situation, insofar as both the areas of ideational reproduction (culture in the narrower sense, the "spiritual world") and of material reproduction ("civilization") form a historically distinguishable and comprehensible unity.[8] There is, however, another fairly widespread usage of the concept of culture, in which the spiritual world is lifted out of its social context, making cul-

94

ture a (false) collective noun and attributing (false) universality to it. This second concept of culture (clearly seen in such expressions as "national culture," "Germanic culture," or "Roman culture") plays off the spiritual world against the material world by holding up culture as the realm of authentic values and self-contained ends in opposition to the world of social utility and means. Through the use of this concept, culture is distinguished from civilization and sociologically and valuationally removed from the social process.[9] This concept itself has developed on the basis of a specific historical form of culture, which is termed "affirmative culture" in what follows. By affirmative culture is meant that culture of the bourgeois epoch which led in the course of its own development to the segregation from civilization of the mental and spiritual world as an independent realm of value that is also considered superior to civilization. Its decisive characteristic is the assertion of a universally obligatory, eternally better and more valuable world that must be unconditionally affirmed: a world essentially different from the factual world of the daily struggle for existence, yet realizable by every individual for himself "from within," without any transformation of the state of fact. It is only in this culture that cultural activities and objects gain that value which elevates them above the everyday sphere. Their reception becomes an act of celebration and exaltation.

Although the distinction between civilization and culture may have joined only recently the mental equipment of the social and cultural sciences, the state of affairs that it expresses has long been characteristic of the conduct of life and the weltanschauung of the bourgeois era. "Civilization and culture" is not simply a translation of the ancient relation of purposeful and purposeless, necessary and beautiful. As the purposeless and beautiful were internalized and, along with

95

the qualities of binding universal validity and sublime beauty, made into the cultural values of the bourgeoisie, a realm of apparent unity and apparent freedom was constructed within culture in which the antagonistic relations of existence were supposed to be stabilized and pacified. Culture affirms and conceals the new conditions of social life.

In antiquity, the world of the beautiful beyond necessity was essentially a world of happiness and enjoyment. The ancient theory had never doubted that men's concern was ultimately their worldly gratification, their happiness. Ultimately, not immediately; for man's first concern is the struggle for the preservation and protection of mere existence. In view of the meager development of the productive forces in the ancient economy, it never occurred to philosophy that material practice could ever be fashioned in such a way that it would itself contain the space and time for happiness. Anxiety stands at the source of all idealistic doctrines that look for the highest felicity in ideational practice: anxiety about the uncertainty of all the conditions of life, about the contingency of loss, of dependence, and of poverty, but anxiety also about satiation, ennui, and envy of men and the gods. Nonetheless, anxiety about happiness, which drove philosophy to separate beauty and necessity, preserves the demand for happiness even within the separated sphere. Happiness becomes a preserve, in order for it to be able to be present at all. What man is to find in the philosophical knowledge of the true, the good, and the beautiful is ultimate pleasure, which has all the opposite characteristics of material facticity: permanence in change, purity amidst impurity, freedom amidst unfreedom.

The abstract individual who emerges as the subject of practice at the beginning of the bourgeois epoch also becomes the bearer of a new claim to happiness, merely on the basis of the new constellation of social forces. No longer acting as the representative or delegate of higher social bodies, each separate individual is supposed to take the provision of his needs and the fulfillment of his wants into his own hands and be in immediate relation to his "vocation," to his purpose and goals, without the social, ecclesiastical, and political mediations of feudalism. In this situation the individual was allotted more room for individual requirements and satisfactions: room which developing capitalist production began to fill with more and more objects of possible satisfaction in the form of commodities. To this extent, the bourgeois liberation of the individual made possible a new happiness.

But the universality of this happiness is immediately canceled, since the abstract equality of men realizes itself in capitalist production as concrete inequality. Only a small number of men dispose of the purchasing power required for the quantity of goods necessary in order to secure happiness. Equality does not extend to the conditions for attaining the means. For the strata of the rural and urban proletariat, on whom the bourgeoisie depended in their struggle against the feudal powers, abstract equality could have meaning only as real equality. For the bourgeoisie, when it came to power, abstract equality sufficed for the flourishing of real individual freedom and real individual happiness, since it already disposed of the material conditions that could bring about such satisfaction. Indeed, stopping at the stage of abstract freedom belonged to the conditions of bourgeois rule, which would have been endangered by a transition from abstract to concrete universality. On the other hand, the bourgeoisie could not give up the general character of its demand (that equality be extended to all men) without denouncing itself and openly proclaiming to the ruled strata that, for the majority, everything was still the same with regard to the improvement of the conditions of life. Such a concession became even less likely as growing

97

social wealth made the real fulfillment of this general demand possible while there was in contrast the relatively increasing poverty of the poor in city and country. Thus the demand became a postulate, and its object a mere idea. The vocation of man, to whom general fulfillment is denied in the material world, is hypostatized as an ideal.

The rising bourgeois groups had based their demand for a new social freedom on the universality of human reason. Against the belief in the divinely instituted eternity of a restrictive order they maintained their belief in progress, in a better future. But reason and freedom did not extend beyond these groups' interest, which came into increasing opposition to the interest of the majority. To accusing questions the bourgeoisie gave a decisive answer: affirmative culture. The latter is fundamentally idealist. To the need of the isolated individual it responds with general humanity, to bodily misery with the beauty of the soul, to external bondage with internal freedom, to brutal egoism with the duty of the realm of virtue. Whereas during the period of the militant rise of the new society all of these ideas had a progressive character by pointing beyond the attained organization of existence, they entered increasingly into the service of the suppression of the discontented masses and of mere self-justifying exaltation, once bourgeois rule began to be stabilized. They concealed the physical and psychic vitiation of the individual.

But bourgeois idealism is not merely ideology, for it expresses a correct objective content. It contains not only the justification of the established form of existence, but also the pain of its establishment: not only quiescence about what is, but also remembrance of what could be. By making suffering and sorrow into eternal, universal forces, great bourgeois art has continually shattered in the hearts of men the facile

98

resignation of everyday life. By painting in the luminous colors of this world the beauty of men and things and transmundane happiness, it has planted real longing alongside poor consolation and false consecration in the soil of bourgeois life. This art raised pain and sorrow, desperation and loneliness, to the level of metaphysical powers and set individuals against one another and the gods in the nakedness of physical immediacy, beyond all social mediations. This exaggeration contains the higher truth that such a world cannot be changed piecemeal, but only through its destruction. Classical bourgeois art put its ideal forms at such a distance from everyday occurrence that those whose suffering and hope reside in daily life could only rediscover themselves through a leap into a totally other world. In this way art nourished the belief that all previous history had been only the dark and tragic prehistory of a coming existence. And philosophy took this idea seriously enough to be concerned about its realization. Hegel's system is the last protest against the degradation of the idea: against playing officiously with the mind as though it were an object that really has nothing to do with human history. At least idealism maintained that the materialism of bourgeois practice is not the last word and that mankind must be led beyond it. Thus idealism belongs to a more progressive stage of development than later positivism, which in fighting metaphysical ideas eliminates not only their metaphysical character, but their content as well. It thus links itself inevitably to the status quo.

Culture is supposed to assume concern for the individual's claim to happiness. But the social antagonisms at the root of culture let it admit this claim only in an internalized and rationalized form. In a society that reproduces itself through economic competition, the mere demand for a happier social existence constitutes rebellion. For if men value the enjoyment of worldly happiness, then they certainly cannot value acquisitive activity, profit, and the authority of the economic powers that preserve the existence of this society. The claim to happiness has a dangerous ring in an order that for the majority means need, privation, and toil. The contradictions of such an order provide the impetus to the idealization of that claim. But the real gratification of individuals cannot be contained by an idealistic dynamic which either continually postpones gratification or transmutes it into striving for the unattained. It can only be realized *against* idealist culture, and only *against* this culture is it propagated as a general demand: the demand for a real transformation of the material conditions of existence, for a new life, for a new form of labor and of enjoyment. Thus it has remained active in the revolutionary groups that have fought the expanding new system of injustice since the waning of the Middle Ages. And while idealism surrenders the earth to bourgeois society and makes its ideas unreal by finding satisfaction in heaven and the soul, materialist philosophy takes seriously the concern for happiness and fights for its realization in history. In the philosophy of the Enlightenment, this connection becomes clear.

> False philosophy can, like theology, promise us an eternal happiness and, cradling us in beautiful chimeras, lead us there at the expense of our days or our pleasure. Quite different and wiser, true philosophy affords only a temporal happiness. It sows roses and flowers in our path and teaches us to pick them.[10]

Idealist philosophy, too, admits the centrality of human happiness. But in its controversy with stoicism, the Enlightenment adopted precisely that form of the claim to happiness which is incompatible with idealism and with which affirmative culture cannot deal:

And how we shall be anti-Stoics! These philosophers are strict, sad, and hard; we shall be tender, joyful, and agreeable. All soul, they abstract from their body; all body, we shall abstract from our soul. They show themselves inaccessible to pleasure and pain; we shall be proud to feel both the one and the other. Aiming at the sublime, they elevate themselves above all occurrences and believe themselves to be truly men only insofar as they cease to exist. Ourselves, we shall not control what governs us, although circumstances will not command our feelings. By acknowledging their lordship and our bondage, we shall try to make them agreeable to us, in the conviction that it is here that the happiness of life resides. Finally, we shall believe ourselves that much happier, the more we feel nature, humanity, and all social virtues. We shall recognize none but these, nor any life other than this one.[11]

* * *

In its idea of pure humanity, affirmative culture took up the historical demand for the general liberation of the individual. "If we consider mankind as we know it according to the laws which it embodies, we find nothing higher in man than humanity."[12] This concept is meant to comprise everything that is directed toward "man's noble education to reason and freedom, to more refined senses and instincts, to the most delicate and the heartiest health, to the fulfillment and domination of the earth."[13] All human laws and forms of government are to have the exclusive purpose of "enabling man, free from attack by others, to exercise his powers and acquire a more beautiful and freer enjoyment of life."[14] The highest point which man can attain is a community of free and rational persons in which each has the same opportunity to unfold and fulfill all of his powers. The concept of the person, in which the struggle against repressive collectivities has remained active through the present, disregards social conflicts and conventions and addresses itself to all individuals. No one relieves the individual of the burden of his existence, but no one prescribes his rights and sphere of action — no one except the "law in his own breast."

> Nature intended that man generate entirely out of himself everything going beyond the mechanical organization of his animal existence, and that he partake of no other happiness or perfection than that which he provides for himself, free of instinct, by means of his own reason.[15]

All wealth and all poverty derive from him and react back upon him. Each individual is immediate to himself: without worldly or heavenly mediations. And this immediacy also holds for his relations to others. The clearest representation of this idea of the person is to be found in classical literature since Shakespeare. In its dramas, individuals are so close to one another that between them there is nothing that is in principle ineffable or inexpressible. Verse makes possible what has already become impossible in prosaic reality. In poetry men can transcend all social isolation and distance and speak of the first and last things. They overcome the factual loneliness in the glow of great and beautiful words; they may even let loneliness appear in its metaphysical beauty. Criminal and saint, prince and servant, sage and fool, rich and poor join in discussion whose free flow is supposed to give rise to truth. The unity represented by art and the pure humanity of its persons are unreal; they are the counterimage of what occurs in social reality. The critical and revolutionary force of the ideal, which in its very unreality keeps alive the best desires of men amidst a bad reality, becomes clearest in those times when the satiated social strata have accomplished the betrayal of their own ideals. The ideal, to be sure, was conceived in such a fashion that its regressive and apologetic, rather than its progressive and critical, characteristics predominated. Its realization is supposed to be effected through the cultural education of individuals. Culture means not so much a better world as a nobler one: a world to be brought about not through the overthrow of the material order of life but through events in the individual's soul. Humanity becomes an inner state. Freedom, goodness, and beauty become spiritual qualities: understanding for everything human, knowledge about the greatness of all times, appreciation of everything difficult and sublime, respect for history in which all of this has become what it is. This inner state is to be the source of action that does not come into conflict with the given order. Culture belongs not to him who comprehends the truths of humanity as a battle cry, but to him in whom they have become a posture which leads to a mode of proper behavior: exhibiting harmony and reflectiveness even in daily routine. Culture should ennoble the given by permeating it, rather than putting something new in its place. It thus exalts the individual without freeing him from his factual debasement. Culture speaks of the dignity of "man" without concerning itself with a concretely more dignified status for men. The beauty of culture is above all an inner beauty and can only reach the external world from within. Its realm is essentially a realm of the *soul.*

That culture is a matter of spiritual (*seelisch*) values is constitutive of the affirmative concept of culture at least since Herder. Spiritual values belong to the definition of culture in contrast to mere civilization. Alfred Weber was merely summing up a conceptual scheme with a long history when he wrote:

> Culture . . . is merely spiritual expression and spiritual will
> and thus the expression and will of an "essence" that lies be-
> hind all intellectual mastery of existence, of a "soul" that, in
> its striving for expression and in its willing, pays no regard
> to purposiveness and utility. . . . From this follows the
> concept of culture as the prevailing form in which the spirit-
> ual is expressed and released in the materially and spiritually
> given substance of existence.[16]

The soul posited by this interpretation is other and more
than the totality of psychic forces and mechanisms (such as
might be the object of empirical psychology). Rather, this
noncorporeal being of man is asserted as the real substance
of the individual.

The character of the soul as substance has since Descartes
been founded upon the uniqueness of the ego as *res cogitans*.
While the entire world outside the ego becomes in principle
one of measurable matter with calculable motion, the ego is
the only dimension of reality to evade the materialistic rationality of the rising bourgeoisie. By coming into opposition
to the corporeal world as a substance differing from it in essence, the ego is subjected to a remarkable division into two
regions. The ego as the subject of thought (*mens*, mind) remains, in the independence of self-certainty, on this side of
the being of matter — its a priori, as it were — while Descartes
attempts to explain materialistically the ego as soul (*anima*),
as the subject of "passions" (love and hate, joy and sorrow,
shame, jealousy, regret, gratitude, and so forth). The passions
of the soul are traced to blood circulation and its transformation in the brain. This reduction does not quite succeed. To
be sure, all muscular movements and sense perceptions are
thought to depend on the nerves, which "are like small fila-
ments or small pipes that all come from the brain," but the
nerves themselves contain "a certain very fine air or wind

called animal spirits."[17] Despite this immaterial residue, the tendency of the interpretation is clear: the ego is either mind (thought, *cogito me cogitare*) or, insofar as it is not merely thought (*cogitatio*), it is no longer authentically ego, but rather corporeal. In the latter case, the properties and activities ascribed to it belonged to *res extensa*.[18] Yet they do not quite admit of being dissolved into matter. The soul remains an unmastered intermediate realm between the unshakable self-certainty of pure thought and the mathematical and physical certainty of material being. Already in the original project of rationalism there is no room in the system for what is later considered actually to compose the soul, viz. the individual's feelings, appetites, desires, and instincts. The position within rationalism of empirical psychology, i.e. of the discipline really dealing with the human soul, is characteristic, for it exists although reason is unable to legitimate it.

Kant polemized against the treatment of empirical psychology within rational metaphysics (by Baumgarten). Empirical psychology must be "completely banished from the domain of metaphysics; it is indeed already completely excluded by the very idea of the latter science." But, he goes on, "in conformity, however, with scholastic usage we must allow it some sort of a place (although as an episode only) in metaphysics, and this from economical motives, because it is not yet so rich as to be able to form a subject of study by itself, and yet is too important to be entirely excluded and forced to settle elsewhere. . . . It is thus merely a stranger who is taken in for a short while until he finds a home of his own, in a complete anthropology."[19] And in his metaphysics lectures of 1792–93 Kant expressed himself even more sceptically about this "stranger": "Is an empirical psychology possible as science? No — our knowledge of the soul is entirely too limited."[20]

Rationalism's estrangement from the soul points to an important state of affairs. For in fact the soul does not enter into the social labor process. Concrete labor is reduced to abstract labor that makes possible the exchange of the products of labor as commodities. The idea of the soul seems to allude to those areas of life which cannot be managed by the abstract reason of bourgeois practice. It is as though the processing of matter is accomplished only by a part of the *res cogitans:* by technical reason. Beginning with the division of labor in manufacture and brought to completion in machine industry, "the intellectual [*geistigen*] potencies of the material process of production" come into opposition to the immediate producers as "the property of another and as a power that rules them."[21] To the extent that thought is not immediately technical reason, it has freed itself since Descartes from conscious connection with social practice and tolerates the reification that it itself promotes. When in this practice human relations appear as material relations, as the very laws of things, philosophy abandons the individual to this appearance by retreating and re-establishing itself at the level of the transcendental constitution of the world in pure subjectivity. Transcendental philosophy does not make contact with reification, for it investigates only the process of cognition of the immemorially (*je schon*) reified world.

The soul is not comprehended by the dichotomy of *res cogitans* and *res extensa,* for it cannot be understood merely as one or the other. Kant destroyed rational psychology without arriving at an empirical psychology. For Hegel, every single attribute of the soul is comprehended from the standpoint of mind (*Geist*), into which the soul passes over (*übergeht*); for mind reveals itself to be the soul's true content. The soul is essentially characterized by its "not yet being mind."[22] Where Hegel treats psychology, i.e. the human soul, in his doctrine of subjective mind, the guiding principle is no longer soul but mind. Hegel deals with the soul principally as part of "anthropology," where it is still completely "bound to the attributes of nature."[23] He examines planetary life on a general scale, natural racial distinctions, the ages of man, magic, somnambulism, various forms of psychopathic self-images, and — only for a few pages — the "real soul." For him the latter is nothing but the transition to the ego of consciousness, wherewith the anthropological doctrine of soul is already left behind, and the phenomenology of mind arrived at. The soul is thus allotted to physiological anthropology on the one hand and the philosophy of mind on the other. Even in the greatest system of bourgeois rationalism there is no place for the independence of the soul. The authentic objects of psychology, feelings, instincts, and will, are conceived only as forms of the existence of mind.

With its concept of the soul, however, affirmative culture means precisely what is not mind. Indeed, the concept of soul comes into ever sharper contradiction to the concept of mind. What is meant by soul "is forever inaccessible to the lucid mind, to the understanding, or to empirical, factual research. . . . One could sooner dissect with a knife a theme by Beethoven or dissolve it with an acid than analyze the soul with the means of abstract thought."[24] In the idea of the soul, the noncorporeal faculties, activities, and properties of man (according to the traditional classifications, reason, will, and appetite) are combined in an indivisible unity that manifestly endures through all of the individual's behavior and, indeed, constitutes his individuality.

The concept of the soul typical of affirmative culture was not developed by philosophy, and the examples from Descartes, Kant, and Hegel were intended only to illustrate philosophy's embarrassment with regard to the soul.[25] This concept found its first positive expression in the literature of the Renaissance. Here the soul is in the first instance an unexplored part of the world to be discovered and enjoyed. To it are extended those demands with whose proclamation the new society accompanied the rational domination of the world by liberated man: freedom and the intrinsic worth of the individual. The riches of the soul, of the "inner life," were thus the correlate of the new-found riches of external life. Interest in the neglected "individual, incomparable, living states" of the soul belonged to the program of "living out one's life fully and entirely."[26] Concern with the soul "reacts upon the increasing differentiation of individualities and augments man's consciousness of enjoying life with a natural development rooted in man's essence."[27] Seen from the standpoint of the consummated affirmative culture of the eighteenth and nineteenth centuries, this spiritual demand appears as an unfulfilled promise. The idea of "natural development" remains, but it signifies primarily inner development. In the external world the soul cannot freely "live itself out." The organization of this world by the capitalist labor process has turned the development of the individual into economic competition and left the satisfaction of his needs to the commodity market. Affirmative culture uses the soul as a protest against reification, only to succumb to it in the end. The soul is sheltered as the only area of life that has not been drawn into the social labor process.

> The word "soul" gives the higher man a feeling of his inner existence, separated from all that is real or has evolved, a very definite feeling of the most secret and genuine potentialities of his life, his destiny, his history. In the early stages of the languages of all cultures, the word "soul" is a sign that encompasses everything that is not world.[28]

108

And in this — negative — quality it now becomes the only still immaculate guarantor of bourgeois ideals. The soul glorifies resignation. The ideal that man, individual, irreplaceable man, beyond all natural and social distinctions, be the ultimate end; that truth, goodness, and justice hold between men; that all human weaknesses be expiated by humanity — this ideal can be represented, in a society determined by the economic law of value, only by the soul and as spiritual occurrence. All else is inhuman and discredited. The soul alone obviously has no exchange value. The value of the soul does not enter into the body in such a way as to congeal into an object and become a commodity. There can be a beautiful soul in an ugly body, a healthy one in a sick body, a noble one in a common body — and vice versa. There is a kernel of truth in the proposition that what happens to the body cannot affect the soul. But in the established order this truth has taken on a terrible form. The freedom of the soul was used to excuse the poverty, martyrdom, and bondage of the body. It served the ideological surrender of existence to the economy of capitalism. Correctly understood, however, spiritual freedom does not mean the participation of man in an eternal beyond where everything is righted when the individual can no longer benefit from it. Rather, it anticipates the higher truth that in this world a form of social existence is possible in which the economy does not preempt the entire life of individuals. Man does not live by bread alone; this truth is thoroughly falsified by the interpretation that spiritual nourishment is an adequate substitute for too little bread.

The soul appears to escape reification just as it does the law of value. As a matter of fact, it can almost be defined by the assertion that through its means all reified relations are dissolved into human relations and negated. The soul institutes an all-encompassing inner community of men that spans the centuries. "The first thought in the first human soul links up with the last thought in the last human soul."[29] In the realm of culture spiritual education and spiritual greatness overcome the inequality and unfreedom of everyday competition, for men participate in culture as free and equal beings. He who looks to the soul sees through economic relations to men in themselves. Where the soul speaks, the contingent position and merit of men in the social process are transcended. Love breaks through barriers between rich and poor, high and lowly. Friendship keeps faith even with the outcast and despised, and truth raises its voice even before the tyrant's throne. Despite all social obstacles and encroachments, the soul develops in the individual's interior. The most cramped surroundings are large enough to expand into an infinite environment for the soul. In its classical era, affirmative culture continually poetized the soul in such a manner.

The individual's soul is first set off from, and against, his body. Its adoption as the decisive area of life can have two meanings: the release of sensuality (as the irrelevant area of life) or, to the contrary, the subjection of sensuality to the domination of the soul. Affirmative culture unequivocally took the second course. Release of sensuality would be release of enjoyment, which presupposes the absence of guilty conscience and the real possibility of gratification. In bourgeois society, such a trend is increasingly opposed by the necessity of disciplining discontented masses. The internalization of enjoyment through spiritualization therefore becomes one of the decisive tasks of cultural education. By being incorporated into spiritual life, sensuality is to be harnessed and transfigured. From the coupling of sensuality and the soul proceeds the bourgeois idea of love.

The spiritualization of sensuality fuses matter with heaven and death with eternity. The weaker the belief in a heavenly beyond, the stronger the veneration of the spiritual beyond. The idea of love absorbs the longing for the permanence of worldly happiness, for the blessing of the unconditional, for the conquest of termination. In bourgeois poetry, lovers love in opposition to everyday inconstancy, to the demands of reality, to the subjugation of the individual, and to death. Death does not come from outside, but from love itself. The liberation of the individual was effected in a society based not on solidarity but on conflict of interests among individuals. The individual has the character of an independent, self-sufficient monad. His relation to the (human and non-human) world is either abstractly immediate (the individual constitutes the world immemorially in itself as knowing, feeling, and willing ego) or abstractly mediated (i.e. determined by the blind laws of the production of commodities and of the market). In neither case is the monadic isolation of the individual overcome. To do so would mean the establishment of real solidarity and presupposes the replacement of individualist society by a higher form of social existence.

The idea of love, however, requires that the individual overcome monadic isolation and find fulfillment through the surrender of individuality in the unconditional solidarity of two persons. In a society in which conflict of interest is the *principium individuationis,* this complete surrender can appear in pure form only in death. For only death eliminates all of the external conditions that destroy permanent solidarity and in the struggle with which individuals wear themselves out. It appears not as the cessation of existence in nothingness, but rather as the only possible consummation of love and thus as its deepest significance.

While in art love is elevated to tragedy, it threatens to become mere duty and habit in everyday bourgeois life. Love contains the individualistic principle of the new society: it

111

demands exclusiveness. The latter appears in the requirement of unconditional fidelity which, originating in the soul, should also be obligatory for sensuality. But the spiritualization of sensuality demands of the latter what it cannot achieve: withdrawal from change and fluctuation and absorption into the unity and indivisibility of the person. Just at this point, inwardness and outwardness, potentiality and reality are supposed to be found in a pre-established harmony which the anarchic principle of society destroys everywhere. This contradiction makes exclusive fidelity untrue and vitiates sensuality, which finds an outlet in the furtive improprieties of the petit bourgeois.

Purely private relationships such as love and friendship are the only realm in which the dominion of the soul is supposed to be immediately confirmed in reality. Otherwise the soul has primarily the function of elevating men to the ideal without urging the latter's realization. The soul has a tranquilizing effect. Because it is exempted from reification, it suffers from it least, consequently meeting it with the least resistance. Since the soul's meaning and worth do not fall within historical reality, it can maintain itself unharmed in a bad reality. Spiritual joys are cheaper than bodily ones; they are less dangerous and are granted more willingly. An essential difference between the soul and the mind is that the former is not oriented toward critical knowledge of truth. The soul can understand what the mind must condemn. Conceptual knowledge attempts to distinguish the one from the other and resolves contradiction only on the basis of the "dispassionately proceeding necessity of the object," while the soul rapidly reconciles all "external" antitheses in some "internal" unity. If there is a Western, Germanic, Faustian soul, then a Western, Germanic, and Faustian culture belongs to it, and feudal, capitalist, and socialist societies are nothing but manifestations of such souls. Their firm antitheses dissolve into the beautiful and profound unity of culture. The reconciliatory nature of the soul manifests itself clearly where psychology is made the organon of the social and cultural sciences, without foundation in a theory of society that penetrates behind culture. The soul has a strong affinity with historicism. As early as Herder we find the idea that the soul, freed from rationalism, should be capable of universal empathy (einfühlen). He adjures the soul,

> Entire nature of the soul that rules all things, that models all other inclinations and psychic forces after itself and tinges even the most indifferent actions — in order to feel these, do not answer in words, but penetrate into the epoch, into the region of heaven, into all of history, feel yourself into everything. . . .[30]

With its property of universal empathy the soul devalues the distinction between true and false, good and bad, or rational and irrational that can be made through the analysis of social reality with regard to the attainable potentialities of the organization of material existence. Every historical epoch, then, as Ranke stated, manifests but another facet of the same human spirit. Each one possesses its own meaning, "and its value rests not on what results from it, but on its very existence, on its own self."[31] Soul has nothing to do with the correctness of what it expresses. It can do honor to a bad cause (as in Dostoevski's case).[32] In the struggle for a better human future, profound and refined souls may stand aside or on the wrong side. The soul takes fright at the hard truth of theory, which points up the necessity of changing an impoverished form of existence. How can an external transformation determine the authentic, inner substance of man? Soul lets one be soft and compliant, submitting to the facts; for, after all, they do not really matter. In this way the soul was able to become a useful factor in the technique of mass domination when, in the epoch of authoritarian states, all available forces had to be mobilized against a real transformation of social existence. With the help of the soul, the bourgeoisie in advanced capitalist society buried its ideals of an earlier period. That soul is of the essence makes a good slogan when only power is of the essence.

But the soul really is essential — as the unexpressed, unfulfilled life of the individual. The culture of souls absorbed in a false form those forces and wants which could find no place in everyday life. The cultural ideal assimilated men's longing for a happier life: for humanity, goodness, joy, truth, and solidarity. Only, in this ideal, they are all furnished with the affirmative accent of belonging to a higher, purer, nonprosaic world. They are either internalized as the duty of the individual soul (to achieve what is constantly betrayed in the external existence of the whole) or represented as objects of art (whereby their reality is relegated to a realm essentially different from that of everyday life). There is a good reason for the exemplification of the cultural ideal in art, for only in art has bourgeois society tolerated its own ideals and taken them seriously as a general demand. What counts as utopia, phantasy, and rebellion in the world of fact is allowed in art. There affirmative culture has displayed the forgotten truths over which "realism" triumphs in daily life. The medium of beauty decontaminates truth and sets it apart from the present. What occurs in art occurs with no obligation. When this beautiful world is not completely represented as something long past (the classic artistic portrayal of victorious humanity, Goethe's *Iphigenie,* is a "historical" drama), it is deprived of concrete relevance by the magic of beauty.

In the medium of beauty, men have been permitted to partake of happiness. But even beauty has been affirmed with good conscience only in the ideal of art, for it contains a dangerous violence that threatens the given form of existence. The immediate sensuousness of beauty immediately suggests sensual happiness. According to Hume the power to stimulate pleasure belongs to the essential character of beauty. Pleasure is not merely a by-product of beauty, but constitutes its very essence.[33] And for Nietzsche beauty reawakens "aphrodisiac bliss." He polemizes against Kant's definition of the beautiful as the object of completely disinterested pleasure (*Wohlgefallen*) and opposes to it Stendhal's assertion that beauty is "une promesse de bonheur."[34] Therein lies its danger in a society that must rationalize and regulate happiness. Beauty is fundamentally shameless.[35] It displays what may not be promised openly and what is denied the majority. In the region of mere sensuality, separated from its connection with the ideal, beauty falls prey to the general devaluation of this sphere. Loosed from all spiritual and mental demands, beauty may be enjoyed in good conscience only in well delimited areas, with the awareness that it is only for a short period of relaxation or dissipation.

Bourgeois society has liberated individuals, but as persons who are to keep themselves in check. From the beginning, the prohibition of pleasure was a condition of freedom. A society split into classes can afford to make man into a means of pleasure only in the form of bondage and exploitation. Since in the new order the regulated classes rendered services not immediately, with their persons, but only mediated by the production of surplus value for the market, it was considered inhuman to exploit an underling's body as a source of pleasure, i.e., to use men directly as means (Kant). On the other hand, harnessing their bodies and intelligence for profit was considered a natural activation of freedom. Correspondingly, for the poor, hiring oneself out to work in a factory became a moral duty, while hiring out one's body as a means to pleasure was depravity and "prostitution." Also, in this society, poverty is a condition of profit and power, yet dependence takes place in the medium of abstract freedom. The sale of labor power is supposed to occur due to the poor man's own decision. He labors in the service of his employer, while he may keep for himself and cultivate as a sacred preserve the abstraction that is his person-in-itself, separated from its socially valuable functions. He is supposed to keep it pure. The prohibition against marketing the body not merely as an instrument of labor but as an instrument of pleasure as well is one of the chief social and psychological roots of bourgeois patriarchal ideology. Here reification has firm limits important to the system. Nonetheless, insofar as the body becomes a commodity as a manifestation or bearer of the sexual function, this occurs subject to general contempt. The taboo is violated. This holds not only for prostitution but for all production of pleasure that does not occur for reasons of "social hygiene" in the service of reproduction.

Those social strata, however, which are kept back in semi-medieval forms, pushed to the lowest margin of society, and thoroughly demoralized, provide, even in these circumstances, an anticipatory memory. When the body has completely become an object, a beautiful thing, it can foreshadow a new happiness. In suffering the most extreme reification man triumphs over reification. The artistry of the beautiful body, its effortless agility and relaxation, which can be displayed today only in the circus, vaudeville, and burlesque, herald the joy to which men will attain in being liberated from the ideal, once mankind, having become a true subject, succeeds in the mastery of matter. When all links to the affirmative ideal have been dissolved, when in the context of an existence marked by knowledge it becomes possible to have real enjoyment without any rationalization and without the least puritanical guilt feeling, when sensuality, in other words, is entirely released by the soul, then the first glimmer of a new culture emerges.

But in affirmative culture, the "soulless" regions do not belong to culture. Like every other commodity of the sphere of civilization, they are openly abandoned to the economic law of value. Only spiritual beauty and spiritual enjoyment are left in culture. According to Shaftesbury, it follows from the inability of animals to know and enjoy beauty

"that neither can man by the same sense or brutish part conceive or enjoy beauty; but all the beauty and good he enjoys is in a nobler way, and by the help of what is noblest, his mind and reason." . . . When you place a joy elsewhere than in the mind, the enjoyment itself will be no beautiful subject, nor of any graceful or agreeable appearance.[36]

Only in the medium of ideal beauty, in art, was happiness permitted to be reproduced as a cultural value in the totality of social life. Not so in the two areas of culture which in other respects share with art in the representation of ideal truth: philosophy and religion. In its idealist trend, philosophy became increasingly distrustful of happiness, and religion accorded it a place only in the hereafter. Ideal beauty was the form in which yearning could be expressed and happiness enjoyed. Thus art became the presage of possible truth. Classical German aesthetics comprehended the relation between beauty and truth in the idea of an aesthetic education of the human species. Schiller says that the "political problem" of a better organization of society "must take the path through the aesthetic realm, because it is through beauty that one arrives at freedom."[37] And in his poem *"Die Künstler"* ("The

117

Artists") he expresses the relation between the established and the coming culture in the lines: "What we have here perceived as beauty/ We shall some day encounter as truth" (*"Was wir als Schönheit hier empfunden/ Wird einst als Wahrheit uns entgegengehn"*). With respect to the extent of socially permitted truth and to the form of attained happiness, art is the highest and most representative area within affirmative culture. "Culture: dominion of art over life" — this was Nietzsche's definition.[38] What entitles art to this unique role?

Unlike the truth of theory, the beauty of art is compatible with the bad present, despite and within which it can afford happiness. True theory recognizes the misery and lack of happiness prevailing in the established order. Even when it shows the way to transformation, it offers no consolation that reconciles one to the present. In a world without happiness, however, happiness cannot but be a consolation: the consolation of a beautiful moment in an interminable chain of misfortune. The enjoyment of happiness is compressed into a momentary episode. But the moment embodies the bitterness of its disappearance. Given the isolation of lone individuals, there is no one in whom one's own happiness can be preserved after the moment passes, no one who is not subject to the same isolation. Ephemerality which does not leave behind solidarity among the survivors must be eternalized in order to become at all bearable. For it recurs in every moment of existence and in each one, as it were, it anticipates death. Because every moment comprehends death, the beautiful moment must be eternalized in order to make possible anything like happiness. In the happiness it proffers, affirmative culture eternalizes the beautiful moment; it immortalizes the ephemeral.

One of the decisive social tasks of affirmative culture is

based on this contradiction between the insufferable mutability of a bad existence and the need for happiness in order to make such existence bearable. Within this existence the resolution can be only illusory. And the possibility of a solution rests precisely on the character of artistic beauty as *illusion*. On the one hand the enjoyment of happiness is permitted only in spiritualized, idealized form. On the other, idealization annuls the meaning of happiness. For the ideal cannot be enjoyed, since all pleasure is foreign to it and would destroy the rigor and purity that must adhere to it in idealless reality if it is to be able to carry out its internalizing, disciplining function. The ideal emulated by the person who renounces his instincts and places himself under the categorical imperative of duty (this Kantian ideal is merely the epitome of all affirmative tendencies of culture) is insensitive to happiness. It can provide neither happiness nor consolation since it never affords gratification in the present. If the individual is ever to come under the power of the ideal to the extent of believing that his concrete longings and needs are to be found in it — found moreover in a state of fulfillment and gratification, then the ideal must give the illusion of granting present satisfaction. It is this illusory reality that neither philosophy nor religion can attain. Only art achieves it — in the medium of beauty. Goethe disclosed the deceptive and consoling role of beauty when he wrote:

> The human mind finds itself in a glorious state when it admires, when it worships, when it exalts an object and is exalted by it. Only it cannot long abide in this condition. The universal left it cold, the ideal elevated it above itself. Now, however, it would like to return to itself. It would like to enjoy again the earlier inclination that it cherished toward the individual without returning to a state of limitation, and does not want to let the significant, that which exalts the

mind, depart. What would become of the mind in this condition if beauty did not intervene and happily solve the rid-
dle! Only beauty gives life and warmth to the scientific; and
by moderating the high and significant and showering it with
heavenly charm, beauty brings us closer to it. A beautiful
work of art has come full circle; it is now a sort of individual
that we can embrace with affection, that we can appropriate.[39]

What is decisive in this connection is not that art represents
ideal reality, but that it represents it as beautiful reality.
Beauty gives the ideal the character of the charming, the
gladdening, and the gratifying — of happiness. It alone per-
fects the illusion of art. For only through it does the illusory
world arouse the appearance of familiarity, of being present:
in short, of reality. Illusion (*Schein*) really enables something
to appear (*erscheinen*): in the beauty of the work of art, longing is momentarily fulfilled. The percipient experiences happiness. And once it has taken form in the work, the beautiful
moment can be continually repeated. It is eternalized in the
art work. In artistic enjoyment, the percipient can always reproduce such happiness.

Affirmative culture was the historical form in which were
preserved those human wants which surpassed the material
reproduction of existence. To that extent, what is true of the
form of social reality to which it belonged holds for it as well:
right is on its side. Certainly, it exonerated "external conditions" from responsibility for the "vocation of man," thus
stabilizing their injustice. But it also held up to them as a task
the image of a better order. The image is distorted, and the
distortion falsified all cultural values of the bourgeoisie. Nevertheless it is an image of happiness. There is an element of
earthly delight in the works of great bourgeois art, even when
they portray heaven. The individual enjoys beauty, goodness,

splendor, peace, and victorious joy. He even enjoys pain and suffering, cruelty and crime. He experiences liberation. And he understands, and encounters understanding for and in response to, his instincts and demands. Reification is transpierced in private. In art one does not have to be "realistic," for man is at stake, not his occupation or status. Suffering is suffering and joy is joy. The world appears as what it is behind the commodity form: a landscape is really a landscape, a man really a man, a thing really a thing.

In the form of existence to which affirmative culture belongs, "happiness in existing . . . is possible only as happiness in illusion."[40] But this illusion has a real effect, producing satisfaction. The latter's meaning, though, is decisively altered; it enters the service of the status quo. The rebellious idea becomes an accessory in justification. The truth of a higher world, of a higher good than material existence, conceals the truth that a better material existence can be created in which such happiness is realized. In affirmative culture even unhappiness becomes a means of subordination and acquiescence. By exhibiting the beautiful as present, art pacifies rebellious desire. Together with the other cultural areas it has contributed to the great educational achievement of so disciplining the liberated individual, for whom the new freedom has brought a new form of bondage, that he tolerates the unfreedom of social existence. The potentiality of a richer life, a potentiality disclosed with the help of modern thought, and the impoverished actual form of life have come into open opposition, repeatedly compelling this thought to internalize its own demands and deflect its own conclusions. It took a centuries-long education to help make bearable the daily reproduced shock that arises from the contradiction between the constant sermon of the inalienable freedom, majesty, and dignity of the person, the magnificence and autonomy of rea-

121

son, the goodness of humanity and of impartial charity and justice, on the one hand, and the general degradation of the majority of mankind, the irrationality of the social life process, the victory of the labor market over humanity, and of profit over charity, on the other. "The entire counterfeit of transcendence and of the hereafter has grown up on the basis of an *impoverished* life . . . ,"[41] but the injection of cultural happiness into unhappiness and the spiritualization of sensuality mitigate the misery and the sickness of that life to a "healthy" work capacity. This is the real miracle of affirmative culture. Men can feel themselves happy even without being so at all. The effect of illusion renders incorrect even one's own assertion that one is happy. The individual, thrown back upon himself, learns to bear and, in a certain sense, to love his isolation. Factual loneliness is sublimated to metaphysical loneliness and, as such, is accorded the entire aura and rapture of inner plenitude alongside external poverty. In its idea of personality affirmative culture reproduces and glorifies individuals' social isolation and impoverishment.

The personality is the bearer of the cultural ideal. It is supposed to represent happiness in the form in which this culture proclaims it as the highest good: private harmony amidst general anarchy, joyful activity amidst bitter labor. The personality has absorbed everything good and cast off or refined everything bad. It matters not that man lives. What matters is only that he live as well as possible. That is one of the precepts of affirmative culture. "Well" here refers essentially to culture: participating in spiritual and mental values, patterning individual existence after the humanity of the soul and the breadth of the mind. The happiness of unrationalized enjoyment has been omitted from the ideal of felicity. The latter may not violate the laws of the established order and, indeed, does not need to violate them, for it is to be realized immanently. The personality, which in developed affirmative culture is supposed to be the "highest happiness" of man, must respect the foundations of the status quo: deference to given relations of domination belongs to its virtues. It may only kick over the traces if it remains conscious of what it is doing and takes it back afterward.

It was not always so. Formerly, at the beginning of the new era, the personality showed another face. Like the soul whose completed human embodiment it was supposed to be, it belonged in the first instance to the ideology of the bourgeois liberation of the individual. The person was the source of all forces and properties that made the individual capable of mastering his fate and shaping his environment in accordance with his needs. Jacob Burckhardt depicted this idea of the personality in his description of the "uomo universale" of the Renaissance.[42] If the individual was addressed as a personality, this was to emphasize that all that he made of himself he owed only to himself, not to his ancestors, his social status, or God. The distinguishing mark of the personality was not soul (in the sense of the "beautiful soul") but power, influence, fame: a life as extensive and as full of deeds as possible.

In the concept of personality which has been representative of affirmative culture since Kant, there is nothing left of this expansive activism. The personality remains lord of its existence only as a spiritual and ethical subject. "Freedom and independence from the mechanism of nature as a whole," which is now the token of its nature,[43] is only an "intelligible" freedom that accepts the given circumstances of life as the material of duty. Space for external fulfillment has shrunk; space for inner fulfillment has expanded considerably. The individual has learned to place all demands primarily upon himself. The rule of the soul has become more exacting inwardly and more modest outwardly. The person is no longer a springboard for attacking the world, but rather a protected line of retreat behind the front. In its inwardness, as an ethical person, it is the individual's only secure possession, the only one he can never lose.[44] It is no longer the source of conquest, but of renunciation. Personality characterizes above all him who renounces, who ekes out fulfillment within given conditions, no matter how poor they might be. He finds happiness in the Establishment. But even in this impoverished form, the idea of personality contains a progressive aspect: the individual is still the ultimate concern. To be sure, culture individuates men to the isolation of self-contained personalities whose fulfillment lies within themselves. But this corresponds to a method of discipline still liberal in nature, for it exempts a concrete region of private life from domination. It lets the individual subsist as a person as long as he does not disturb the labor process, and lets the immanent laws of this labor process, i.e. economic forces, take care of men's social integration.

*   *   *

Changes occur as soon as the preservation of the established form of the labor process can no longer gain its end with merely partial mobilization (leaving the individual's private life in reserve), but rather requires "total mobilization," through which the individual must be subjected in all spheres of his existence to the discipline of the authoritarian state. Now the bourgeoisie comes into conflict with its own culture. Total mobilization in the era of monopoly capitalism is incompatible with the progressive aspects of culture centered about the idea of personality. The self-abolition of affirmative culture begins.

The loud pugnacity of the authoritarian state against the

124

"liberal ideals" of humanity, individuality, and rationality and against idealist art and philosophy cannot conceal that what is occurring is a process of self-abolition. Just as the social reorganization involved in passing from parliamentary democracy to an authoritarian leadership-state is only a reorganization within the established order, so the cultural reorganization in which liberalist idealism changes into "heroic realism" takes place within affirmative culture itself. Its nature is to provide a new defense of old forms of existence. The basic function of culture remains the same. Only the ways in which it exercises this function change.

The identity of content preserved within a complete change of form is particularly visible in the idea of internalization. The latter, involving the conversion of explosive instincts and forces into spiritual dimensions, had been one of the strongest levers of the disciplining process.[45] Affirmative culture had canceled social antagonisms in an abstract internal community. As persons, in their spiritual freedom and dignity, all men were considered of equal value. High above factual antitheses lay the realm of cultural solidarity. During the most recent period of affirmative culture, this abstract internal community (abstract because it left the real antagonisms untouched) has turned into an equally abstract external community. The individual is inserted into a false collectivity (race, folk, blood, and soil). But this externalization has the same function as internalization: renunciation and subjection to the status quo, made bearable by the real appearance of gratification. That individuals freed for over four hundred years march with so little trouble in the communal columns of the authoritarian state is due in no small measure to affirmative culture.

The new methods of discipline would not be possible without casting off the progressive elements contained in the earlier stages of culture. Seen from the standpoint of the most recent development, the culture of those stages seems like a happy past. But no matter how much the authoritarian reorganization of existence actually serves only the interests of small social groups, it presents itself, like its predecessor, as the way in which the social totality preserves itself in the changed situation. To that extent it represents — in a bad form and to the increasing unhappiness of the majority — the interest of all individuals whose existence is bound up with the preservation of this order. And it is this order in which idealist culture was implicated. This double contradiction is in part the source of the weakness with which culture today protests against its new form.

The extent to which idealist inwardness is related to heroic outwardness is shown by their united front against the mind. Along with the high esteem for the mind which was characteristic of several areas and bearers of affirmative culture, a deep contempt for the mind was always present in bourgeois practice. It could find its justification in philosophy's lack of concern for the real problems of men. But there were still other reasons why affirmative culture was essentially a culture of the soul and not of the mind. Even before its decline the mind was always somewhat suspect. It is more tangible, more demanding, and nearer to reality than the soul. Its critical lucidity and rationality and its contradiction of irrational facticity are difficult to hide and to silence. Hegel goes poorly with an authoritarian state; he was for the mind, while the moderns are for the soul and for feeling. The mind cannot escape reality without denying itself; the soul can, and is supposed to do so. It is precisely because the soul dwells beyond the economy that the latter can manage it so easily. The soul derives its value from its property of not being subjected to the law of value. An individual full of soul is more compliant, acquiesces more humbly to fate, and is better at obeying authority. For he gets to keep for himself the entire wealth of his soul and can exalt himself tragically and heroically. The intensive education to inner freedom that has been in progress since Luther is now, when inner freedom abolishes itself by turning into outer unfreedom, bearing its choicest fruit. While the mind falls prey to hate and contempt, the soul is still cherished. Liberalism is even reproached with no longer caring for "soul and ethical content." "Greatness of soul and personality with strong character," and "the infinite expansion of the soul" are extolled as the "deepest spiritual feature of classic art."[46] The festivals and celebrations of the authoritarian state, its parades, its physiognomy, and the speeches of its leaders are all addressed to the soul. They go to the heart, even when their intent is power.

The outlines of the heroic form of affirmative culture were most clearly drawn during the period of ideological preparation for the authoritarian state. Noteworthy is hostility to the "academic and artistic [*museal*] establishment" and to the "grotesque forms of edification" it has taken on.[47] This cultural establishment is judged and rejected from the standpoint of the requisites of total mobilization. It

represents nothing other than one of the last oases of bourgeois security. It provides the apparently most plausible excuse for avoiding political decision.

Cultural propaganda is

a sort of opium that veils danger and calls forth the deceptive consciousness of order. But this is an unbearable luxury in a situation in which the need of the day is not to speak of tradition, but to create it. We live in a period of history in which everything depends on an immense mobilization and concentration of available forces."[48]

127

Mobilization and concentration for what? What Ernst Jünger could still designate as the salvation of the "totality of our life," as the creation of a heroic world of labor, and so forth, reveals itself in action increasingly as the reshaping of all of human existence in the service of the most powerful economic interests. They also determine the demands for a new culture. The requisite intensification and expansion of labor discipline make occupation with the "ideals of an objective science and of an art existing for its own sake" appear a waste of time. It seems desirable to cast off ballast in this area. "Our entire so-called culture cannot prevent even the smallest neighboring state from violating the border," which is really what is primary. The world must know that the government would not hesitate for a minute "to auction off all art treasures in the museums if national defense required it."[49] This attitude determines the shape of the new culture that is to replace the old. It must be represented by young and reckless leadership. "The less education of the usual kind possessed by this stratum, the better it will be."[50]

The cynical suggestions offered by Jünger are vague and restricted primarily to art. "Just as the victor writes history, i.e., creates his myth, so he decides what is to count as art."[51] Even art must enter the service of national defense and of labor and military discipline. (Jünger mentions city planning: the dismemberment of large city blocks in order to disperse the masses in the event of war and revolution, the military organization of the countryside, and so forth.) Insofar as such culture aims at the enrichment, beautification, and security of the authoritarian state, it is marked by its social function of organizing the whole society in the interest of a few economically powerful groups and their hangers-on. Hence its attributes of humility, sacrifice, poverty, and dutifulness on the one hand, and extreme will to power, impulse to expansion, and technical and military perfection on the other. "The task of total mobilization is the transformation of life into energy as manifested in economics, technology, and transportation by the whirring of wheels or, on the battlefield, by fire and movement."[52] The idealist cult of inwardness and the heroic cult of the state serve a fundamentally identical social order to which the individual is now completely sacrificed. Whereas formerly cultural exaltation was to satisfy the personal wish for happiness, now the individual's happiness is to disappear completely in the greatness of the folk. While culture formerly appeased the demand for happiness in real illusion, it is now to teach the individual that he may not advance such a claim at all: "The given criterion lies in the worker's way of life. What is necessary is not to improve this way of life, but to lend it an ultimate and decisive significance."[53] Here, too, "exaltation" replaces transformation. Demolishing culture in this way is thus an expression of the utmost intensification of tendencies fundamental to affirmative culture.

Overcoming these tendencies in any real sense would lead not to demolishing culture as such but to abolishing its affirmative character. Affirmative culture was the counterimage of an order in which the material reproduction of life left no space or time for those regions of existence which the ancients had designated as the "beautiful." It became customary to see the entire sphere of material reproduction as essentially tainted with the blemish of poverty, severity, and injustice and to abandon or suppress any demands protesting it. The orientation of all traditional cultural philosophy, i.e. setting culture apart from civilization and from the material life process, is based upon acknowledging as perpetual this historical situation. The latter is metaphysically exculpated by the theory of culture according to which life must be "deadened to a certain extent" in order "to arrive at goods of independent value."[54]

The integration of culture into the material life process is considered a sin against the mind and the soul. As a matter of fact, its occurrence would only make explicit what has long been in effect blindly, since not only the production but also the reception of cultural goods is already governed by the law of value. Yet the reproach is justified to the extent that until now such resorption has taken place only in the form of utilitarianism. The latter is simply the obverse of affirmative culture. Its concept of utility is nothing but that of the businessman who enters happiness in his books as an inevitable expense: as necessary regimen and recreation. Happiness is calculated at the outset with regard to its utility just as the chance of profit is weighed in relation to risk and cost. It is thus smoothly integrated into the economic principle of this society. In utilitarianism the interest of the individual remains linked to the basic interest of the established order. His happiness is harmless, and this harmlessness is preserved even in the organization of leisure in the authoritarian state. Whatever joy is permitted is now organized. The idyllic countryside, the site of Sunday happiness, is transformed into drilling grounds, the picnic of the petit bourgeois is replaced by scouting. Harmlessness generates its own negation.

From the standpoint of the interest of the status quo, the real abolition of affirmative culture must appear utopian. For it goes beyond the social totality in which culture has been enmeshed. Insofar as in Western thought culture has meant affirmative culture, the abolition of its affirmative character will appear as the abolition of culture as such. To the extent that culture has transmuted fulfillable, but factually unfulfilled, longings and instincts, it will lose its object. The assertion that today culture has become unnecessary contains a dynamic, progressive element. It is only that culture's lack of object in the authoritarian state derives not from fulfillment but from the awareness that even keeping alive the desire for fulfillment is dangerous in the present situation. When culture gets to the point of having to sustain fulfillment itself and no longer merely desire, it will no longer be able to do so in contents that, as such, bear an affirmative character. "Gratitude" will then perhaps really be its essence, as Nietzsche asserted of all beautiful and great art.[55] Beauty will find a new embodiment when it no longer is represented as real illusion but, instead, expresses reality and joy in reality. A foretaste of such potentialities can be had in experiencing the unassuming display of Greek statues or the music of Mozart or late Beethoven. Perhaps, however, beauty and its enjoyment will not even devolve upon art. Perhaps art as such will have no objects. For the common man it has been confined to museums for at least a century. The museum was the most suitable place for reproducing in the individual withdrawal from facticity and the consolation of being elevated to a more dignified world — an experience limited by temporal restriction to special occasions. This museum-like quality was also present in the ceremonious treatment of the classics, where dignity alone was enough to still all explosive elements. What a classic writer or thinker did or said did not have to be taken too seriously, for it belonged to another world and could not come into conflict with this one. The authoritarian state's polemic against the cultural (*museal*) establishment contains an element of correct knowledge. But when it opposes "grotesque forms of edification," it only wants to replace obsolete methods of affirmation with more modern ones.

Every attempt to sketch out the counterimage of affirmative culture comes up against the ineradicable cliché about the fools' paradise. It would be better to accept this cliché than the one about the transformation of the earth into a gigantic community center, which seems to be at the root of some theories of culture. There is talk of a "general diffusion of cultural values," of the "right of all members of the nation [*Volk*] to cultural benefits," of "raising the level of the nation's physical, spiritual, and ethical culture."[56] But all this would be merely raising the ideology of a conflicted society to the conscious mode of life of another, making a new virtue out of its necessity. When Kautsky speaks of the "coming happiness," he means primarily "the gladdening effects of scientific work," and "sympathetic enjoyment in the areas of science and art, nature, sport, and games."[57] "Everything hitherto created in the way of culture should be . . . put at the disposal of the masses," whose task is "to conquer this entire culture for themselves."[58] This can mean nothing other than winning the masses to the social order that is affirmed by the "entire culture." Such views miss the main point: the abolition of this culture. It is not the primitive, materialistic element of the idea of fools' paradise that is false, but its perpetuation. As long as the world is mutable there will be enough conflict, sorrow, and suffering to destroy the idyllic picture. As long as there is a realm of necessity, there will be enough need. Even a nonaffirmative culture will be burdened with mutability and necessity: dancing on the volcano, laughter in sorrow, flirtation with death. As long as this is true, the reproduction of life will still involve the reproduction of culture: the molding of unfulfilled longings and the purification of unfulfilled instincts. In affirmative culture, renunciation is linked to the external vitiation of the individual, to his compliance with a bad order. The struggle against ephemerality does not liberate sensuality but devalues it and is, indeed, possible only on the basis of this devaluation. This unhappiness is not metaphysical. It is the product of an irrational social organization. By eliminating affirmative culture, the abolition of this social organization will not eliminate individuality, but realize it. And "if we are ever happy at all, we can do nothing other than promote culture."[59]

Originally published in German in Zeitschrift für Sozialforschung, *vol. VI (1937).*

FROM the beginning the critical theory of society was constantly involved in philosophical as well as social issues and controversies. At the time of its origin, in the thirties and forties of the nineteenth century, philosophy was the most advanced form of consciousness, and by comparison real conditions in Germany were backward. Criticism of the established order there began as a critique of that consciousness, because otherwise it would have confronted its object at an earlier and less advanced historical stage than that which had already attained reality in countries outside Germany. Once critical theory had recognized the responsibility of economic conditions for the totality of the established world and comprehended the social framework in which reality was organized, philosophy became superfluous as an independent scientific discipline dealing with the structure of reality. Furthermore, problems bearing on the potentialities of man and of reason could now be approached from the standpoint of economics.

Philosophy thus appears within the economic concepts of materialist theory, each of which is more than an economic concept of the sort employed by the academic discipline of economics. It is more due to the theory's claim to explain the totality of man and his world in terms of his social being. Yet it would be false on that account to reduce these concepts to philosophical ones. To the contrary, the philosophical contents relevant to the theory are to be educed from the economic structure. They refer to conditions that, when forgotten, threaten the theory as a whole.

In the conviction of its founders the critical theory of society is essentially linked with materialism. This does not mean that it thereby sets itself up as a philosophical system in opposition to other philosophical systems. The theory of society is an economic, not a philosophical, system. There are two basic elements linking materialism to correct social theory: concern with human happiness, and the conviction that it can be attained only through a transformation of the material conditions of existence. The actual course of the transformation and the fundamental measures to be taken in order to arrive at a rational organization of society are prescribed by analysis of economic and political conditions in the given historical situation. The subsequent construction of the new society cannot be the object of theory, for it is to occur as the free creation of the liberated individuals. When reason has been realized as the rational organization of mankind, philosophy is left without an object. For philosophy, to the extent that it has been, up to the present, more than an occupation or a discipline within the given division of labor, has drawn its life from reason's not yet being reality.

Reason is the fundamental category of philosophical thought, the only one by means of which it has bound itself to human destiny. Philosophy wanted to discover the ultimate and most general grounds of Being. Under the name of reason it conceived the idea of an authentic Being in which all significant antitheses (of subject and object, essence and appearance, thought and being) were reconciled. Connected with this idea was the conviction that what exists is not immediately and already rational but must rather be brought to reason. Reason represents the highest potentiality of man and of existence; the two belong together. For when reason is accorded the status of substance, this means that at its highest level, as authentic reality, the world no longer stands opposed to the rational thought of men as mere material objectivity (*Gegenständlichkeit*). Rather, it is now comprehended by thought and defined as a concept (*Begriff*). That is, the external, antithetical character of material objectivity is overcome in a process through which the identity of subject and object is established as the rational, conceptual structure that is common to both. In its structure the world is considered accessible to reason, dependent on it, and dominated by it. In this form philosophy is idealism; it subsumes being under thought. But through this first thesis that made philosophy into rationalism and idealism it became critical philosophy as well. As the given world was bound up with rational thought and, indeed, ontologically dependent on it, all that contradicted reason or was not rational was posited as something that had to be overcome. Reason was established as a critical tribunal. In the philosophy of the bourgeois era reason took on the form of rational subjectivity. Man, the individual, was to examine and judge everything given by means of the power of his knowledge. Thus the concept of reason contains the concept of freedom as well. For such examination and judgment would be meaningless if man were not free to act in accordance with his insight and to bring what confronts him into accordance with reason.

> Philosophy teaches us that all properties of mind subsist only through freedom, that all are only means for freedom, and that all seek and produce only freedom. To speculative phi-

136

losophy belongs the knowledge that freedom is that alone which is true of mind.[1]

Hegel was only drawing a conclusion from the entire philosophical tradition when he identified reason and freedom. Freedom is the "formal element" of rationality, the only form in which reason can be.[2]

With the concept of reason as freedom, philosophy seems to reach its limit. What remains outstanding to the realization of reason is not a philosophical task. Hegel saw the history of philosophy as having reached its definitive conclusion at this point. However, this meant for mankind not a better future but the bad present that this condition perpetuates. Kant had, of course, written essays on universal history with cosmopolitan intent, and on perpetual peace. But his transcendental philosophy aroused the belief that the realization of reason through factual transformation was unnecessary, since individuals could become rational and free within the established order. In its basic concepts this philosophy fell prey to the order of the bourgeois epoch. In a world without reason, reason is only the semblance of rationality; in a state of general unfreedom, freedom is only a semblance of being free. This semblance is generated by the internalization of idealism. Reason and freedom become tasks that the individual is to fulfill within himself, and he can do so regardless of external conditions. Freedom does not contradict necessity, but, to the contrary, necessarily presupposes it. Only he is free who recognizes the necessary as necessary, thereby overcoming its mere necessity and elevating it to the sphere of reason. This is equivalent to asserting that a person born crippled, who cannot be cured at the given state of medical science, overcomes this necessity when he gives reason and freedom scope within his crippled existence, i.e. if from the start he always posits his needs, goals, and actions only as the needs, goals, and actions

137

of a cripple. Idealist rationalism canceled the given antithesis of freedom and necessity so that freedom can never trespass upon necessity. Rather, it modestly sets up house within necessity. Hegel once said that this suspension of necessity "transfigures necessity into freedom."[3]

Freedom, however, can be the truth of necessity only when necessity is already true "in itself." Idealist rationalism's attachment to the status quo is distinguished by its particular conception of the relation of freedom and necessity. This attachment is the price it had to pay for the truth of its knowledge. It is already given in the orientation of the subject of idealist philosophy. This subject is rational only insofar as it is entirely self-sufficient. All that is "other" is alien and external to this subject and as such primarily suspect. For something to be true, it must be certain. For it to be certain, it must be posited by the subject as its own achievement. This holds equally for the *fundamentum inconcussum* of Descartes and the synthetic a priori judgments of Kant. Self-sufficiency and independence of all that is other and alien is the sole guarantee of the subject's freedom. What is not dependent on any other person or thing, what possesses itself, is free. Having excludes the other. Relating to the other in such a way that the subject really reaches and is united with it (or him) counts as loss and dependence. When Hegel ascribed to reason, as authentic reality, movement that "remains within itself," he could invoke Aristotle. From the beginning, philosophy was sure that the highest mode of being was being-within-itself (*Beisichselbstsein*).

This identity in the determination of authentic reality points to a deeper identity, property. Something is authentic when it is self-reliant, can preserve itself, and is not dependent on anything else. For idealism this sort of being is attained when the subject has the world so that it cannot be deprived of it, that it disposes of it omnipresently, and that it appropriates it to the extent that in all otherness the subject is only with itself. However, the freedom attained by Descartes' *ego cogito,* Leibniz's monad, Kant's transcendental ego, Fichte's subject of original activity, and Hegel's world-spirit is not the freedom of pleasurable possession with which the Aristotelian God moved in his own happiness. It is rather the freedom of interminable, arduous labor. In the form that it assumed as authentic Being in modern philosophy, reason has to produce itself and its reality continuously in recalcitrant material. It exists only in this process. What reason is to accomplish is neither more nor less than the constitution of the world for the ego. Reason is supposed to create the universality and community in which the rational subject participates with other rational subjects. It is the basis of the possibility that, beyond the encounter of merely self-sufficient monads, a common life develops in a common world. But even this achievement does not lead beyond what already exists. It changes nothing. For the constitution of the world has always been effected prior to the actual action of the individual; thus he can never take his most authentic achievement into his own hands. The same characteristic agitation, which fears really taking what is and making something else out of it, prevails in all aspects of this rationalism. Development is proclaimed, but true development is "not a transformation, or becoming something else."[4] For at its conclusion it arrives at nothing that did not already exist "in itself" at the beginning. The absence of concrete development appeared to this philosophy as the greatest benefit. Precisely at its maturest stage, the inner statics of all its apparently so dynamic concepts become manifest.

Undoubtedly all these characteristics make idealist rationalism a bourgeois philosophy. And yet, merely on account of the single concept of reason, it is more than ideology, and in devoting oneself to it one does more than struggle against ideology. The concept of ideology has meaning only when oriented to the interest of theory in the transformation of the social structure. Neither a sociological nor a philosophical but rather a political concept, it considers a doctrine in relation not to the social conditions of its truth or to an absolute truth but rather to the interest of transformation.[5] Countless philosophical doctrines are mere ideology and, as illusions about socially relevant factors, readily integrate themselves into the general apparatus of domination. Idealist rationalism does not belong to this class, precisely to the extent that it is really idealistic. The conception of the domination of Being by reason is, after all, not only a postulate of idealism. With a sure instinct, the authoritarian state has fought classical idealism. Rationalism saw into important features of bourgeois society: the abstract ego, abstract reason, abstract freedom. To that extent it is correct consciousness. Pure reason was conceived as reason "independent" of all experience. The empirical world appears to make reason dependent; it manifests itself to reason with the character of "foreignness" (*Fremdartigkeit*).[6] Limiting reason to "pure" theoretical and practical achievement implies an avowal of bad facticity — but also concern with the right of the individual, with that in him which is more than "economic man," with what is left out of universal social exchange. Idealism tries to keep at least thought in a state of purity. It plays the peculiar double role of opposing both the true materialism of critical social theory and the false materialism of bourgeois practice. In idealism the individual protests the world by making both himself and the world free and rational in the realm of thought. This philosophy is in an essential sense individualistic. However, it comprehends the individual's uniqueness in terms of his self-sufficiency and "property"; all attempts to use the subject, construed in this sense, as the basis for constructing an intersubjective world have a dubious character. The alter ego always could be linked to the ego only in an abstract manner: it remained a problem of pure knowledge or pure ethics. Idealism's purity, too, is equivocal. To be sure, the highest truths of theoretical and of practical reason were to be pure and not based on facticity. But this purity could be saved only on the condition that facticity be left in impurity; the individual is surrendered to its untruth. Nevertheless, concern for the individual long kept idealism from giving its blessing to the sacrifice of the individual to the service of false collectives.

Rationalism's protest and critique remain idealistic and do not extend to the material conditions of existence. Hegel termed philosophy's abiding in the world of thought an "essential determination." Although philosophy reconciles antitheses in reason, it provides a "reconciliation not in reality, but in the world of ideas."[7] The materialist protest and materialist critique originated in the struggle of oppressed groups for better living conditions and remain permanently associated with the actual process of this struggle. Western philosophy had established reason as authentic reality. In the bourgeois epoch the reality of reason became the task that the free individual was to fulfill. The subject was the locus of reason and the source of the process by which objectivity was to become rational. The material conditions of life, however, allotted freedom to reason only in pure thought and pure will. But a social situation has come about in which the realization of reason no longer needs to be restricted to pure thought and will. If reason means shaping life according to men's free decision on the basis of their knowledge, then the demand for reason henceforth means the creation of a social organization in which individuals can collectively regulate their lives in accordance with their needs. With the realization of reason in such a society, philosophy would disappear. It was the task of social theory to demonstrate this possibility and lay the foundation for a transformation of the economic structure. By so doing, it could provide theoretical leadership for those strata which, by virtue of their historical situation, were to bring about the change. The interest of philosophy, concern with man, had found its new form in the interest of critical social theory. There is no philosophy alongside and outside this theory. For the philosophical construction of reason is replaced by the creation of a rational society. The philosophical ideals of a better world and of true Being are incorporated into the practical aim of struggling mankind, where they take on a human form.

What, however, if the development outlined by the theory does not occur? What if the forces that were to bring about the transformation are suppressed and appear to be defeated? Little as the theory's truth is thereby contradicted, it nevertheless appears then in a new light which illuminates new aspects and elements of its object. The new situation gives a new import to many demands and indices of the theory, whose changed function accords it in a more intensive sense the character of "critical theory."[8] Its critique is also directed at the avoidance of its full economic and political demands by many who invoke it. This situation compels theory anew to a sharper emphasis on its concern with the potentialities of man and with the individual's freedom, happiness, and rights contained in all of its analyses. For the theory, these are exclusively potentialities of the concrete social situation. They become relevant only as economic and political questions and as such bear on human relations in the productive process, the distribution of the product of social labor, and men's active participation in the economic and political administration of the whole. The more elements of the theory become reality — not only as the old order's evolution confirms the theory's predictions, but as the transition to the new order begins — the more urgent becomes the question of what the theory intended as its goal. For here, unlike in philosophical systems, human freedom is no phantom or arbitrary inwardness that leaves everything in the external world as it was. Rather, freedom here means a real potentiality, a social relationship on whose realization human destiny depends. At the given stage of development, the constructive character of critical theory emerges anew. From the beginning it did more than simply register and systematize facts. Its impulse came from the force with which it spoke against the facts and confronted bad facticity with its better potentialities. Like philosophy, it opposes making reality into a criterion in the manner of complacent positivism. But unlike philosophy, it always derives its goals only from present tendencies of the social process. Therefore it has no fear of the utopia that the new order is denounced as being. When truth cannot be realized within the established social order, it always appears to the latter as mere utopia. This transcendence speaks not against, but for, its truth. The utopian element was long the only progressive element in philosophy, as in the constructions of the best state and the highest pleasure, of perfect happiness and perpetual peace. The obstinacy that comes from adhering to truth against all appearances has given way in contemporary philosophy to whimsy and uninhibited opportunism. Critical theory preserves obstinacy as a genuine quality of philosophical thought.

The current situation emphasizes this quality. The reverse suffered by the progressive forces took place at a stage where the economic conditions for transformation were present.

The new social situation expressed in the authoritarian state could be easily comprehended and predicted by means of the concepts worked out by the theory. It was not the failure of economic concepts that provided the impetus behind the new emphasis of the theory's claim that the transformation of economic conditions involves the transformation of the entirety of human existence. This claim is directed rather against a distorted interpretation and application of economics that is found in both practice and theoretical discussion. The discussion leads back to the question: In what way is the theory more than economics? From the beginning the critique of political economy established the difference by criticizing the entirety of social existence. In a society whose totality was determined by economic relations to the extent that the uncontrolled economy controlled all human relations, even the noneconomic was contained in the economy. It appears that, if and when this control is removed, the rational organization of society toward which critical theory is oriented is more than a new form of economic regulation. The difference lies in the decisive factor, precisely the one that makes the society rational — the subordination of the economy to the individuals' needs. The transformation of society eliminates the original relation of substructure and superstructure. In a rational reality, the labor process should not determine the general existence of men; to the contrary, their needs should determine the labor process. Not that the labor process is regulated in accordance with a plan, but the interest determining the regulation becomes important: it is rational only if this interest is that of the freedom and happiness of the masses. Neglect of this element despoils the theory of one of its essential characteristics. It eradicates from the image of liberated mankind the idea of happiness that was to distinguish it from all previous mankind. Without freedom and happiness in the social relations of men, even the greatest increase of production and the abolition of private property in the means of production remain infected with the old injustice.

Critical theory has, of course, distinguished between various phases of realization and pointed out the unfreedoms and inequalities with which the new era inevitably will be burdened. Nevertheless, the transformed social existence must be determined by its ultimate goal even at its inception. In its concept of an ultimate goal, critical theory did not intend to replace the theological hereafter with a social one — with an ideal that appears in the new order as just another hereafter in virtue of its exclusive opposition to the beginning and its telescoping distance. By defending the endangered and victimized potentialities of man against cowardice and betrayal, critical theory is not to be supplemented by a philosophy. It only makes explicit what was always the foundation of its categories: the demand that through the abolition of previously existing material conditions of existence the totality of human relations be liberated. If critical theory, amidst today's desperation, indicates that the reality it intends must comprise the freedom and happiness of individuals, it is only following the direction given by its economic concepts. They are constructive concepts, which comprehend not only the given reality but, simultaneously, its abolition and the new reality that is to follow. In the theoretical reconstruction of the social process, the critique of current conditions and the analysis of their tendencies necessarily include future-oriented components. The transformation toward which this process tends and the existence that liberated mankind is to create for itself determine at the outset the establishment and unfolding of the first economic categories. Theory can invoke no facts in confirmation of the theoretical elements that point toward future freedom. From the viewpoint of theory all that is already attained is given only as something threatened and in the process of disappearing; the given is a positive fact, an element of the coming society, only when it is taken into the theoretical construction as something to be transformed. This construction is neither a supplement to nor an extension of economics. It is economics itself insofar as it deals with contents that transcend the realm of established economic conditions.

Unconditional adherence to its goal, which can be attained only in social struggle, lets theory continually confront the already attained with the not yet attained and newly threatened. The theory's interest in great philosophy is part of the same context of opposition to the established order. But critical theory is not concerned with the realization of ideals brought into social struggles from outside. In these struggles it identifies on one side the cause of freedom and on the other the cause of suppression and barbarism. If the latter seems to win in reality, it might easily appear as though critical theory were holding up a philosophical idea against factual development and its scientific analysis. Traditional science was in fact more subject to the powers that be than was great philosophy. It was not in science but in philosophy that traditional theory developed concepts oriented to the potentialities of man lying beyond his factual status. At the end of the *Critique of Pure Reason*, Kant cites the three questions in which "all the interest" of human reason "coalesces": What can I know?; What should I do?; What may I hope?[9] And in the introduction to his lectures on logic, he adds a fourth question encompassing the first three: What is man?[10] The answer to this question is conceived not as the description of human nature as it is actually found to be, but rather as the demonstration of what are found to be human potentialities. In the bourgeois period, philosophy distorted the meaning of both question and

146

answers by equating human potentialities with those that are real within the established order. That is why they could be potentialities only of pure knowledge and pure will.

The transformation of a given status is not, of course, the business of philosophy. The philosopher can only participate in social struggles insofar as he is not a professional philosopher. This "division of labor," too, results from the modern separation of the mental from the material means of production, and philosophy cannot overcome it. The abstract character of philosophical work in the past and present is rooted in the social conditions of existence. Adhering to the abstractness of philosophy is more appropriate to circumstances and closer to truth than is the pseudophilosophical concreteness that condescends to social struggles. What is true in philosophical concepts was arrived at by abstracting from the concrete status of man and is true only in such abstraction. Reason, mind, morality, knowledge, and happiness are not only categories of bourgeois philosophy, but concerns of mankind. As such they must be preserved, if not derived anew. When critical theory examines the philosophical doctrines in which it was still possible to speak of man, it deals first with the camouflage and misinterpretation that characterized the discussion of man in the bourgeois period.

With this intention, several fundamental concepts of philosophy have been discussed in this journal [*Zeitschrift für Sozialforschung*]: truth and verification, rationalism and irrationalism, the role of logic, metaphysics and positivism, and the concept of essence. These were not merely analyzed sociologically, in order to correlate philosophical dogmas with social loci. Nor were specific philosophical contents "resolved" into social facts. To the extent that philosophy is more than ideology, every such attempt must come to nought. When critical theory comes to terms with philosophy, it is interested

147

in the truth content of philosophical concepts and problems. It presupposes that they really contain truth. The enterprise of the sociology of knowledge, to the contrary, is occupied only with the untruths, not the truths of previous philosophy. To be sure, even the highest philosophical categories are connected with social facts, even if only with the most general fact that the struggle of man with nature has not been undertaken by mankind as a free subject but instead has taken place only in class society. This fact comes to expression in many "ontological differences" established by philosophy. Its traces can perhaps be found even in the very forms of conceptual thought: for example, in the determination of logic as essentially the logic of predication, or judgments about given objects of which predicates are variously asserted or denied. It was dialectical logic that first pointed out the shortcomings of this interpretation of judgment: the "contingency" of predication and the "externality" of the process of judgment, which let the subject of judgment appear "outside" as self-subsistent and the predicate "inside" as though in our heads.[11] Moreover, it is certainly true that many philosophical concepts are mere "foggy ideas" arising out of the domination of existence by an uncontrolled economy and, accordingly, are to be explained precisely by the material conditions of life.

But in its historical forms philosophy also contains insights into human and objective conditions whose truth points beyond previous society and thus cannot be completely reduced to it. Here belong not only the contents dealt with under such concepts as reason, mind, freedom, morality, universality, and essence, but also important achievements of epistemology, psychology, and logic. Their truth content, which surmounts their social conditioning, presupposes not an eternal consciousness that transcendentally constitutes the individual conscious-

148

ness of historical subjects but only those particular historical subjects whose consciousness expresses itself in critical theory. It is only with and for this consciousness that the "surpassing" content becomes visible in its real truth. The truth that it recognizes in philosophy is not reducible to existing social conditions. This would be the case only in a form of existence where consciousness is no longer separated from being, enabling the rationality of thought to proceed from the rationality of social existence. Until then truth that is more than the truth of what is can be attained and intended only in opposition to established social relations. To this negative condition, at least, it is subject.

In the past, social relations concealed the meaning of truth. They formed a horizon of untruth that deprived the truth of its meaning. An example is the concept of universal consciousness, which preoccupied German Idealism. It contains the problem of the relation of the subject to the totality of society: How can universality as community (*Allgemeinheit*), become the subject without abolishing individuality? The understanding that more than an epistemological or metaphysical problem is at issue here can be gained and evaluated only outside the limits of bourgeois thought. The philosophical solutions met with by the problem are to be found in the history of philosophy. No sociological analysis is necessary in order to understand Kant's theory of transcendental synthesis. It embodies an epistemological truth. The interpretation given to the Kantian position by critical theory[12] does not affect the internal philosophical difficulty. By connecting the problem of the universality of knowledge with that of society as a universal subject, it does not purport to provide a better philosophical solution. Critical theory means to show only the specific social conditions at the root of philosophy's inability to pose the problem in a more compre-

149

hensive way, and to indicate that any other solution lay beyond that philosophy's boundaries. The untruth inherent in all transcendental treatment of the problem thus comes into philosophy "from outside"; hence it can be overcome only outside philosophy. "Outside" does not mean that social factors affect consciousness from without as though the latter existed independently. It refers rather to a division within the social whole. Consciousness is "externally" conditioned by social existence to the very extent that in bourgeois society the social conditions of the individual are eternal to him and, as it were, overwhelm him from without. This externality made possible the abstract freedom of the thinking subject. Consequently, only its abolition would enable abstract freedom to disappear as part of the general transformation of the relationship between social being and consciousness.

If the theory's fundamental conception of the relation of social existence to consciousness is to be followed, this "outside" must be taken into consideration. In previous history there has been no pre-established harmony between correct thought and social being. In the bourgeois period, economic conditions determine philosophical thought insofar as it is the emancipated, self-reliant individual who thinks. In reality, he counts not in the concretion of his potentialities and needs but only in abstraction from his individuality, as the bearer of labor power, i.e. of useful functions in the process of the realization of capital. Correspondingly, he appears in philosophy only as an abstract subject, abstracted from his full humanity. If he pursues the idea of man, he must think in opposition to facticity. Wishing to conceive this idea in its philosophical purity and universality, he must abstract from the present state of affairs. This abstractness, this radical withdrawal from the given, at least clears a path along which the individual in bourgeois society can seek the truth and adhere to what is known. Beside concreteness and facticity, the thinking subject also leaves its misery "outside." But it cannot escape from itself, for it has incorporated the monadic isolation of the bourgeois individual into its premises. The subject thinks within a horizon of untruth that bars the door to real emancipation.

This horizon explains some of the characteristic features of bourgeois philosophy. One of them affects the idea of truth itself and would seem to relativize "sociologically" all its truths from the start: the coupling of truth and certainty. As such, this connection goes all the way back to ancient philosophy. But only in the modern period has it taken on the typical form that truth must prove itself as the guaranteed property of the individual, and that this proof is considered established only if the individual can continually reproduce the truth as his own achievement. The process of knowledge is never terminated, because in every act of cognition the individual must once again re-enact the "production of the world" and the categorical organization of experience. However, the process never gets any further because the restriction of "productive" cognition to the transcendental sphere makes any new form of the world impossible. The constitution of the world occurs behind the backs of the individuals; yet it is their work.

The corresponding social factors are clear. The progressive aspects of this construction of the world, namely the foundation of knowledge on the autonomy of the individual and the idea of cognition as an act and task to be continually re-enacted, are made ineffective by the life process of bourgeois society. But does this sociological limitation affect the true content of the construction, the essential connection of knowledge, freedom, and practice? Bourgeois society's domination reveals itself not only in the dependence of thought but also in the (abstract) independence of its contents. For this society determines consciousness such that the latter's activity and contents survive in the dimension of abstract reason; abstractness saves its truth. What is true is so only to the extent that it is not the truth about social reality. And just because it is not the latter, because it transcends this reality, it can become a matter for critical theory. Sociology that is interested only in the dependent and limited nature of consciousness has nothing to do with truth. Its research, useful in many ways, falsifies the interest and the goal of critical theory. In any case, what was linked, in past knowledge, to specific social structures disappears with them. In contrast, critical theory concerns itself with preventing the loss of the truths which past knowledge labored to attain.

This is not to assert the existence of eternal truths unfolding in changing historical forms of which they need only to be divested in order for their kernel of truth to be revealed. If reason, freedom, knowledge, and happiness really are transformed from abstract concepts into reality, then they will have as much and as little in common with their previous forms as the association of free men with competitive, commodity-producing society. Of course, to the identity of the basic social structure in previous history certainly corresponds an identity of certain universal truths, whose universal character is an essential component of their truth content. The struggle of authoritarian ideology against abstract universals has clearly exhibited this. That man is a rational being, that this being requires freedom, and that happiness is his highest good are all universal propositions whose progressive impetus derives precisely from their universality. Universality gives them an almost revolutionary character, for they claim that all, and not merely this or that particular person, should be rational, free, and happy. In a society whose reality gives the lie to all these universals, philosophy cannot make them concrete. Under such conditions, adherence to universality is more important than its philosophical destruction.

Critical theory's interest in the liberation of mankind binds it to certain ancient truths. It is at one with philosophy in maintaining that man can be more than a manipulable subject in the production process of class society. To the extent that philosophy has nevertheless made its peace with man's determination by economic conditions, it has allied itself with repression. That is the bad materialism that underlies the edifice of idealism: the consolation that in the material world everything is in order as it is. (Even when it has not been the personal conviction of the philosopher, this consolation has arisen almost automatically as part of the mode of thought of bourgeois idealism and constitutes its ultimate affinity with its time.) The other premise of this materialism is that the mind is not to make its demands in this world, but is to orient itself toward another realm that does not conflict with the material world. The materialism of bourgeois practice can quite easily come to terms with this attitude. The bad materialism of philosophy is overcome in the materialist theory of society. The latter opposes not only the production relations that gave rise to bad materialism, but every form of production that dominates man instead of being dominated by him: this idealism underlies its materialism. Its constructive concepts, too, have a residue of abstractness as long as the reality toward which they are directed is not yet given. Here, however, abstractness results not from avoiding the status quo, but from orientation toward the future status of man. It cannot be supplanted by another, correct theory of the established order (as idealist abstractness was replaced by the critique of political economy). It cannot be succeeded by a

153

new theory, but only by rational reality itself. The abyss between rational and present reality cannot be bridged by conceptual thought. In order to retain what is not yet present as a goal in the present, phantasy is required. The essential connection of phantasy with philosophy is evident from the function attributed to it by philosophers, especially Aristotle and Kant, under the title of "imagination." Owing to its unique capacity to "intuit" an object though the latter be not present and to create something new out of given material of cognition, imagination denotes a considerable degree of independence from the given, of freedom amid a world of unfreedom. In surpassing what is present, it can anticipate the future. It is true that when Kant characterizes this "fundamental faculty of the human soul" as the a priori basis of all knowledge,[13] this restriction to the a priori diverts once again from the future to what is always past. Imagination succumbs to the general degradation of phantasy. To free it for the construction of a more beautiful and happier world remains the prerogative of children and fools. True, in phantasy one can imagine anything. But critical theory does not envision an endless horizon of possibilities.

The freedom of imagination disappears to the extent that real freedom becomes a real possibility. The limits of phantasy are thus no longer universal laws of essence (as the last bourgeois theory of knowledge that took seriously the meaning of phantasy so defined them[14]), but technical limits in the strictest sense. They are prescribed by the level of technological development. What critical theory is engaged in is not the depiction of a future world, although the response of phantasy to such a challenge would not perhaps be quite as absurd as we are led to believe. If phantasy were set free to answer, with precise reference to already existing technical material, the fundamental philosophical questions asked

154

by Kant, all of sociology would be terrified at the utopian character of its answers. And yet the answers that phantasy could provide would be very close to the truth, certainly closer than those yielded by the rigorous conceptual analyses of philosophical anthropology. For it would determine what man is on the basis of what he really can be tomorrow. In replying to the question, "What may I hope?", it would point less to eternal bliss and inner freedom than to the already possible unfolding and fulfillment of needs and wants. In a situation where such a future is a real possibility, phantasy is an important instrument in the task of continually holding the goal up to view. Phantasy does not relate to the other cognitive faculties as illusion to truth (which in fact, when it plumes itself on being the only truth, can perceive the truth of the future only as illusion). Without phantasy, all philosophical knowledge remains in the grip of the present or the past and severed from the future, which is the only link between philosophy and the real history of mankind.

Strong emphasis on the role of phantasy seems to contradict the rigorously scientific character that critical theory has always made a criterion of its concepts. This demand for scientific objectivity has brought materialist theory into unusual accord with idealist rationalism. While the latter could pursue its concern with man only in abstraction from given facts, it attempted to undo this abstractness by associating itself with science. Science never seriously called use-value into question. In their anxiety about scientific objectivity, the Neo-Kantians are at one with Kant, as is Husserl with Descartes. How science was applied, whether its utility and productivity guaranteed its higher truth or were instead signs of general inhumanity — philosophy did not ask itself these questions. It was chiefly interested in the methodology of the sciences. The critical theory of society maintained primarily

155

that the only task left for philosophy was elaborating the most general results of the sciences. It, too, took as its basis the viewpoint that science had sufficiently demonstrated its ability to serve the development of the productive forces and to open up new potentialities of a richer existence. But while the alliance between idealist philosophy and science was burdened from the beginning with sins engendered by the dependence of the sciences on established relations of domination, the critical theory of society presupposes the disengagement of science from this order. Thus the fateful fetishism of science is avoided here in principle. But this does not dispense the theory from a constant critique of scientific aims and methods which takes into account every new social situation. Scientific objectivity as such is never a sufficient guarantee of truth, especially in a situation where the truth speaks as strongly against the facts and is as well hidden behind them as today. Scientific predictability does not coincide with the futuristic mode in which the truth exists. Even the development of the productive forces and the evolution of technology know no uninterrupted progression from the old to the new society. For here, too, man himself is to determine progress: not "socialist" man, whose spiritual and moral regeneration is supposed to constitute the basis for planning the planners (a view that overlooks that "socialist" planning presupposes the disappearance of the abstract separation both of the subject from his activity and of the subject as universal from each individual subject), but the association of those men who bring about the transformation. Since what is to become of science and technology depends on them, science and technology cannot serve a priori as a conceptual model for critical theory.

Critical theory is, last but not least, critical of itself and of the social forces that make up its own basis. The philosophical element in the theory is a form of protest against the new "Economism," which would isolate the economic struggle and separate the economic from the political sphere. At an early stage, this view was countered with the criticism that the determining factors are the given situation of the entire society, the interrelationships of the various social strata, and relations of political power. The transformation of the economic structure must so reshape the organization of the entire society that, with the abolition of economic antagonisms between groups and individuals, the political sphere becomes to a great extent independent and determines the development of society. With the disappearance of the state, political relations would then become, in a hitherto unknown sense, general human relations: the organization of the administration of social wealth in the interest of liberated mankind.

The materialist theory of society is originally a nineteenth-century theory. Representing its relation to rationalism as one of "inheritance," it conceived this inheritance as it manifested itself in the nineteenth century. Much has changed since then. At that time the theory had comprehended, on the deepest level, the possibility of a coming barbarity, but the latter did not appear to be as imminent as the "conservative" abolition of what the nineteenth century represented: conservative of what the culture of bourgeois society, for all its poverty and injustice, had accomplished nonetheless for the development and happiness of the individual. What had already been achieved and what still remained to be done was clear enough. The entire impetus of the theory came from this interest in the individual, and it was not necessary to discuss it philosophically. The situation of inheritance has changed in the meantime. It is not a part of the nineteenth century, but authoritarian barbarity, that now separates the previous reality of reason from the form intended by the theory. More and more, the culture that was to have been abolished recedes into the past. Overlaid by an actuality in which the complete sacrifice of the individual has become a pervasive and almost unquestioned fact of life, that culture has vanished to the point where studying and comprehending it is no longer a matter of spiteful pride, but of sorrow. Critical theory must concern itself to a hitherto unknown extent with the past — precisely insofar as it is concerned with the future.

In a different form, the situation confronting the theory of society in the nineteenth century is being repeated today. Once again real conditions fall beneath the general level of history. Fettering the productive forces and keeping down the standard of life is characteristic of even the economically most developed countries. The reflection cast by the truth of the future in the philosophy of the past provides indications of factors that point beyond today's anachronistic conditions. Thus critical theory is still linked to these truths. They appear in it as part of a process: that of bringing to consciousness potentialities that have emerged within the maturing historical situation. They are preserved in the economic and political concepts of critical theory.

Originally published in German in Zeitschrift für Sozialforschung, *vol. VI (1937).*

V. ON HEDONISM

THE idealist philosophy of the bourgeois era attempted to comprehend the universal, which was supposed to realize itself in and through isolated individuals, under the notion of reason. The individual appears as an ego isolated from and against others in its drives, thoughts, and interests. This isolating individuation is overcome and a common world constructed through the reduction of concrete individuality to the subject of mere thought, the rational ego. Operating among men who at first follow only their particular interests, the laws of reason eventually succeed in bringing about community. The universal validity of at least some forms of intuition and of thought can be securely established, and certain general maxims of conduct can be derived from the rationality of the person. Insofar as the individual partakes of universality only as a rational being and not with the empirical manifold of his needs, wants, and capacities, this idea of reason implicitly contains the sacrifice of the individual. His full development could not be admitted into the realm of reason. The gratification of his wants and capacities, his happiness, appears as an arbitrary and subjective element that

159

cannot be brought into consonance with the universal validity of the highest principle of human action.

> For it is every man's own special feeling of pleasure and pain that decides in what he is to place his happiness, and even in the same subject this will vary with the difference of his wants according as this feeling changes, and thus a law which is *subjectively necessary* (as a law of nature) is *objectively* a very *contingent* practical principle, which can and must be very different in different subjects, and therefore can never furnish a law . . .[1]

Happiness is of no matter, for happiness does not lead beyond the individual in all his contingency and imperfection. Hegel saw the history of humanity as burdened with this irredeemable misfortune. Individuals must be sacrificed for the sake of the universal, for there is no pre-established harmony between the general and the particular interest, or between reason and happiness. The progress of reason realizes itself against the happiness of individuals.

> Happy is he who has adapted his existence to his particular character, will, and choice and thus enjoys himself in his existence. History is not the stage of happiness. In it, the periods of happiness are empty pages . . .[2]

The universal follows its course in disregard of individuals, and history, when comprehended, appears as the monstrous Calvary of the spirit.

Hegel fought against eudaemonism in the interest of historical progress. As such, the eudaemonistic principle of "making happiness and pleasure the highest good" is not false, according to Hegel. Rather, the baseness of eudaemonism is that it transposes the fulfillment of desire and the happiness of individuals into a "vulgar world and reality."

In accordance with this eudaemonism, the individual is supposed to be reconciled to this common and base world. The individual should "trust in this world and yield himself to it and be able to devote himself to it without sin."[3] Eudaemonism sins against historical reason, according to Hegel, in that it lets the culmination of human existence be prescribed and tainted by bad empirical reality.

Hegel's critique of eudaemonism expresses insight into the required objectivity of happiness. If happiness is no more than the immediate gratification of particular interests, then eudaemonism contains an irrational principle that keeps men within whatever forms of life are given. Human happiness should be something other than personal contentment. Its own title points beyond mere subjectivity.

Both ancient and bourgeois eudaemonism viewed happiness essentially as such a subjective condition. Insofar as men can and should attain happiness within the status prescribed them by the established social order, this doctrine contains a moment of resignation and approbation. Eudaemonism comes into contradiction with the principle of the critical autonomy of reason.

The contraposition of happiness and reason goes all the way back to ancient philosophy. The relegation of happiness to chance, to that which cannot be controlled and is not dominated, to the irrational power of conditions that are essentially external to the individual, so that happiness at most "supervenes" on its aims and goals — this resigned relationship to happiness is contained in the Greek concept of *tyche*.[4] One is happy in the realm of "external goods," which do not fall within the freedom of the individual, but rather are subject to the opaque contingency of the social order of life. True felicity, the fulfillment of individuals' highest potentialities, thus cannot consist in what is commonly called happiness, but must be sought in the world of the soul and the mind.

It is against this internalization of happiness, which accepts as inevitable the anarchy and unfreedom of the external conditions of existence, that the hedonistic trends of philosophy have protested. By identifying happiness with pleasure, they were demanding that man's sensual and sensuous potentialities and needs, too, should find satisfaction — that in them, too, man should enjoy his existence without sinning against his essence, without guilt and shame. In the principle of hedonism, in an abstract and undeveloped form, the demand for the freedom of the individual is extended into the realm of the material conditions of life. Insofar as the materialistic protest of hedonism preserves an otherwise proscribed element of human liberation, it is linked with the interest of critical theory.

Two types of hedonism are commonly distinguished: the Cyrenaic and the Epicurean trends. The Cyrenaics' point of departure is the thesis that the fulfillment of specific instincts and wants of the individual is associated with the feeling of pleasure. Happiness consists in having these individual pleasures as often as possible.

> Our end is particular pleasure, whereas happiness is the sum total of all individual pleasures, in which are included both past and future pleasures. Particular pleasure is desirable for its own sake, whereas happiness is desirable not for its own sake, but for the sake of particular pleasures.[5]

What the individual instincts and wants may be makes no difference; their moral evaluation is not based upon their "nature." They are a matter of custom, of social convention.[6] Pleasure is all that matters. It is the only happiness that the individual is allotted. ". . . pleasure does not differ from pleasure nor is one pleasure more pleasant than another."[7]

And now the materialist protest against internalization:

> . . . bodily pleasures are far better than mental pleasures, and bodily pains far worse than mental pains . . .[8]

Even rebellion against sacrificing the individual to the hypostatized community is preserved: "It was reasonable . . . for the good man not to risk his life in the defence of his country, for he would never throw wisdom away to benefit the unwise."[9]

This hedonism fails to differentiate not only between individual pleasures but also between the individuals who enjoy them. They are to gratify themselves just as they are, and the world is to become an object of possible enjoyment just as it is. In its relegation of happiness to immediate abandon and immediate enjoyment, hedonism accords with circumstances located in the structure of antagonistic society itself; they become clear only in their developed form.

In this form of society, the world as it is can become an object of enjoyment only when everything in it, men and things, is accepted as it appears. Its essence, that is, those potentialities which emerge as the highest on the basis of the attained level of the productive forces and of knowledge, is not present to the subject of enjoyment. For since the life process is not determined by the true interests of individuals creating, in solidarity, their existence through contending with nature, these potentialities are not realized in the decisive social relations. They can only appear to consciousness as lost, atrophied, and repressed. Any relationship to men and things going beyond their immediacy, any deeper understanding, would immediately come upon their essence, upon that which they could be and are not, and would then suffer from their appearance. Appearance becomes visible in the light of unrealized potentialities. Then it is no longer one beautiful moment among others so much as something evanescent which is lost and cannot be restored. Faults and blemishes of the objects of enjoyment are then burdened with the general ugliness and general unhappiness, whereas in immediacy they can even become a source of pleasure. Contingency in relations to men and things and the accompanying obstacles, losses, and renunciations become an expression of the anarchy and injustice of the whole, of a society in which even the most personal relations are determined by the economic law of value.

In this society, all human relationships transcending immediate encounter are not relations of happiness: especially not relationships in the labor process, which is regulated with regard not to the needs and capacities of individuals but rather to profit on capital and the production of commodities. Human relations are class relations, and their typical form is the free labor contract. This contractual character of human relationships has spread from the sphere of production to all of social life. Relationships function only in their reified form, mediated through the class distribution of the material output of the contractual partners. If this functional depersonalization were ever breached, not merely by that backslapping familiarity which only underscores the reciprocal functional distance separating men but rather by mutual concern and solidarity, it would be impossible for men to return to their normal social functions and positions. The contractual structure upon which this society is based would be broken.

Contract, however, does not encompass all interpersonal relations. Society has released a whole dimension of relation-

164

ships whose value is supposed to consist precisely in their not being determined by contractual achievements and contractual services. These are relationships in which individuals are in the relation of "persons" to one another and in which they are supposed to realize their personality. Love, friendship, and companionship are such personal relations, to which Western culture has relegated man's highest earthly happiness. But they cannot sustain happiness, precisely when they are what they are intended to be. If they are really to guarantee an essential and permanent community among individuals, they must be based on comprehending understanding of the other. They must contain uncompromising knowledge. To this knowledge the other reveals himself not merely in the uninterrupted immediacy of sensual appearance that can be desired and enjoyed as beautiful, through satisfaction with appearance, but rather in his essence, as he really is. His image will thus include ugliness, injustice, inconstancy, decay, and ephemerality not as subjective properties that could be overcome by understanding concern but rather as the effects of the intervention of social necessities into the personal sphere. These necessities actually constitute the instincts, wants, and interests of the person in this society. Accordingly the very essence of the person expresses itself in modes of behavior to which the other (or the person himself) reacts with disappointment, concern, sympathy, anxiety, infidelity, jealousy, and sorrow. Culture has transfigured these feelings and given them tragic consecration. In fact, they subvert reification. In the behavior to which they are a response, the individual wants to release himself from a situation whose social law he has hitherto obeyed, whether marriage, occupation, or any other obligation in which he has accepted morality. He wants to follow his passions. In an order of unfreedom, however, passion is deeply disorderly and hence immoral. When not diverted toward generally desired goals, it leads to unhappiness.

This is not the only way in which personal relations are linked to pain and unhappiness. The development of personality also means the development of knowledge: insight into the structures of the reality in which one lives. These structures being what they are, every step of cognition removes the individual from immediate abandonment to appearance and from ready acceptance of the ideology that conceals its essence. Thus knowledge destroys proffered happiness. If the individual really acts on his knowledge, he is led either to struggle against the status quo or to renunciation. Knowledge does not help him attain happiness, yet without if he reverts to reified relationships. This is an inescapable dilemma. Enjoyment and truth, happiness and the essential relations of individuals are disjunctions.

By not concealing this dichotomy, consistent hedonism fulfilled a progressive function. It did not pretend that, in an anarchic society, happiness could be found in a developed, harmonic "personality" based on the highest achievements of culture. Hedonism is useless as ideology and in no way admits of being employed to justify an order associated with the suppression of freedom and the sacrifice of the individual. For such a purpose it must first be morally internalized or revised in a utilitarian sense. Hedonism advocates happiness equally for all individuals. It does not hypostatize a community in which happiness is negated without regard to the individuals. It is meaningful to speak of the progress of universal reason realizing itself in the face of the unhappiness of individuals, but general happiness apart from the happiness of individuals is a meaningless phrase.

Hedonism is the opposite pole to the philosophy of reason.

In abstract fashion, both movements of thought have preserved potentialities of existing society that point to a real human society. The philosophy of reason has emphasized the development of the productive forces, the free rational shaping of the conditions of life, the domination of nature, and the critical autonomy of the associated individuals. Hedonism has stressed the comprehensive unfolding and fulfillment of individual wants and needs, emancipation from an inhuman labor process, and liberation of the world for the purposes of enjoyment. In society up to the present, the two doctrines have been incompatible, as are the principles that they represent. The idea of reason aims at universality, at a society in which the antagonistic interests of "empirical" individuals are canceled. To this community, however, the real fulfillment of individuals and their happiness remains alien and external; they must be sacrificed. There is no harmony between the general and the particular interest, between reason and happiness. If the individual believes that both interests are in accord, he becomes the victim of a necessary and salutary illusion; reason outwits the individuals. The true interest (of universality) reifies itself in opposition to the individuals and becomes a power that overwhelms them.

Hedonism wants to preserve the development and gratification of the individual as a goal within an anarchic and impoverished reality. But the protest against the reified community and against the meaningless sacrifices which are made to it leads only deeper into isolation and opposition between individuals as long as the historical forces that could transform the established society into a true community have not matured and are not comprehended. For hedonism, happiness remains something exclusively subjective. The particular interest of the individual, just as it is, is affirmed as the true interest and is justified against every and all community. This is the limit of hedonism: its attachment to the individualism of competition. Its concept of happiness can be derived only by abstracting from all universality and community. Abstract happiness corresponds to the abstract freedom of the monadic individual. The concrete objectivity of happiness is a concept for which hedonism finds no evidence.

This inevitable entanglement of even the most radical eudaemonism is a proper target of Hegel's critique. For it reconciles particular happiness with general unhappiness. Hedonism is not untrue because the individual is supposed to seek and find his happiness in a world of injustice and of misery. To the contrary, the hedonistic principle as such rebels often enough against this order. If it were ever to take hold of the masses, they would scarcely tolerate unfreedom and would be made completely unsuited for heroic domestication. The apologetic aspect of hedonism is located at a deeper level. It is to be found in hedonism's abstract conception of the subjective side of happiness, in its inability to distinguish between true and false wants and interests and between true and false enjoyment. It accepts the wants and interests of individuals as simply given and as valuable in themselves. Yet these wants and interests themselves, and not merely their gratification, already contain the stunted growth, the repression, and the untruth with which men grow up in class society. The affirmation of the one already contains the affirmation of the other.

The inability of hedonism to apply the category of truth to happiness, its fundamental relativism, is not a logical or epistemological fault of a philosophical system. It can be neither corrected within the system nor eliminated by a more comprehensive and better philosophical system. It originates in the form of social relations to which hedonism is linked, and all attempts to avoid it through immanent differentiation lead to new contradictions.

The second type of hedonism, the Epicurean, represents such an attempt at immanent differentiation. The identification of the highest good with pleasure is retained, but a specific kind of pleasure is, as "true" pleasure, opposed to all others. The undifferentiated gratification of whatever wants are given is all too often obviously followed by pain, whose magnitude is the basis for a differentiation of individual pleasures. There are wants and desires whose satisfaction is succeeded by pain that only serves to stimulate new desires, detroying man's peace of mind and health. Therefore

> . . . we do not choose every pleasure whatsoever, but ofttimes pass over many pleasures when a greater annoyance ensues from them. And ofttimes we consider pains superior to pleasures when submission to the pains for a long time brings us as a consequence a greater pleasure.[10]

Reason, whose foresight makes possible a comparison of the values of momentary pleasure and later pain, becomes the adjudicator of pleasure. It may itself even become the highest pleasure.

> It is not an unbroken succession of drinking-bouts and of revelry, not sexual love, not the enjoyment of the fish and other delicacies . . . which produce a pleasant life; it is sober reasoning, searching out the grounds of every choice and avoidance, and banishing those beliefs through which the greatest tumults take possession of the soul.[11]

Reason grants man that moderate enjoyment which reduces risk and offers the prospect of permanently balanced health. The differentiating evaluation of pleasure ensues therefore with regard to the greatest possible security and permanence of pleasure. This method expresses fear of the insecurity and badness of the conditions of life, the invincible limitation of enjoyment. It is a negative hedonism. Its principle is less the pleasure to be striven for than the pain to be avoided. The truth against which pleasure is to be measured is only evasion of conflict with the established order: the socially permitted if not desired form of pleasure. The "sage's" tranquility is the goal: an idea in which the concept of pleasure as well as the concept of the sage are deprived of their meaning. Pleasure perishes, inasmuch as the cautious, measured, and withdrawn relationship of the individual to men and things resists their dominion over him precisely where this dominion brings real happiness: as enjoyable abandon. In the antagonistic ordering of existence, happiness is encountered as something withdrawn from the autonomy of the individual, something that can be neither achieved nor controlled by reason. The element of extraneousness, contingency, and gratuitousness is here an essential component of happiness. It is just in this externality, in this innocent, unburdened, harmonious conjunction of the individual with something in the world, that pleasure consists. In the historical situation of individuals up to the present, it is not what reason has achieved nor what the soul experiences that can be called happiness (for these are necessarily tainted with unhappiness). To the contrary, only "externalized" pleasure, i.e. sensuality, can be called happiness. In reified social relationships, sensuality, and not reason, is the "organ" of happiness.

In the antithesis of reason and sensuality (or sensuousness), as it has been worked out in the development of philosophy, sensuality has increasingly acquired the character of a lower, baser human faculty, a realm lying on this side of true and false and of correct and incorrect, a region of dull, undiscriminating instincts. Only in epistemology has the connection between sensuousness and truth been preserved. Here the decisive aspect of sensuality has been retained: receptivity that is open and that opens itself (to experience). This quality contradicts sensuality's allegedly dull instinctual character. Precisely through this receptivity, this open abandon to objects (men and things), sensuality can become a source of happiness. For in it, in complete immediacy, the individual's isolation is overcome. Objects can occur to him here without their essential mediation through the social life process and, consequently, without their unhappy side becoming constitutive of pleasure. In the process of knowledge, in reason, quite the reverse holds. Here the individual's spontaneity necessarily comes up against the object as against something foreign. Reason must overcome the latter quality and comprehend the object in its essence, not only as it is presented and appears but as it has become. The method of reason has always been held to be the way of attaining clarity about the origin and principle of beings. This method implicitly referred to history. To be sure, history was understood not as real history but only transcendentally. Nevertheless, that process of comprehension worthy of the title of reason absorbed enough of the mutability, the insecurity, the conflicts, and suffering of reality to make the application of the term "pleasure" appear false in this realm. When Plato and Aristotle connected reason with pleasure, they did not establish reason as one of (or the best of) the individual pleasures in the sense of the hedonists. Rather, reason appears as the highest human potentiality and therefore, necessarily, as the highest human pleasure. Here, in the fight against hedonism, the concept of pleasure is taken out of the sphere to which the hedonists had relegated it and held up in opposition to this entire sphere.

The situation is different when, as in the case of Epicurus, reason is made a pleasure or pleasure is made reasonable within hedonism itself. This gives rise to that ideal of the satisfied sage in which both pleasure as well as reason have lost their meaning. The sage, then, would be the person whose reason and whose pleasure never go too far. They never are followed through to the end because, if they were, they would come upon knowledge that negates enjoyment. The sage's reason would be so limited from the start that it would only be occupied with the calculation of risks and with the psychic technique of extracting the best from everything. Such reason has abdicated its claim to truth. It appears only as subjective cunning and private expertise, calmly acquiescing in the persistence of general unreason and enjoying not so much what is allotted or occurs to it as itself.

Hedonism embodies a correct judgment about society. That the receptivity of sensuality and not the spontaneity of reason is the source of happiness results from antagonistic work relations. They are the real form of the attained level of human reason. It is in them that the extent of possible freedom and possible happiness is decided. If this form is one in which the productive forces are disposed of in the interest of the smallest social groups, in which the majority of men are separated from the means of production, and in which labor is performed not in accordance with the capacities and needs of individuals but according to the requirements of the process of profitable production, then happiness cannot be general within it. Happiness is restricted to the sphere of consumption. Radical hedonism was formulated in the ancient world and draws a moral conclusion from the slave economy. Labor and happiness are essentially separated. They belong to different modes of existence. Some men are slaves in their essence, others are free men. In the modern epoch the principle of labor has become general. Everyone is supposed to work and everyone is supposed to be rewarded in accordance with his work. But since the distribution of social labor proceeds according to the opaque necessity of the capitalist law of value, no rational relation is established between production and consumption, between labor and enjoyment. Gratification occurs as a contingency that is to be accepted. Reason rules only behind the backs of individuals in the reproduction of the whole that takes place despite anarchy. For the individual in pursuit of his own interests, reason's role is at most a personal calculation in choosing among given possibilities. And it is in this atrophied form that reason depreciated to the idea of the sage. If reason cannot be effective in the process of production as free communal decision about the state of human existence (within specific historical and natural conditions), then it can certainly not be effective in the process of consumption.

The restriction of happiness to the sphere of consumption, which appears separated from the process of production, stabilizes the particularity and the subjectivity of happiness in a society in which rational unity of the process of production and consumption, of labor and enjoyment, has not been brought about. The rejection by idealistic ethics of hedonism just because of the latter's essential particularity and subjectivity is founded upon a justified criticism: Does not happiness, with its immanent demand for increase and permanence, require that, within happiness itself, the isolation of individuals, the reification of human relations, and the contingency of gratification be done away with? Must not happiness become compatible with truth? On the other hand, none other than isolation, reification, and contingency have been the dimensions of happiness in previous society. Hedonism, therefore, has been right precisely in its falsehood insofar as it has preserved the demand for happiness against every idealization of unhappiness. The truth of hedonism would be its abolition by and preservation in a new principle of social organization, not in a different philosophical principle.

Philosophy has attempted in various ways to save the objectivity of happiness and to comprehend it under the category of truth and universality. Such attempts are to be found in ancient eudaemonism, in the Catholic philosophy of the Middle Ages, in humanism, and in the French Enlightenment. If inquiry into the possible objectivity of happiness is not extended to the structure of the social organization of humanity, its result is bound to run aground on social contradictions. Inasmuch, however, as the philosophical critique at least refers decisively to the historical problem at hand as a task of historical practice, we shall discuss in what follows the first and most important controversy with hedonism.

Plato's critique of hedonism (on two different levels in the *Gorgias* and *Philebus*) worked out for the first time the concept of true and false wants and true and false pleasure. Here truth and falsehood are categories that are supposed to be applicable to every individual pleasure. The critique takes its departure from the essential conjunction of pleasure and pain. Every pleasure is connected with pain, since pleasure is the removal and fulfillment of a want (lack, privation) that as such is felt as painful. Pleasure, therefore, cannot be "the good" or happiness, because it contains its own opposite: unless it were possible to find an "unmixed" pleasure, one essentially separated from pain. In the *Philebus* (51 b ff.) what remains as unmixed, true pleasure is in the last analysis only pleasure in lines, sounds, and colors that are "beautiful in themselves," in other words, enjoyment released from all painful desire and restricted to inorganic objects. This enjoyment is obviously too empty to be happiness. Designating inorganic entities as the object of pure pleasure shows decisively that in the given form of existential relations true pleasure is not only separated from the soul, which, as the seat of desire and longing, is necessarily also the source of pain, but is also separated from all essential personal relationships. Unmixed pleasure is to be had only in those things which are most removed from the social life process. The receptivity of open abandonment to the object of enjoyment, which Plato recognizes as the precondition of pleasure, remains only in complete externality, in which all essential relations between man and man are silenced. Happiness is thus situated at the antipode of internalization and inwardness.

Plato's earlier solution of the problem of true pleasure takes another direction. In the *Gorgias* he proceeds directly to the question of the social order within which the individual is to fulfill himself. This order itself as the highest norm against which individual pleasures are to be measured is not a subject of discussion; it is accepted in its given form. Bad wants and bad pleasures are those which destroy the just order of the soul and which prevent the individual from attaining his true potentialities. It is the community, however, within which individuals live and through which alone "the heavens and the earth, gods and men are bound together" (508 a) that decides these potentialities and thus the truth and falsehood of wants and pleasures. The concept of the order of the soul turns into that of the order of the community and the concept of the individually "just" into that of justice (504). Whether the individuals enjoy the right pleasure depends on the right ordering of the polis. The generality of happiness is posed as a problem. Only those wants may be satisfied which make the individual a good citizen. They are true wants, and the pleasure associated with their gratification is true pleasure. The others are not to be fulfilled. It is the task of the statesman to look after the general interest and to bring the satisfaction of particular interests into accord with it. The possibility of such harmony, the authentic social question, is not pursued further in the *Gorgias* (although the critique of major Greek statesmen at least suggests social criticism).

Inasmuch as true and false pleasure are contraposed, happiness is subjected to the criterion of truth. If human existence is to come in pleasure to its highest fulfillment, to felicity, then not every sensation of pleasure can in itself be happiness. Plato's critique of hedonism traces the givens of wants and of pleasures back to the individuals who "have" them. This conceptual regress is made necessary by the fact that both the sick and the healthy, the good and the bad, the crazy and the normal feel pleasure in like manner (at least with respect to the fact of pleasure).[12] What is common to all of these cannot be the highest. There must be a truth of happiness on the basis of which the happiness of the individual can be judged. Pleasure must be susceptible to distinction according to truth and falsehood and to justice and injustice if (in case pleasure is happiness) the happiness of men is not to be inseparably associated with unhappiness. The basis of such a distinction, however, cannot lie in the individual sensation of pleasure as such, for both the sick and the healthy and the bad and the good feel real pleasure. Nevertheless, just as an idea can be false even though it be a real idea, so too a pleasure can be false without the reality of the sensation of pleasure being denied (*Philebus* 36). This is more than a mere analogy. Here a cognitive function in the strictest sense is attributed to pleasure, for it reveals beings as objects of enjoyment. On the basis of its "intentional" character, pleasure is thus made accessible to the question of truth. A pleasure is untrue when the object that it intends is not "in itself" pleasurable (according to the exposition of the *Philebus,* when it can only be encountered mixed with pain). But the question of truth does

176

not regard only the object but also the subject of pleasure. This is made possible through Plato's interpretation of pleasure as belonging not merely to sensuousness (*aesthesis*) alone but also to the psyche (*Philebus* 33 f.). Psychic forces (such as desire, expectation, memory) are necessary for every sensation of pleasure, so that in pleasure the whole man is involved. With respect to the latter the question of truth arrives at the same point that had been reached in the *Gorgias:* that "good" men have true pleasure and "bad" men have false pleasure (*Philebus* 40 b, c).

The essential connection of the good of man with the truth of pleasure at which Plato's discussion of hedonism arrives makes of pleasure a moral problem. For it is the concrete form of the "community" that ultimately decides on this connection. Pleasure is subject to the claim of society and enters the realm of duty — duty to oneself and to others. The truth of the particular interest and its gratification is determined by the truth of the general interest. The agreement of the two is not immediate. Rather, it is mediated through the subjection of the particular to the requirements of generality. Within a society that requires morality (as an objective, general code of ethics opposed to the subjective wants and interests of individuals) for its existence, an amoral attitude is intolerable, for the latter destroys the bases of communal order. The amoral man violates the law of a society that, even if in a bad form, guarantees the preservation of social life. He does so, furthermore, without linking himself to a better, true society. For he remains in the given, "corrupted" structure of instincts and wants. Morality is the expression of the antagonism between the particular and the general interest. It is the code of those demands which are a matter of life and death for the society's self-preservation.[13] Insofar as particular interests are not really incorporated into and fulfilled in the society, such demands appear to the individual as commands coming from outside himself. If left to itself, pleasure as the immediate gratification of the merely particular interest must come into conflict with the interest of the hypostatized social community. In contrast to the isolated individual, society represents what is historically right. It demands the repression of all pleasure that violates the decisive social taboo. It forbids the satisfaction of those wants which would shatter the foundations of the established order.

The moralization of pleasure is called for by the existence of antagonistic society. It is the historical form in which this society unites the satisfaction of particular wants and instincts with the general interest, and it has had a progressive function in the development of the social labor process.[14] The hedonistic protest of the individual who is isolated in his particular interest is amoral. The amoral, beyond-good-and-evil attitude can be progressive only within a historical practice that leads beyond the already attained form of this process and fights for a new, true community against the established one. Only then does this attitude represent more than a merely particular interest. Isolated from the historical struggle for a better organization of the conditions of life, in which the individual has to engage himself in concrete social groups and tasks and thus gives up his amorality, amoral thought and action can, of course, escape from morality (if its subject is economically independent enough). But the ruling social law maintains its power over the amoral individual both in his wants and in the objects of their satisfaction. They originated under this law, and only the latter's transformation could overcome morality. Amoral rebellion, however, stops short of this decisive sphere. It wants to avoid morality as well as its social basis within the given order. Dodging the latter's contradictions, this amoral rebellion really remains beyond good and evil. It puts itself beyond the bounds of even that morality which links the established order with a more rational and happy society.

The attempt to save the objectivity of happiness, expressed for the first time in Plato's critique of hedonism, takes two directions in the advance toward an objective formulation of the concept of happiness. On the one hand, the gratification of the individual, his best possible existence, is measured against the "essence of man" in such a way that the highest potentialities open to man in his historical situation take precedence in development and gratification over all others in which man is not free but rather dependent on what is "external." On the other hand, the essence of man can develop only within society, whose actual organization participates in determining the realization of those potentialities and therefore also determines happiness. In Platonic and Aristotelian ethics both aspects, the personal and the social, are still joined. In the ethics of the modern period, in the form in which they have become prevalent since the Reformation, society is to a great extent relieved of responsibility for human potentialities. The latter are supposed to subsist exclusively in the individual himself, in his autonomy. The unconditioned freedom of the person becomes the measure of the "highest good." Since, however, this freedom is only abstract in the real world and coexists with social unfreedom and unhappiness, it becomes, in idealist ethics, programmatically separated from happiness. The latter increasingly takes on the character of irrational, bodily gratification, of mere enjoyment and therefore of inferiority:

> . . . reason can never be persuaded that the existence of a man who merely lives for *enjoyment* . . . has a worth in itself. . . . Only through what he does without reference to enjoyment, in full freedom and independently of what nature can procure for him passively, does he give an absolute

179

worth to his being, as the existence of a person; and happiness, with the whole abundance of its pleasures, is far from being an unconditioned good.[15]

The duress of the disciplining process of modern society comes to expression: the happiness of the individual is at best a worthless accident of his life. In the determination of the highest good, happiness is completely subordinated to virtue. Happiness may be only the "morally conditioned although necessary consequence" of morality. A "necessary connection" between the ethics of conviction and happiness becomes possible only through the assumption of a "purely intellectual determining principle" of human action and of an "intelligible author of nature."[16] The harmony of virtue and happiness belongs to those beautiful relations for whose realization the world beyond is necessary.

The unconditional manner, however, in which German idealism adhered to the principle of freedom as the condition of the highest good serves to emphasize more than ever the inner connection between happiness and freedom. The concrete form of human freedom determines the form of human happiness. Comprehension of the connection between happiness and freedom was already expressed in the ancient critique of hedonism. Happiness, as the fulfillment of all potentialities of the individual, presupposes freedom: at root, it is freedom. Conceptual analysis reveals them to be ultimately identical. Because freedom does not reign in the material conditions of the external world, because there happiness and contingency are almost identical, and because on the other hand the individual's freedom was maintained as a condition of the "highest good," felicity could not be made to reside in the external world. This motive is at work in Platonic and Aristotelian ethics. In the moral critique of the bourgeois period, too, hedonism is rejected from the standpoint of the concept of freedom. Kant rejected the principle of pleasure as something merely contingent which contradicted the autonomy of the person. And Fichte called pleasure essentially "involuntary" since it presupposes an agreement of the "external world" with the instincts and wants of the subject, whose realization does not fall within the range of the subject's freedom. In the happiness of pleasure, the individual is thus "alienated from himself."[17] This position presupposes that the subject's unfreedom in relation to the good things of the external world cannot be abolished and that the free person is therefore necessarily debased if his happiness is located in this relation. For the ancient critique the highest good was still supposed really to be the highest happiness. But now factual unfreedom is ontologized, and both freedom and happiness are so internalized that in the process happiness is excluded. The attempt to include happiness in the autonomous development of the person is abandoned, and a virtue is made out of the abstract freedom that accompanies social unfreedom.

The gratification of instincts and wants falls into ill repute; in any case, it lies beneath the human sphere with which philosophy is to concern itself. Moral commands can be followed without one's wants having been fulfilled to more than the physiological minimum; with this proposition, to be sure, a decisive achievement of modern society receives philosophical recognition. Man educated to internalization will not be easily induced, even under extreme wretchedness and injustice, to struggle against the established order.

In the moral concept of the highest good an untruth of hedonism is supposed to be eliminated: the mere subjectivity of happiness. Happiness remains an "element" of the highest good, but it stays subject to the universality of the moral law. This law is a law of reason: happiness is linked to knowledge and taken out of the dimension of mere feeling. Real happiness presupposes knowledge of the truth: that men know what they can attain as the highest potential of their existence, that they know their true interest. Individuals can feel happy and yet not be happy, because they do not even know real happiness. How, though, is one to judge of the reality of happiness? What is the criterion of its truth? In the ancient critique of hedonism this question became the political question of the right organization of the polis. The Christian ethics of the Middle Ages saw the answer to it in divine justice. The rigoristic morality of the bourgeois period made freedom the criterion of truth. But this was defined as the abstract freedom of the rational being and, in contrast to it, happiness remained external and contingent. The moral interpretation of happiness, its subjection to a universal law of reason, tolerated both the essential isolation of the autonomous person and his actual limitation.

Critical theory[18] comes to the question of the truth and universality of happiness in the elucidation of the concepts with which it seeks to determine the rational form of society. One of these determinations circumscribing the association of free men contains the explicit demand that each individual share in the social product according to his needs. With the comprehensive development of individuals and of the productive forces, society can inscribe on its banner, "From each according to his abilities, to each according to his needs." Here reappears the old hedonistic definition which seeks happiness in the comprehensive gratification of needs and wants. The needs and wants to be gratified should become the regulating principle of the labor process. But the wants of liberated men and the enjoyment of their satisfaction will have a different form from wants and satisfaction in a state of unfreedom, even if they are physiologically the same. In a social organization that opposes atomized individuals to one another in classes and leaves their particular freedom to the mechanism of an uncontrolled economic system, unfreedom is already operative in the needs and wants themselves: how much more so in enjoyment. The way want and enjoyment appear here, they do not even require general freedom. The development of the productive forces, the growing domination of nature, the extension and refinement of the production of commodities, money, and universal reification have created, along with new needs, new possibilities for enjoyment. But these given possibilities for enjoyment confront men who objectively, due to their economic status, as well as subjectively, due to their education and disciplining, are largely incapable of enjoyment. From the discrepancy between what exist as objects of possible enjoyment and the way in which these objects are understood, taken, and used arises the question of the truth of the condition of happiness in this society. Acts intending enjoyment do not achieve the fulfillment of their own intention; even when they fulfill themselves, they remain untrue.

Enjoyment is an attitude or mode of conduct toward things and human beings. The former, unless they have been made generally available by nature or by social regulation, are commodities accessible to corresponding purchasing power. For the great majority of humanity, only the very cheapest portion of these commodities is available. They become objects of enjoyment as commodities, and their origin is preserved within them — even enjoyment has a class character. The cheap is not as good as the dear. Precisely insofar as they lie outside the labor process, relations between men are essentially relations between members of the same class. For the majority, one's partner in pleasure will also be one's partner in the poverty of the same class. These conditions of life are a paltry showplace for happiness. The continual pressure under which the great masses must be kept for the reproduction of this society has only been augmented by the monopolistic accumulation of wealth. Any growth of enjoyment would endanger necessary discipline and make difficult the punctual and reliable coordination of the masses who keep the apparatus of the whole in operation. The economic regulation of enjoyment is supplemented by the police and the administration of justice. Pleasure wants essentially its own augmentation and refinement. The unfolding of the personality must not be merely spiritual. Industrial society has differentiated and intensified the objective world in such a manner that only an extremely differentiated and intensified sensuality can respond adequately to it. Modern technology contains all the means necessary to extract from things and bodies their mobility, beauty, and softness in order to bring them closer and make them available. Both the wants corresponding to these potentialities and the sensual organs through which they can be assimilated have been developed. What man can perceive, feel, and do in the midst of advanced civilization corresponds to the newly opened-up wealth of the world. But only those groups with the greatest purchasing power can take advantage of the expanded capacities and their gratification. The development of sensuality is only one part of the development of the productive forces; the need to fetter them is rooted in the antagonistic social system within which this development has taken place. There are many ways in which the ruled strata can be educated to diversion and substitute gratification. Here sports and a wide variety of permitted popular entertainment fulfill their historical function. In authoritarian states sadistic terror against enemies of the regime has found unforeseen modes of organized discharge. At the movies the common man can regularly participate in the glamour of the world of the stars and yet be aware at the same time that it is only a film and that there, too, there is splendor, bitterness, trouble, guilt, atonement, and the triumph of the good. The labor process, in which the laborer's organs atrophy and are coarsened, guarantees that the sensuousness of the lower strata does not develop beyond the technically necessary minimum. What is allowed beyond this as immediate enjoyment is circumscribed by the penal code.

It is not only the masses, however, in whom enjoyment cannot achieve the fulfillment of all subjective and objective potentialities, as it intends. Where the prevailing social relationship is the relation of men to one another as owners of commodities and where the value of every commodity is determined by the abstract labor time applied to it, enjoyment has no value in itself. For all that it is in this society, it is in separation from labor. In enjoyment the individual expends no labor power, nor does he reproduce labor power. He behaves as and acknowledges himself to be a private person. When value, the standard of the equity of exchange, is created only by abstract labor, then pleasure may not be a value. For if it were, social justice would be called into question. Indeed, it would reveal itself as striking injustice. The legitimation of pleasure as a value would, in fact, invert what is "all the news that's fit to print."

> For every modern man the value of a thing is the value of the labor that was necessary to produce it. Value is thus coated with the laborer's sweat, which pastes up the flaming sword that separates culture from paradise. It is dangerous to associate conceptually pleasure and pain with value. For the question then arises whether those who produce values have more pleasure or more pain. And one could come upon the thought that value may be in inverse proportion to pleasure.[19]

The danger of this conceptual association was recognized as early as at the origins of bourgeois society. The worthlessness of mere pléasure was inculcated by all means into the consciousness of individuals.

Nowhere does the connection between the devaluation of enjoyment and its social justification manifest itself as clearly as in the interpretation of sexual pleasure. The latter — pragmatically or morally — is rationalized and appears as a mere means to an end lying outside of itself, in the service of a smooth subordination of the individual to the established form of the labor process. As a hygienic value sexual pleasure is supposed to contribute to physical and mental health, which promotes the normal functioning of man within the given order. According to Spinoza, "sensual pleasure" may only "be sought as means," and above all as hygienic means. We may "indulge ourselves with pleasures only insofar as they are necessary for preserving health."[20] Leibniz declares that "voluptuousness of the senses must be used, according to the rules of reason, as a nourishment, medication, or tonic."[21] Fichte brings sexuality into immediate conjunction with the renovation of the social labor process:

> The real station, the honor and worth of the human being, and quite particularly of man in his morally natural existence, consists without doubt in his capacity as original progenitor to produce out of himself new men, new commanders of nature: beyond his earthly existence and for all eternity to establish new masters of nature. . . . It would consequently be absolute dishonor, the abnegation of authentic human and manly honor, if the capacity bestowed for the exercise of that privilege were made into a means of sensual pleasure. What is above all of nature and intended to reproduce dominion over her would become secondary and subject to one of nature's urges: pleasure. . . . [This absolute worthlessness is] lewdness — the use of the faculty of generation for mere pleasure, without intending its purpose or consciously willing it.[22]

Only when sexual relations are placed under the express purpose of the production of new labor power for the process of the social domination of nature is their enjoyment worthy of a human being and sanctioned. Later representatives of idealist ethics turned away from such frankness. Hermann Cohen considers the mere procreation of men an "animalistic" process and demands the purification of sexual pleasure by means of a truly ethical purpose. Only in love based on fidelity is sexual intercourse raised to the sphere of morality, making "sexual love" into a "characteristic of the pure will to the formation of ethical self-consciousness."[23] In the authoritarian phase of the bourgeois order, the attachment of love to the form of marriage comes into open contradiction to the state's need of a strong military and economic reserve army. The "experience of love" is "not unconditionally bound to marriage." But love should be "the presupposition and condition of marriage and of childbearing in marriage." Not the begetting of children as such, but the procreation of industrious and useful children is decisive. "Racial hygiene, social anthropology, and other medical-anthropological disciplines [give consideration] in a very meritorious way to valuable aspects even of human procreation."[24]

The unpurified, unrationalized release of sexual relationships would be the strongest release of enjoyment as such and the total devaluation of labor for its own sake. No human being could tolerate the tension between labor as valuable in itself and the freedom of enjoyment. The dreariness and injustice of work conditions would penetrate explosively the consciousness of individuals and make impossible their peaceful subordination to the social system of the bourgeois world.

The function of labor within this society determines its attitude with respect to enjoyment. The latter may not be meaningful in itself or remain unrationalized. Instead it must

187

receive its value from elsewhere. "Pleasure . . . and pain are withdrawn from any justification or motivation by the will to labor; rather, they provide this will with the stimulus to labor," which would then be subsumed under the principle of the satisfaction of wants. "Hedonism is the limit of a self-justification of the will to labor"[25] and contradicts the basic interest of the established order. The internalization and spiritualization by means of which enjoyment is refined to the level of culture, which helps reproduce the whole and thus proves its social value, is subject to this conviction. For the immediate producer the restriction of enjoyment operates immediately, without any moral mediation, through the working day, which leaves only a brief period of "leisure time" for enjoyment and puts it in the service of relaxation and the recreation of energy or labor power. The usufructuaries of the labor process are affected by the same valuation. That their enjoyment consists of doing and having what actually produces no value, creates a kind of social guilt feeling that leads to a rationalization of enjoyment. As representation, relaxation, and display of the splendor of those who are on top and bear the greatest responsibility, this enjoyment is discharged almost as a burden or duty.

The creation of social guilt feeling is a decisive achievement of education. The prevailing law of value is mirrored in the continually renewed conviction that everyone, left completely to himself, must earn a living in the general competitive struggle, if only in order to be enabled to continue to earn it in the future, and that everyone is rewarded in proportion to the labor power he has expended. Happiness, however, cannot be earned in this fashion. The goal of labor is not supposed to be happiness, and its remuneration is not enjoyment but profit or wages, i.e. the possibility of working more in the future. For the perpetuation of this labor process,

those instincts and wants which could undermine the normal
relation of labor and enjoyment (as the extent of the absence
of labor) and the institutions that secure it (such as the family
or marriage) must be diverted or repressed. This diversion
and repression is not always linked to cultural progress. Many
instincts and wants first become false and destructive due to
the false forms into which their satisfaction is channeled,
while the attained level of objective development would permit their true gratification — true because they could fulfill
themselves in their original intention of "unmixed" pleasure.
Such are the repressed cruelty that leads to sadistic terror and
the repressed self-abandon that leads to masochistic subjection. In their authentic intention as forms of the sexual instinct they can result in augmented pleasure not only for the
subject but for the object as well. They are then no longer
connected with destruction.[26] But precisely the increased differentiation of pleasure is intolerable in a society that requires
such wants to be gratified in a repressed form. Augmented
pleasure would represent immediately increased liberation of
the individual, for it would demand freedom in the choice of
object, in the knowledge and in the realization of his potentialities, and freedom of time and of place. All these demands
violate the law of life of the established society. The taboo on
pleasure has been most stubbornly maintained due to the in-
nermost connection of happiness and freedom. This taboo has
extended far into the ranks of the historical opposition to the
given order, distorting the problem and its solutions.[27]

The designation of happiness as the condition of the comprehensive gratification of the individual's needs and wants
is abstract and incorrect as long as it accepts needs and wants
as ultimate data in their present form. For as such they are
beyond neither good and evil nor true and false. As historical
facts they are subject to questioning as to their "right": Are

they of such a sort that their gratification can fulfill the subjective and objective potentialities of individuals? For many forms of want characteristic of the prevailing human condition, this question would have to be answered in the negative in view of the already attained stage of social development. For the latter makes possible a truer happiness than that which men attain for themselves today. Pleasure in the abasement of another as well as self-abasement under a stronger will, pleasure in the manifold surrogates for sexuality, in meaningless sacrifices, in the heroism of war are false pleasures because the drives and needs that fulfill themselves in them make men less free, blinder, and more wretched than they have to be. They are the drives and needs of individuals who were raised in an antagonistic society. To the extent to which they do not completely disappear in a new form of social organization, modes of their gratification are conceivable in which the most extreme potentialities of men can really unfold happiness. This liberation of potentialities is a matter of social practice. What men, with their developed sensuous and psychic organs and the wealth created by their work, can undertake to attain the highest measure of happiness rests with this practice. Understood in this way, happiness can no longer or in any way be merely subjective: it enters the realm of men's communal thought and action.

Where society utilizes the developed productive forces only in fettered form, it is not just the gratifications but the very wants themselves that are falsified. Insofar as they extend beyond the subsistence minimum, they come to expression only in proportion to their effective demand. Class situation, especially the situation of the individual in the labor process, is active in them, for this situation has formed the (bodily and spiritual) organs and capacities of men and the horizon of their demands. Since these appear as wants only in their stunted form, with all their repressions, renunciations, adaptations, and rationalizations, they can normally be satisfied within the given social framework. Because they are themselves already unfree, the false happiness of their fulfillment is possible in unfreedom.

In critical theory, the concept of happiness has been freed from any ties with bourgeois conformism and relativism. Instead, it has become a part of general, objective truth, valid for all individuals insofar as all their interests are preserved in it. Only in view of the historical possibility of general freedom is it meaningful to designate as untrue even actual, really perceived happiness in the previous and present conditions of existence. It is the individual's interest that expresses itself in his wants, and their gratification corresponds to this interest. That there is any happiness at all in a society governed by blind laws is a blessing. Through this happiness, the individual in this society can feel secure and protected from ultimate desperation. Rigoristic morality sins against the cheerless form in which humanity has survived. All hedonism is right in opposing it. Only today, at the highest stage of development of the established order, when the objective forces making for a higher order of humanity have become mature, and only in connection with the theory and practice linked to such a transformation, may the critique of the totality of the established order also take as its object the happiness that this order provides. It appears that individuals raised to be integrated into the antagonistic labor process cannot be judges of their own happiness. They have been prevented from knowing their true interest. Thus it is possible for them to designate their condition as happy and, without external compulsion, embrace the system that oppresses them. The results of modern plebiscites prove that men separated from possible truth can be brought to vote against themselves. As long as individuals see their interest only as getting along within the given order, such plebiscites pose no problems for the authoritarian apparatus. Terror merely supplements the delusions of the governed. Appeal to interest is untrue.

In view of the possibility of a happier real state of humanity the interest of the individual is no longer an ultimate datum. There are true and false interests even with regard to the individual. His factual, immediate interest is not in itself his true interest. It is not as though the true interest were that which demanded, on the grounds of lesser risk and greater chance of enjoyment, the sacrifice of an immediate interest. Such calculation of happiness stays within the general framework of false interest and can at best facilitate the choice of the better false happiness. It cannot be in the true interest of the individual to want his own and others' vitiation — not even in the true interest of those whose power can only be maintained at the cost of such vitiation. At the attained level of development power can no longer enjoy the world which it dominates. For if it were to cease working and continually renewing the bloody and destructive process of its mere reproduction, it would be instantly lost. Even the powers that be have something to gain.

That the true interest of individuals is the interest of freedom, that true individual freedom can coexist with real general freedom and, indeed, is possible only in conjunction with it, that happiness ultimately consists in freedom — these are not propositions of philosophical anthropology about the nature of man but descriptions of a historical situation which humanity has achieved for itself in the struggle with nature. The individuals whose happiness is at stake in making good use of this situation have grown up in the school of capitalism. To the high intensification and differentiation of their abilities and of their world corresponds the social shackling of this development. Insofar as unfreedom is already present in wants and not just in their gratification, they must be the first to be liberated — not through an act of education or of the moral renewal of man but through an economic and political process encompassing the disposal over the means of production by the community, the reorientation of the productive process toward the needs and wants of the whole society, the shortening of the working day, and the active participation of the individuals in the administration of the whole. When all present subjective and objective potentialities of development have been unbound, the needs and wants themselves will change. Those based on the social compulsion of repression, on injustice, and on filth and poverty would necessarily disappear. There may still be the sick, the insane, and the criminal. The realm of necessity persists; struggle with nature and even among men continues. Thus the reproduction of the whole will continue to be associated with privations for the individual. Particular interest will not coincide immediately with true interest. The difference between particular and true interest, nevertheless, is something other than the difference between particular interest and a hypostatized general interest that suppresses the individuals. In his relation to an authentic general interest, the individual would relate to truth; the demands and decisions of the whole would then preserve the individual interest and eventually promote his happiness. If the true interest, furthermore, must be represented by a general law forbidding specific wants and gratifications, such a law will no longer be a front for the particular interest of groups that maintain their power against the general interest through usurpation. Rather, it will express the rational decision of free individuals. Having come of age, men themselves will have to confront and deal with their wants. Their responsibility will be infinitely greater, because they will no longer have the false pleasure of masochistic security in the strong protection of a heteronomous power. The internal, real union of duty and happiness (and not a union effected in the world beyond), which idealist ethics had doubted, is possible only in freedom. This was Kant's intention when he founded the concept of duty on the autonomy of the person. Through its limitation to the freedom of the pure will, autonomy limits itself in favor of a social order that it could only admit in an abstract form.

If individuals, having attained majority, reject particular wants or a particular pleasure as bad, this would occur on the basis of the autonomous recognition of their true interest: the preservation of general freedom. Consequently it would occur in the interest of happiness itself, which can only exist in general freedom as the fulfillment of all developed potentialities. It was the ancient desideratum of hedonism to join in thought both happiness and truth. The problem was insoluble. For as long as an anarchic, unfree society determined the truth, the latter could only manifest itself either in the particular interest of the isolated individual or in the necessities of the hypostatized general interest, the society. In the first case its form (generality) was lost; in the second, its content (particularity). The truth to which the liberated individual relates in happiness is both general and particular. The subject is no longer isolated in its interest against others. His life can be happy beyond the contingency of the moment, because his conditions of existence are no longer determined by a labor process which creates wealth only through the perpetuation of poverty and privation. Instead they are regulated through the rational self-administration of the whole in which the subject participates actively. The individual can relate to others as equals and to the world as his world, no longer alienated from him. Mutual understanding will no longer be permeated by unhappiness, since insight and passion will no longer come into conflict with a reified form of human relationship.

General happiness presupposes knowledge of the true interest: that the social life-process be administered in a manner which brings into harmony the freedom of individuals and the preservation of the whole on the basis of given objective historical and natural conditions. With the development of social antagonisms the connection of happiness with knowledge was obscured. The abstract reason of isolated individuals is certainly powerless over a happiness abandoned to contingency. But this very social development has also brought forth the forces which can once again bring about that connection. For the immediate producers, isolating individuation has already been abolished extensively within unfreedom: the individual has no property to preserve that can only be enjoyed at the expense of others. His interest drives him not to competition or into interest groups based in turn upon competition but rather to militant solidarity. The first goal of struggle is only a particular social group's interest in better, more humane conditions of life. But this particular interest cannot be pursued without bettering and making more humane the conditions of life of the whole and liberating the entire society. In the monopolistic phase of bourgeois society, when the preservation of the general interest on the part of the groups fighting for transformation is obvious enough, the efforts of the beneficiaries of the Establishment are directed toward splitting that solidarity. Bureaucratization, increase of wage differentials, and immediate corruption of the workers are intended to root contradictions even among these strata. Their true interest requires not piecemeal change but the reconstruction of the productive process. When this has been achieved, general reason can no longer outwit the particular

195

interest behind the backs of the individuals. To the contrary, the particular interest becomes the active and cognitive force of the process through which generality, embodied in the community, is advanced. Only at this point in society is "the truth of *particular* satisfactions . . . the *general* satisfaction that, as happiness, the thinking will sets itself as goal."[28]

Hegel pointed out that general progress comes about in history only through particular interests, for only particular interest can stir the individual to the passion of historical struggle. "The particular interest of passion is therefore inseparable from the activity of the universal; for it is from the particular and determinate and from its negation, that the universal results."[29] When this inseparability rests on the cunning of reason, it entails the unhappiness of individuals. In the passion with which they pursue their particular interests, they wear themselves out and are destroyed. Hegel called it a "horrible comfort" that "historical men have not been what is called happy."[30] If no higher form of historical reason is possible than the antagonistic organization of humanity, then this horror cannot be thought away. It is true, of course, that men intend not happiness but, in each case, specific ends whose fulfillment then brings happiness. In the specific goals which are aimed at in solidary struggle for a rational society, happiness is no longer merely an attendant contingency. It is built into the very structure of the new order of the conditions of existence that have been demanded. Happiness ceases to be a mere subjective state of feeling when general concern for the potentialities of individuals is effective at the level of the liberated needs and wants of the subjects.

For Hegel, then, the struggle for the higher generality, or form of society, of the future becomes in the present the cause of particular individuals and groups, and this constitutes the tragic situation of world-historical persons. They attack social conditions in which — even if badly — the life of the whole reproduces itself. They fight against a concrete form of reason without empirical proof of the practicability of the future form which they represent. They offend against that which, within limits at least, has proven true. Their rationality necessarily operates in a particular, irrational, explosive form, and their critique of decadence and anarchy appears anarchic and destructive. Individuals who hold so fast to the Idea[31] that it permeates their existence are unyielding and stubborn. Common sense cannot distinguish between them and criminals, and in fact in the given order they are criminals like Socrates in Athens.[32] Universality and reason have become their own passion. The formalistic conformist, for whom one want is just as valid as another, knows of them as selfish characters who are dangerous. He sees how the critique of the appearance of freedom in the present and the knowledge of the future reality of freedom already constitute their happiness, because in them the blunt separation of here and there, today and tomorrow, the exclusive, defensive ego-feeling of bourgeois existence is overcome — but he cannot understand it. Whatever he may say, they are to him exalted, at best religious. For of themselves, thinks the conformist, people have only their own advantage in mind. Their paradoxical situation is apparent only to few.

Just as the attainable form of happiness can only be realized through the particular interest of only those social strata whose liberation leads not to the domination of particular interests over the community but to the general liberation of humanity, the same holds for the correct knowledge required by this form. This interest requires its ideology as a veil over the structure of truth in order to justify itself as a general interest. This interest, by its very nature, implies thinking to the end all realizable potentialities (which in the bourgeois period found their social limit in the danger of a material transformation of the whole) and keeping to the goal of their realization. The loss of correct knowledge would entail the loss of happiness as well, for the compulsion and necessity of an uncontrollable situation would once again win its contingent power over men. Freedom of knowledge is a part of real freedom, which can only exist together with common decision and action on the basis of what is known to be true. The essential role of truth for the happiness of individuals makes the characterization of happiness as pleasure and enjoyment appear insufficient. When knowledge of truth is no longer linked to knowledge of guilt, poverty, and injustice, it is no longer forced to remain external to a happiness ceded to immediate, sensual relationships. Even the most personal human relations can be opened to happiness in a really guiltless knowledge. Perhaps they would thereby become, in fact, that free community in life of which idealist morality had expected the highest unfolding of individuality. Knowledge will no longer disturb pleasure. Perhaps it can even become pleasure, which the ancient idea of *nous* had dared to see as the highest determination of knowledge. The bogey of the unchained voluptuary who would abandon himself only to his sensual wants is rooted in the separation of intellectual from material productive forces and the separation of the labor process from the process of consumption. Overcoming this separation belongs to the preconditions of freedom. The development of material wants must go together with the development of psychic and mental wants. The organization of technology, science, and art changes with their changed utilization and changed content. When they are no longer under the compulsion of a system of production based on the unhappiness of the majority, and of the pressures of rationalization, internalization, and sublimation, then mind and spirit can only mean an augmentation of happiness. Hedonism is both abolished and preserved in critical theory and practice. If freedom prevails in the spiritual and mental side of life, i.e. in culture, and if culture is no longer subject to the compulsion of internalization, then it becomes meaningless to restrict happiness to sensual pleasure.

The reality of happiness is the reality of freedom as the self-determination of liberated humanity in its common struggle with nature. "The truth of particular satisfactions is the *general* [*allgemeine*] satisfaction that, as happiness, the thinking will sets itself as goal." But this happiness is at first "generality of content only as representation, as abstraction, only as something that *should* be." Its truth is "the *universal* [*allgemeine*] determinacy of the will in itself, i.e. its own self-determination: *freedom*."[33] For idealism, freedom was also reason: "the substance of" and "that alone which is true of spirit."[34] In their completed form both, happiness and reason, coincide. Hegel did not believe that the realization of this form by bringing about a new form of the social organization of humanity could become the task of historical practice. Under the title of the "ideal," however, he represented happiness as a "stage of world development" that is simultaneously one of reason and freedom: as the abolition of the antithesis, characteristic of the bourgeois stage of development, between individuals isolated in their particular interests, on the one hand, and the hypostatized general interest as the state that perpetuates itself through the sacrifice of individuals, on the other.

In the ideal . . . particular individuality is supposed to remain precisely in undissolved harmony with the substantial; and insofar as the ideal partakes of the freedom and independence of subjectivity, to that extent the surrounding world of conditions and developmental structures may not possess any essential objectivity belonging to itself quite apart from the subjective and the individual. For the ideal individual should be self-contained. The objective world should still be part of what is incontestably his and not move or develop by itself, detached from the individuality of subjects. Otherwise the subject becomes merely subordinate to a world that is complete in itself.[35]

Originally published in German in Zeitschrift für Sozialforschung, *vol. VII (1938).*

VI. INDUSTRIALIZATION AND CAPITALISM
IN THE WORK OF MAX WEBER

INDUSTRIALIZATION and capitalism become problematic in
Max Weber's work in two respects: as the historical fate of
the West, and as the contemporary fate of the Germany created by Bismarck. As the fate of the West, they are the decisive realizations of that Western rationality, that idea of
reason, which Weber traces in its open and veiled, progressive
and repressive, manifestations. As the fate of modern Germany, these manifestations determine for him the politics of
the Reich, primarily as the historical task of the German
bourgeoisie — in the transformation of the conservative-
feudal state, then in democratization, finally in the struggle
against revolution and socialism. It is essentially the idea of a
fateful connection between industrialization, capitalism, and
national self-preservation that motivates Max Weber's pas-
sionate and — let us be frank — spiteful fight against the socialist efforts of 1918. According to him, socialism contradicts the
idea of occidental reason, as well as that of the national state;
hence it is a world-historical error, if not a world-historical
crime. (We might ask, what Max Weber would have said had
he lived to see that it is not the West, but the East, which, in
the name of socialism, has developed modern occidental ra-

tionality in its extreme form.) Whatever capitalism may do to man, it must, according to Weber, first and before all evaluation, be understood as necessary reason.

Philosophical, sociological-historical, and political motives are fundamentally connected in Weber's analysis of industrial capitalism. His theory of the intrinsic value-freedom, or ethical neutrality, of science reveals itself as that which it is in practice: an attempt to make science "free" to accept obligatory valuations that are imposed on it from the outside. This function of Weber's theory of knowledge has been clear ever since his inaugural address at Freiburg in 1895, which with ruthless frankness subordinates value-free economics to the claims of national power politics. Sometime later (at the meeting of the *Verein für Sozialpolitik* in 1909) he himself made it as explicit as possible:

> The reason why I argue on every occasion so sharply and even, perhaps, pedantically against the fusion of Is and Ought is not because I underestimate Ought questions, but, on the contrary, because I cannot stand it when problems of world-moving importance, of the greatest intellectual and spiritual bearing, in a certain sense the highest problems that can move a human breast are transformed here into questions of technical-economic "productivity" and are made into the topic of discussion of a *technical* discipline, such as economics is.[1]

But the Ought that is thus taken out of science (a mere "technical discipline") is thereby simultaneously protected from science and shielded from scientific criticism: the "value of that ideal itself can never be derived"[2] from the material of scientific work itself.

It is precisely Max Weber's analysis of industrial capitalism, however, which shows that the concept of scientific neutrality, or, better, impotence, vis-à-vis the Ought, cannot be maintained: pure value-free philosophical-sociological concept formation becomes, *through its own process,* value criticism. Inversely, the pure value-free scientific concepts reveal the valuation that is contained in them: they become the critique of the given, in the light of what the given does to men (and things). The Ought shows itself in the Is: the indefatigable effort of conceptual thinking makes it appear. In *Wirtschaft und Gesellschaft,* that work of Max Weber which is most free from values and where the method of formal definitions, classifications, and typologies celebrates true orgies, formalism attains the incisiveness of content. This authentic concretion is the result of Weber's mastery of an immense material, of scholarship that seems unimaginable today, of knowledge that can afford to abstract because it can distinguish the essential from the inessential and reality from appearance. With its abstract concepts, formal theory reaches the goal at which a positivistic, pseudoempirical sociology hostile to theory aims in vain: the real definition of reality. The concept of industrial capitalism thus becomes concrete in the formal theory of *rationality* and of *domination* which are the two fundamental themes of *Wirtschaft und Gesellschaft.*

Let us try first to present the connection between capitalism, rationality, and domination in the work of Max Weber. In its most general form this connection may be formulated as follows: the specifically Western idea of reason realizes itself in a system of material and intellectual culture (economy, technology, "conduct of life," science, art) that develops to the full in industrial capitalism, and this system tends toward a specific type of domination which becomes the fate of the contemporary period: total bureaucracy. The comprehensive and basic concept is the idea of reason as Western rationality. We begin with this concept.

For Weber, there is a rationality that has come into effect

only in the West, that has formed (or has at least helped form) capitalism, and that has decided our foreseeable future. The effort to determine this rationality in its many (and often contradictory) manifestations occupies a large part of Weber's work. The "spirit of capitalism," as described in the first volume of his collected essays in the sociology of religion, is one of these manifestations; the preface to this work points out programmatically that the rationality formulated and acted on in capitalism fundamentally distinguishes Western industrialization from all other forms of economy and technology.

Let us first list the elements that are characteristic of Max Weber's concept of reason. (1) There is the progressive mathematization of experience and knowledge, a mathematization which, starting from the natural sciences and their extraordinary successes, extends to the other sciences and to the "conduct of life" itself (universal quantification). (2) There is the insistence on the necessity of rational experiments and rational proofs in the organization of science as well as in the conduct of life. (3) There is the result of this organization which is decisive for Weber, namely, the genesis and solidification of a universal, technically trained organization of officials that becomes the "absolutely *inescapable* condition of our entire existence."[3] With this last characteristic, the transition from theoretical to practical reason, to the historical form of reason is effected. The consciousness of its specific historicity was contained in the beginning in Weber's conception of reason, with, or precisely due to, its abstractness. However, we shall see that it is not sustained in the entire course of his analysis and miscarries at the decisive point. In his sociology, formal rationality turns into *capitalist* rationality. Thus it appears as the methodical taming of the irrational "acquisitive drive," the taming that finds its typical expression in "innerworldly asceticism."

In this "taming," occidental reason becomes the *economic* reason of capitalism, that is, the striving for ever renewed gain within the continuous, rational, capitalist enterprise. Rationality thus becomes the condition of profitability, which in turn is oriented toward systematic, methodical calculation, "capital accounting."[4]

The basis of this rationality is abstraction which, at once theoretical and practical, the work of both scientific and social organization, determines the capitalist period: through the reduction of quality to quantity. As universal functionalization (which finds its economic expression in exchange value), it becomes the precondition of calculable *efficiency* — of universal efficiency, insofar as functionalization makes possible the domination of all particular cases and relations (through their reduction to quantities and exchange values). Abstract reason becomes concrete in the calculable and calculated *domination* of nature and man. The reason envisaged by Weber thus is revealed as *technical* reason, as the production and transformation of material (things and men) through the methodical-scientific apparatus. This apparatus has been built with the aim of calculable efficiency; its rationality organizes and controls things and men, factory and bureaucracy, work and leisure. But *to what purpose* does it control them? Up to this point, Weber's concept of reason has been "formal," that is, has been defined as quantifying abstraction from all particulars, an abstraction that rendered possible the universally calculable efficiency of the capitalist apparatus. But now the limits of formal reason emerge: neither the specific purpose of the scientific-technical construction nor its material (its subjects and its objects) can be deduced from the concept of reason; they explode from the start this formal, "value-free" concept.

In capitalist rationality, as analyzed by Weber, these elements that are prior and "external" to reason and that thus materially delimit it appear in two historical facts: (1) provision for human needs — the aim of economic activity — is carried out in the framework of *private enterprise* and its calculable chances of gain, that is, within the framework of the *profit* of the individual entrepreneur or enterprise; (2) consequently, the existence of those whose needs are to be satisfied depends on the profit opportunities of the capitalist enterprise. This dependence is embodied, in its extreme form, in the "free" labor that is at the disposal of the entrepreneur.

In terms of Weber's conception, these facts are pregiven to formal reason from the outside, but as historical facts, they limit the general validity of the concept itself. According to Weber, the focal reality of capitalist rationality is the *private* enterprise; the entrepreneur is a free person, responsible by and to himself for his calculations and their risks. In this function, he is *bourgeois,* and the bourgeois conduct of life finds its representative expression in innerworldly asceticism. Is this conception still valid today? Is the bourgeoisie, in which Weber saw the bearer of industrial development, still its bearer in the late capitalist phase? Is late capitalist rationality still that which derives from innerworldly asceticism? I think the answer to these questions must be in the negative. In the development of capitalistic rationality itself, the forms ascribed to it by Weber have disintegrated and become obsolete, and their disintegration makes the rationality of capitalistic industrialization appear in a very different light: in the light of its *ir*rationality. To mention only one aspect: "innerworldly asceticism" is no longer a motivating force in late capitalism; it has become a fetter that serves the maintenance of the system. Keynes denounced it as such, and it is a danger to the "affluent society" wherever it could hinder the production and consumption of superfluous goods. To be sure, even late capitalism is built on "renunciation": the struggle for existence and the exploitation of labor must be intensified more and more if increased accumulation is to be possible. "Planned obsolescence," methodical irrationality, becomes a social necessity. But this is no longer the conduct of life of the bourgeoisie as the class that develops the productive forces. It is rather the stigma of productive destruction under total administration. And the capital accounting of mathematized profitability and efficiency celebrates its greatest triumphs in the calculation of kill and overkill, of the risk of our own annihilation compared with that of the annihilation of the enemy.

In the unfolding of capitalist rationality, *irrationality* becomes *reason:* reason as frantic development of productivity, conquest of nature, enlargement of the mass of goods (and their accessibility for broad strata of the population); irrational because higher productivity, domination of nature, and social wealth become destructive forces. This destruction is not only figurative, as in the betrayal of so-called higher cultural values, but literal: the struggle for existence intensifies both within national states and internationally, and pent-up aggression is discharged in the legitimation of medieval cruelty (torture) and in the scientifically organized destruction of men. Did Max Weber foretell this development? The answer is No if the accent is placed on "tell." But this development is implied in his conceptual scheme — implied at such a deep level that it appears as inexorable, final, and thereby, in turn (in the bad sense), rational.

In the course of Weber's analysis, the value-free concept of capitalist rationality becomes a critical concept — critical in the sense not only of "pure science," but also of an evaluative, goal-positing critique of reification.

But then the critique stops, accepts the allegedly inexorable, and turns into apologetics — worse, into the denunciation of the possible alternative, that is, of a qualitatively different historical rationality. With clairvoyance, Weber himself recognized the limit of his conceptual scheme. He defined himself as a "bourgeois" and identified his work with the historical mission of the bourgeoisie; in the name of this alleged mission, he accepted the alliance of representative strata of the German bourgeoisie with the organizers of reaction and repression. For political adversaries on the radical left, he recommended the lunatic asylum, the zoo, and the revolver shot. He raged against the intellectuals who had sacrificed their lives for the revolution.[5] The personal serves us here only as illustration of the conceptual; it serves to show how the concept of reason itself, in its critical content, remains ultimately tied to its origin: "reason" remains *bourgeois* reason, and, indeed, only one part of the latter, viz. capitalist technical reason.

Let us try now to reconstruct the inner development of the Weberian concept of capitalist reason. The Freiburg inaugural address envisions capitalist industrialization wholly as a form of power politics, that is, as imperialism. Only the development of large-scale industry can guarantee the independence of the nation in the ever more intense international competitive struggle. Imperialist power politics requires intensive and extensive industrialization, and vice versa. The economy must serve the *raison d'état* of the national state and must work with the latter's means. Such means are colonization and military power, means for the realization of the extrascientific aims and values to which value-free economics must subordinate itself. As historical reason, the reason of state demands rule by that class which is capable of carrying out industrialization and thus effecting the growth of the nation, i.e. rule by the *bourgeoisie*. It is dangerous when an "economically declining class is in power"[6] (as the Junkers in Germany). Under the pressure of extrascientific, political valuation, economic science thus becomes, with Weber, the political-sociological critique of the state erected by Bismarck. And this critique anticipates the future in an unheard-of way: in Germany, the historically appointed class, the bourgeoisie, is "immature"; in its weakness it longs for a new Caesar who would do the deed for it.[7]

The coming to power of the bourgeois class meant, at that time, the democratization of the still prebourgeois state. But, owing to its political immaturity, the German bourgeoisie can neither realize nor hinder this democratization and calls for caesarism. Democracy, the political form corresponding to capitalist industrialization, threatens to change into plebiscitary dictatorship; bourgeois reason conjures up irrational *charisma*. This dialectic of bourgeois democracy if not of bourgeois reason continued to trouble Weber, and is incisively expressed in *Wirtschaft und Gesellschaft*. We shall return to it. Here it should be observed that Weber, more correctly than most contemporary socialists, also foresaw the later development of the other class that underlies capitalism, the proletariat, and therewith repeated almost unchanged what Bismarck had said as early as 1865. "The danger does not lie with the masses,"[8] Weber declared in his 1895 inaugural address. It is not the ruled classes who will hinder imperialistic politics, let alone cause it to fail. It is rather "the ruling and rising classes" who represent this threat to the nation's chances for survival in international competition.

The conservative character of the masses, the caesaristic tendencies of the ruling classes: *these* changes of late capitalism Max Weber did foresee. He did not, as Marxist theory does, root them in the structure of capitalism itself. "Political immaturity" is a poor category as long as it does not define the factors behind the fact — in this case the impossibility for capitalist production of preserving the free market through free competition. Capitalist production itself runs up against its limits in the democratic institutions of the market society. Domination is concentrated in and above the bureaucracy, as the necessary apex of regimentation. What appeared as political immaturity within the context of liberalistic capitalism becomes, in organized capitalism, political maturity.

And the harmlessness of the ruled classes? Even while Weber was still living, they were, for a historical instant, ready to cause imperialistic politics to fail. After that, however, the political maturity of the bourgeoisie and the intellectual efficiency of capitalist productivity took things in hand and confirmed Weber's prediction.

Let us now look at his concept of capitalism where (apparently) it is removed from the concrete context of imperialistic power politics and developed in its value-free scientific purity: in *Wirtschaft und Gesellschaft*. Here capitalism, as a form of "rational economic acquisition," is defined in the first instance as a "particular form of monetary calculation":

> Capital accounting is the valuation and calculation of profit opportunities and . . . proceeds by means of comparing the respective monetary values of total (fixed and liquid) assets at the beginning and end of a single profit-oriented undertaking or, in the case of a continuous profit-making enterprise, of comparing the initial and final balance sheets for an accounting period.[9]

The effort — one is tempted to say the provocative effort — to define capitalism in a purely scientific manner and to abstract from everything human and historical shows forth even in the forbidding syntax (at least in German). What is at issue here is business and nothing else. In contrast to this attitude, Weber's emphasis on the next page seems almost shocking: "Capital accounting in its *formally* most rational mode thus presupposes *the struggle of man with man*."[10] What capital accounting does to men finds sharper expression in its abstract definition than in the latter's concretion: inhumanity is included in the rationality of the initial and final balance sheets.

The "formally most rational" mode of capital accounting is the one into which man and his "purposes" enter only as variables in the calculation of the chances of gain and profit. In this formal rationality, mathematization is carried to the point of the calculus with the real *negation of life* itself; at the extreme, risk of death from hunger, it becomes a motive for economic activity on the part of those who have nothing:

> . . . decisive as [an] element of the motivation of economic activity under the conditions of a market economy [is] *normally* . . . for those without property . . . the fact that they run the risk, both for themselves and their personal dependents, such as children, wives, sometimes parents, whose maintenance the individual typically takes over, of going without any provision . . .[11]

Again and again, Weber defines *formal* rationality in contrast to a *material* (substantive) rationality, in which the economic maintenance of men is considered "from the point of view of certain valuational postulates (of whatever kind)."[12]

Formal rationality is thus in conflict not only with "traditional" value orientations and goals, but also with revolutionary ones. As an example, Max Weber mentions the antinomy between formal rationality on the one hand and, on the other, of attempts to abolish the separation of powers ("soviet republic, government by a convention or committee of public safety"[13]) of attempts, in other words, to change radically the existing form of domination. But is the formal rationality that finds expression in a capitalist economy really so formal? Here, once more, is its definition:

> The term "formal rationality of economic action" will be used to designate the extent of quantitative calculation or accounting which is technically possible and which is actually applied. A system of economic activity will be called "formally" rational according to the degree in which the provision for needs, which is essential to every rational economy, is capable of being expressed in numerical, calculable terms, and is so expressed.[14]

According to this definition, a totally planned economy, that is, a noncapitalist economy, would evidently be *more* rational, in the sense of formal rationality, than the capitalist economy. For the latter sets itself the limits of calculability in the particular interest of the private enterprise and in the "freedom" (however regimented) of the market. If Weber declares such a planned economy retrogressive or even realistically impossible, he does so in the first place for a technological reason: in modern industrial society, the separation of the workers from the means of production has become a *technical* necessity requiring the individual and private direction and control of the means of production, that is, the authority of the personally responsible entrepreneur in the enterprise. The highly *material*, historical fact of the private-capitalist enterprise thus becomes (in Weber's sense) a *formal* structural element of capitalism and of *rational* economic activity itself.

But the rational social function of individual control of production that is based on the separation of labor from the means of production goes beyond this. For Max Weber, it is the guarantor of technically and economically necessary organizational *discipline*, which then becomes the model of the entire discipline required by modern industrial society. Even socialism, according to Weber, has its origin in factory discipline: "From this life situation, from the discipline of the factory, was modern socialism born."[15]

The "subjection to work discipline" characteristic of free enterprise is thus, on the one hand, the rationality of a *personal hierarchy*, but on the other hand, the rational domination of things over man, that is, "of the means over the end (the satisfaction of needs)." In these words, Weber quotes a socialist thesis.[16] He does not contest it but believes that not even a socialist society will change the fundamental fact of the worker's separation from the means of production, because this separation is simply the form of technical progress, of industrialization. Even socialism remains subject to its rationality, for otherwise it cannot remain faithful to its own promise of the general satisfaction of needs and the pacification of the struggle for existence. The control of man by things can be deprived of its irrationality only through the rational control of man by man. The question, therefore, is for socialism, too: "Who, then, is supposed to take over and direct this new economy?"[17]

Industrialization is thus seen as the fate of the modern world, and the fateful question for both capitalist and socialist industrialization is only this: What is the most rational form of dominating industrialization and hence society? ("Most rational" is still used in the sense of that *formal* rationality which is determined only by the calculable and regulated functioning of its own system.) But this formal rationality seems to have changed imperceptibly in the course of the logical development of Weber's analysis. In becoming

a question of domination, of control, this rationality subordinates itself, by virtue of its own inner dynamic, to another,
namely, to the rationality of domination. Precisely insofar as
this formal rationality does not go beyond its own structure
and has nothing but its own system as the norm of its calculations and calculating actions, it is as a whole dependent, determined "from the outside" by something other than itself;
in this fashion reason becomes, in Weber's own definition,
"material."

Industrialization as "fate," domination as "fate" — Max
Weber's concept of "fate" shows in exemplary fashion the
material content of his formal analysis. "Fate" is the law of
an economy and society which are largely independent of
individuals, and violation of this law would mean self-destruc-
tion. But society is not "nature." Who decrees the fate?
Industrialization is a phase in the development of men's capacities and needs, a phase in their struggle with nature and
with themselves. This development can proceed in very different forms and with very different aims; not only the forms
of control but also those of technology and hence of needs and
of their satisfactions are in no way "fatal," but rather *become*
such only when they are socially sanctioned, that is, as the
result of material, economic, and psychological coercion.
Weber's concept of fate is construed "after the fact" of such
coercion: he generalizes the blindness of a society which reproduces itself behind the back of the individuals, of a society
in which the law of domination appears as objective technological law. However, in fact, this law is neither "fatal" nor
"formal." The context of Weber's analysis is the historical
context in which economic reason became the reason of
domination — domination at almost any price. This fate has
become a fate and inasmuch as it has become a fate it can also

be *abolished*. Any scientific analysis that is not committed to this possibility is pledged, not to reason, but to the reason of established domination. For there is no structure that has not been *posited* or *made* and is not as such dependent. In the continuum of history, in which all economic action takes place, all economic reason is always the reason of domination, which historically and socially determines economic action. Capitalism, no matter how mathematized and "scientific," remains the mathematized, technological *domination* of men; and socialism, no matter how scientific and technological, is the construction or demolition of domination.

If in Weber's work the formal analysis of capitalism thus becomes the analysis of forms of domination, this is not due to a discontinuity in concept or method; their purity itself shows itself impure. And this is so, not because Max Weber was a bad or inconsistent sociologist, but because he knew his subject matter: Truth becomes critique and accusation, and accusation becomes the function of true science. If he subjected the science of economics to politics as early as in the inaugural address, this tour de force shows itself, in the light of the whole of Weber's work, as the inner logic of his method. Your science must remain "pure"; only thus can you remain faithful to the truth. But this truth forces you to recognize what determines the objects of your science "from the outside." Over this you have no power. Your freedom from value judgments is as necessary as it is mere appearance. For neutrality is *real* only when it has the power of resisting interference. Otherwise it becomes the victim, as well as the aid, of every power that wants to use it.

The formal rationality of capitalism comes up against its internal limit in two places: in the fact of *private enterprise,* or the private entrepreneur as the actual subject of the calculated nature of economic activity; and in the fact of the worker's separation from the means of production, of *free labor*.

These two facts belong, for Max Weber, to the specific rationality of capitalism;[18] they are technological necessities. For him, they thus are the basis for domination as an integral element of capitalist (and even of economic) rationality in modern industrial society. If this is so, then domination itself must be demonstrated as the form of modern economic rationality; and this is what Weber tries to do in his analysis of *bureaucracy*.

Bureaucratic control is inseparable from increasing industrialization; it extends the maximally intensified efficiency of industrial organization to society as a whole. It is the formally most rational form of control, thanks to its "precision, steadfastness, discipline, rigor, and dependability, in short calculability for both the head [of the organization] and for those having to do with it . . .";[19] and it is all this because it is "domination by virtue of knowledge," ascertainable, calculable, calculating knowledge, specialized knowledge. Properly speaking, it is the *apparatus* that dominates, for the control of this apparatus, based on specialized knowledge, is such only if it is fully adjusted to its technical demands and potentialities. For this reason, domination of the apparatus is "possible for the layman only within limits: in the long run, the technically trained permanent official is usually superior to the layman as a [government] minister."[20]

Again Weber stresses that any "rational socialism" "would simply have to take over and would intensify" bureaucratic administration since this administration is nothing but purely *objective* domination, demanded by the objective circumstances themselves, and equally valid for the most varied political, cultural, and moral aims and institutions. And the objective circumstances themselves are the given, ever more productively and efficiently developing, ever more precisely calculable apparatus.

The specialized scientific administration of the apparatus as formally rational domination: this is the reification of reason, reification *as* reason, the apotheosis of reification. But the apotheosis turns into its negation, is bound to turn into its negation. For the apparatus, which dictates its own objective administration, is itself instrument, means — and there is no such thing as a means "as such." Even the most productive, most reified apparatus is a means to an end outside itself. As far as the economic apparatus of capitalism is concerned, it is not enough to say that this end is the satisfaction of needs. Such a concept is too general, too abstract, in the bad sense of the word. For, as Max Weber himself realized, the satisfaction of needs is far more the by-product than the end of capitalist economic activity. Human needs are necessary and "formally rational" as long as living human beings are still required as consumers (as producers they already are partly unnecessary), and already much is sold to warehouses — stockpiling for annihilation and a subhuman subterranean life. But if the bureaucratic administration of the capitalist apparatus, with all its rationality, remains a means, and thus dependent, then it has, as rationality, its own limit. The bureaucracy subjects itself to an extra- and suprabureaucratic power — to an "unbusinesslike" power. And if rationality is embodied in administration, and *only* in administration, then this legislative power must be irrational. The Weberian conception of reason ends in irrational *charisma*.

Among all of Weber's concepts, that of charisma is perhaps the most questionable. Even as a term it contains the bias that gives every kind of successful, allegedly personal domination an almost religious consecration. The concept itself is under discussion here only insofar as it can illuminate the dialectic of rationality and irrationality in modern society. Charismatic domination appears as a phase in a twofold process of development. On the one hand, charisma tends to turn into the solidified domination of interests and their bureaucratic organization; on the other hand, bureaucratic organization tends to submit to a charismatic leader.

In the chapter "Transformation of Charisma" Max Weber describes how pure charismatic domination tends to transform itself into a "permanent possession"; in this process "it is given over to the conditions of everyday life and to the powers that dominate it, above all to economic interests."[21] What begins as the charisma of the single individual and his personal following ends in domination by a bureaucratic apparatus that has acquired rights and functions and in which the charismatically dominated individuals become regular, tax-paying, dutiful "subjects."

But this rational administration of masses and things cannot do without the irrational charismatic leader. For the administration would tend, precisely to the degree to which it is really rational, to the abolition of domination (and to the administration of *things*). Yet the administrative apparatus has always been built on the basis of domination and has been established to maintain and strengthen domination. To the democratization required by rational administration thus corresponds a parallel limitation and manipulation of democratization. Domination as the privilege of particular interests and self-determination as an expression of the general interest are brought into forced unity. This violent and simultaneously formally rational, i.e. technically efficient, solution of the contradiction has its classical manifestation in plebiscitary democracy,[22] in which the masses periodically depose their leaders and determine their policies — under previously established conditions well controlled by the leaders. For Max Weber, universal suffrage thus is not only the result of domination but also its instrument in the period of its technical perfection. Plebiscitary democracy is the political expression of irrationality-become-reason.

In what way does this dialectic of reason (that is, of *formal* reason) show forth in the development of capitalism? The latter's profane power resists the idea of charisma, and Weber is rather timid when it comes to the application of this term to contemporary industrial society, even though his attitude and even his language during World War I and against the revolution often came very close to succumbing to charismatic illusions. But the actual trend is clearly exhibited by his analysis: the formal reason of the technically perfect administrative apparatus is subordinated to the irrational. Max Weber's analysis of bureaucracy breaks through the ideological camouflage. Far ahead of his time, he showed the illusory character of modern mass democracy with its pretended equalization and adjustment of class conflicts. The bureaucratic administration of industrial capitalism is indeed a "leveling," but what is decisive here is exclusively the *leveling of the dominated* vis-à-vis the ruling, bureaucratically organized group, which may actually, and often even formally, occupy a wholly autocratic position.[23] He stresses again and again that precisely the technically perfect administrative apparatus, *by virtue of its formal rationality,* is a "means of power of the very first rank for him who has the bureaucratic apparatus at his disposal."

The dependence of the material fate of the mass on the continuous, correct functioning of the increasingly bureaucratically organized private-capitalist organizations increases continuously, and the thought of the possibility of their elimination thus becomes ever more utopian.[24]

Total dependence on the functioning of an omnipresent apparatus becomes the "basis of all order" so that the apparatus itself is no longer questioned. "Trained orientation toward obedient subjection to those orders" becomes the cement of a subjugation of which people are no longer conscious because the order to which they subordinate themselves is itself so terrifyingly rational; that is, because it administers to efficiently and puts at one's calculable disposal the world of goods and performances of which the single individual no longer has an overview or a comprehension. Max Weber did not live long enough to see how mature capitalism, in the efficiency of its reason, makes even the planned annihilation of millions of human beings and the planned destruction of human labor the fountainhead of a bigger and better prosperity, how even sheer insanity becomes the basis, not only of the continuation of life, but of the more comfortable life. He did not live to see the "affluent society," in the face of inhuman misery and methodical cruelty outside its borders, squander its unimaginable technical, material, and intellectual power and abuse its power for the purposes of permanent mobilization. Even before the unfolding of the power of this reason he called attention to the danger present in the submission of the rational bureaucratic administrative apparatus, by virtue of its own rationality, to an irrational supreme authority.

In the first place, in the framework of Weber's conceptual scheme, it is almost self-evident that the administration of industrial society requires outside and superior direction: "Every administration requires some kind of domination, since, for its direction, some commanding powers must always be placed in someone's hands."[25] The capitalist entrepreneur is "in the material sense" as little of a trained official as the monarch at the head of the empire. No specialized qualities are required of him: "Bureaucratic domination thus inevitably has at its apex an element that is at least not purely bureaucratic."[26] "Inevitably," because the value-free rationality of administration is dependent upon values and goals that come to it from the outside. In his inaugural address, Weber had defined the power politics of the nation-state as giving economics its values and goals. Capitalism was therewith defined as *imperialism*.

In *Wirtschaft und Gesellschaft* some characteristics of the imperialistic economy are called by their names and summed up in the concept of "politically oriented capitalism." Weber then states: "It is clear from the start that those politically oriented events that offer these (political) possibilities for gain are economically irrational when viewed from the point of view of orientation toward market chances. . . ."[27] As irrational, they can be replaced by others. Control of the capitalistic economy not only requires no specialized qualification, it is also to a great degree fungible.

Capitalism, with all its rationality (or rather just because of its specific rationality), thus terminates in an irrational, "accidental" head — not only in the economy, but also in the control of the bureaucratic administration itself, in governmental administration. (It is difficult not to think here of Hegel's *Philosophy of Right* where the state of civil society, the rational state, culminates in the "accidental" person of the monarch who is determined only by the contingency of birth: in Hegel as in Weber, the analysis of bourgeois reason reveals the latter's limits: bourgeois reason negates itself in its consummation.)

Let us look back briefly at the stages in the development of Weber's concepts (and of their objects). Western capitalism originated under the specific social, political, and economic conditions of the waning Middle Ages and of the Reformation. It developed its "spirit" in that formal rationality that realized itself in the psychological as well as the economic orientation and action of the originators (but not the objects!) of the process of capital. Industrialization has been carried out under this formal reason: technical progress and progressive satisfaction of needs, whatever needs they may be. We have seen that this formal rationality develops on the basis of two very *material* historical facts, which maintain themselves in its progress and which (according to Max Weber) are *conditions* of capitalism, namely (1) the private enterprise and (2) "free labor," the existence of a class that "economically," "under the compulsion of the lash of hunger," is forced to sell its services.[28] As productive forces, these material conditions enter into formal reason. Capitalism expands in the competitive struggle of unequal (but formally free) powers: the struggle for existence of persons, nation-states, and international alliances.

For Max Weber, the contemporary phase of capitalism is dominated by national power politics: capitalism is imperialism. But its administration remains formally rational, i.e. bureaucratic domination. It administers the control of men by things; rational, "value-free" technology is the separation of man from the means of production and his subordination to technical efficiency and necessity — all this within the framework of private enterprise. The machine is the determining factor, but the "lifeless machine is congealed spirit (*Geist*). Only by being this has it the power to force men into its service . . . ."[29] Yet because it is "congealed spirit," it also is domination of man by man; thus *this* technical reason reproduces enslavement. Subordination to technology becomes subordination to domination as such; formal technical rationality turns into material political rationality (or is it the other way around, inasmuch as technical reason was from

222

the beginning the control of "free" labor by private enterprise?). Under the compulsion of reason, the fate is fulfilled that Weber foresaw with remarkable clarity in one of his most telling passages:

> Joined to the dead machine, [bureaucratic organization] is at work to erect the shell of that future bondage to which one day men will perhaps be forced to submit in impotence, as once the fellahs in the ancient Egyptian state—*if a purely, technically good, that is, rational bureaucratic administration and maintenance is the last and only value which is to decide on the manner in which their affairs are directed.*[30]

But it is precisely here, at this most decisive point, where Weber's analysis becomes self-criticism, that one can see how much this analysis has fallen prey to the identification of technical reason with bourgeois capitalist reason. This identification prevents him from seeing that not "pure," formal, technical reason but the reason of domination erects the "shell of bondage," and that the consummation of technical reason can well become the instrument for the *liberation* of man. Put differently: Max Weber's analysis of capitalism was not sufficiently value-free, inasmuch as it took into its "pure" definitions of formal rationality valuations peculiar to capitalism. On this basis, the contradiction developed between formal and material (or substantive) rationality, whose obverse is the "neutrality" of technical reason vis-à-vis all outside material valuations. This neutrality, in turn, made it possible for Weber to accept the (*reified*) interest of the nation and its political power as the values that determine technical reason.

The very concept of technical reason is perhaps ideological. Not only the application of technology but technology itself is domination (of nature and men) — methodical, scientific, calculated, calculating control. Specific purposes and interests of domination are not foisted upon technology "subsequently" and from the outside; they enter the very construction of the technical apparatus. Technology is always a historical-social *project:* in it is projected what a society and its ruling interests intend to do with men and things. Such a "purpose" of domination is "substantive" and to this extent belongs to the very form of technical reason.

Weber abstracted from this ineluctable social material. We have emphasized the right to this abstraction in the analysis of capitalist reason: abstraction becomes *critical* of this reason insofar as it shows the degree to which capitalist rationality itself abstracts from man, to whose needs it is "indifferent," and in this indifference becomes ever more productive and efficient, calculating and methodical, thus erecting the "shell of bondage," furnishing it (quite luxuriously), and universalizing it. Weber's abstractness is so saturated with his material that it pronounces rational judgment on the rational exchange society. In the course of its development, however, this society tends to abolish its own material prerequisites: the private entrepreneur is no longer the subject of economic rationality, answering only to himself, and "free labor" is no longer the enslavement enforced by the threatening "lash of hunger." The exchange society, where everything proceeds so freely and rationally, comes under the control of economic and political monopolies. The market and its liberties, whose ideological character Max Weber demonstrated often enough, is now subjected to frightfully efficient regulation, in which the general interest is markedly shaped by the ruling particular interests. Reification is abolished, but in a very deceptive manner. The separation from the means of production, in which Weber rightly saw a technical necessity, turns into the subjection of the whole to its calculating managers. The formal rationality of capitalism celebrates its triumph in electronic computers, which calculate everything, no matter what the purpose, and which are put to use as mighty instruments of political manipulation, reliably calculating the chances of profit and loss, including the chance of the annihilation of the whole, with the consent of the likewise calculated and obedient population. Mass democracy becomes plebiscitary even within the economy and the sciences: the masses themselves elect their leaders into the shell of bondage.

But if technical reason thus reveals itself as political reason, it does so only because from the beginning it was this technical reason and this political reason, that is, limited in the specific interest of domination. As political reason, technical reason is *historical*. If separation from the means of production is a technical necessity, the bondage that it organizes is *not*. On the basis of its own achievements, that is, of productive and calculable mechanization, this separation contains the potentiality of a qualitatively different rationality, in which separation from the means of production becomes the separation of man from the socially necessary labor that depurposiveness would be no longer "antinomical"; nor would administer automated production, formal and substantive purposiveness would be no longer "antinomical"; nor would formal reason prevail indifferently among and over men. For, as "congealed spirit," the machine is *not neutral;* technical reason is the social reason ruling a given society and can be changed in its very structure. As technical reason, it can become the technique of liberation.

For Max Weber this possibility was utopian. Today it looks as if he was right. But if contemporary industrial society defeats and triumphs over its own potentialities, then this triumph is no longer that of Max Weber's bourgeois reason. It is difficult to see reason at all in the ever more solid "shell of bondage" which is being constructed. Or is there perhaps already in Max Weber's concept of reason the irony that understands but disavows? Does he by any chance mean to say: And this you call "reason"?

First published in German in Max Weber und die Soziologie heute *(1964). This translation is based on a revised form of the essay first published in German in* Kultur und Gesellschaft *(1965).*

. . . sie hätte singen nicht reden sollen diese neue Seele
— Stefan George, "Nietzsche"

FOR here is the "new soul," prophet of the new man — radical break with the past and with the present which is still the rule of the past. And this past is the archetypal one, in the individual as well as in the history of the species: the primal crime and the primal scene. Psychoanalysis in its most extreme and most advanced concepts guides Brown's interpretation of the history of men and of the human condition. Brown likes to quote Adorno: "In psychoanalysis, only the exaggerations are true." For only the exaggerations can shatter the normal complacency of common sense and scientific sense and their comforting limitations and illusions. Only the exaggerations can (perhaps), with the violence of a shock, elucidate the horror of the whole, the depth of the deception, and the incommunicable promise of a future which can come into being (can come into thought) only as the total annihilation of the past and present. Apocalypse and Pentecost: destruction of everything and the redemption of everything: final liberation of the repressed content — abolition of the reality principle, nay, abolition of reality. For what we call reality Brown calls illusion, lie, dream. We are asleep, and being asleep is being dead; we still live in the womb or return into the womb; our genital sexuality is regression to the state before birth; and we are still under the spell of the primal scene: we reenact the father whom we have introjected; our sex life is his, not ours, and our pleasure remains vicarious. Thus if all our life is dream and illusion, then the awakening to real life is the end of our life: death and resurrection in one. The way out of the womb, out of the dream cave is to die in order to be reborn.

Liberation is transubstantiation; resurrection of the body, but the body is "raised a spiritual or symbolic body" (p. 191). "The revolution, the revelation, the apocalypse, is vision; which pronounces a last judgment; and brings about the end" (p. 232). The cave and the womb, Plato and Freud, revolution and revelation, Marx and Christ: the grand union and communion of opposites, the overcoming of all division between male and female, self and outside world, thine and mine, body and spirit — this ultimate reconciliation of opposites, does it convey the image of liberation? Or is it again the past that asserts its power over the image of the future, the old in new clothes? The attempt to answer this question involves heavy responsibility, for Norman Brown has carried the burden of radical thought to the farthest point: the point where sanity must appear as madness, where concepts must turn into fantasies, and the truth must become ridiculous. Once again, the tragedy of man as comedy, as the play of Satyre. Norman Brown's book moves along the limits of communication; he is on the search for a new language, which can break through the falsifying, stultifying, repressive universe of ordinary and academic discourse ("senatorial and senile"). In its best parts, this book is a poem and a song, of the beauty which is *"nichts als des Schrecklichen Anfang, den wir noch grade ertragen. . . .*"[2] The form of the sentence, the proposition which freezes the content is abandoned; the words, freed from the enchaining form, recapture their explosive meaning, a hidden truth.

The normal flux of ordinary and academic discourse is also broken — the argument is developed in relatively self-sufficient fragments, short paragraphs, aphorisms; their inner connection, the flow of the argument is of a musical rather than conceptual order: variations on a theme, progress through repetition, dissonance as element of structural harmony and development. The right of the imagination as cognitive power is thus restored: released from its senatorial and senile garb, thought becomes play, *jeu interdit,* the scandal; the *esprit de sérieux* gives way to the *gaya sciencia,* drunkenness and laughter. Hegel, the most serious of all serious philosophers, knew it well:

> The true is thus the bacchanalian whirl in which no member is not drunken; and because each, as soon as it detaches itself, dissolves immediately — the whirl is just as much transparent and simple repose.[3]

But then comes the hangover; the imagination falters, and the new language looks for support in the old. Support in quotations and references, which are to demonstrate or at least to illustrate the points made; support in returning to the primordial, elemental, subrational; to the infantile stages in the development of the individual and of the species. Psychoanalysis changes its direction and function: the latent content, the unconscious and its prehistory, serve not only as powers to be recognized, comprehended, conquered, but also (and increasingly so in the unfolding of the argument) as normative values, as ends. The grand leap into the realm of freedom and light is thus arrested and becomes a leap backward, into darkness.

*　　*　　*

Norman Brown's demonstrations and illustrations have yet another and very different significance. A large bulk of his reference is to Holy Script, to Christ and his gospel. A few examples may show how central these references are:

> The conclusion of the whole matter is, break down the boundaries, the walls. Down with defense mechanisms, character-armor; disarmament. Ephesians II, 14 . . . (p. 149).

> The real world . . . is the world where thoughts are omnipotent, where no distinction is drawn between wish and deed. As in the New Testament . . . (p. 151).

> The solution to the problem of identity is, get lost. Or as it says in the New Testament . . . (p. 161).

> The solution to the problem of war in the Eucharist, with transubstantiation . . . (p. 173).

> But the unconscious is the true psychic reality; and the unconscious is the Holy Spirit . . . (p. 195).

> Real life is life after death, or resurrection. Colossians III, 3 . . . (p. 207).

> Fulfillment gathers up the past into the present in the form of a recapitulation: that in the dispensation of times there might be a recapitulation of all things in Christ . . . (p. 207).

> Then cometh the end, when he shall have put down all rule and all authority and power. Mere anarchy is loosed upon the world. I Corinthians XV, 24 . . . (p. 243).

Now Brown takes great pains to state again and again that the religious symbolism is to be interpreted symbolically, in the other direction, as it were. Sexual potency is restored at Pentecost; speech resexualized (p. 251); knowledge made carnal, copulation of subject and object (p. 249); and the spirit is phallic (p. 224) — merger of Christ and Dionysus. But the one stays with the other, and the new emphasis does not suffice to reverse the established direction: sexualization of the spirit is also spiritualization of sexuality, and sexuality itself becomes symbolic: "everything is symbolic, including the sexual act" (p. 131). Behind the veil of Brown's sexualized language, de-sexualization prevails. The orgasm provides only "vicarious gratification" (p. 129). Brown's consistent attempt to convey, against overwhelming odds, the new nonrepressive interpretation of the old repressive symbols cannot undo the association of the spirit with the Spirit, the resurrection of the body with the Resurrection. Brown's images of fulfillment suggest total sublimation which drains the unsublimated dimension. Liberation in Nirvana: I like to believe that Norman Brown was aware of this goal of his voyage, and that he communicated his awareness to the reader: his first chapter is headed "Liberty" and his last, "Nothing."

Before examining the reasons for this failure, I shall review briefly the radical origin and intent of Brown's analysis prior to their mystification.

* * *

The truth of the human condition is hidden, repressed — not by a conspiracy of some sort, but by the actual course of history. The first aim, therefore, is the critical destruction of history, and of the manner in which history is written and understood. The facts stand for other facts in the depth of the individual and collective unconscious, and the repressed prehistory of mankind continues to make the history of man. The established facts are symbolic facts, derivatives and distortions of the latent content, which is the unexpurgated drama of sexuality. Consequently, history must be explained symbolically. All literal interpretation of history is falsifica-

231

tion; the "modern historical consciousness is Protestant literalism" which offends against the spirit, kills the spirit. Thus it becomes an "operation with ghosts" (*Geisteswissenschaft*) (pp. 198ff.). "We must rise from history to mystery" (p. 214) — here is the first mystification in Brown's analysis: the "mystery" is initially that of the primal crime and the ambivalent penitence for it; but then the mystery becomes that of the resurrection and redemption, transubstantiation, the Eucharist. The radical destruction of history terminates in the religious tale, in which history is, not *aufgehoben*, but simply negated, abolished. The beginning of Brown's book contained a very different promise: the refusal to accept any mystification, and the resolution to call things by their name, their real name, instead of canceling all names in the impossible unity and union of everything.

In line with this promise, Brown begins with the symbolic interpretation of politics:

> In order to know the reality of politics we have to believe the myth, to believe what we were told as children. Roman history is the story of the brothers Romulus and Remus, the sons of the she-wolf; leaders of gangs of juvenile delinquents . . . ; who achieved the rape of the Sabine women; and whose festival is the Lupercalia; at which youth naked except for girdles made from the skin of victims ran wild through the city; . . . a season fit for killing. *Julius Caesar*, Act I (p. 15).

And Brown continues, summing up the initial exposition: "Politics made out of delinquency. All brothers are brothers in crime; all equal as sinners" after the killing of the father, whom they restored in themselves and whom they continue to obey, the killing of each other. Myth or reality? Fictitious past, or factual history that is still with us? The stuff out of which history is made — the stuff of greatness and progress: Brown quotes Livy:

To expand the population, Romulus followed the model of other founders of cities: he opened an asylum for fugitives. The mob that came in was the first step to the city's future greatness.

The City of Man — "a sanctuary" providing "immunity for a multitude of criminals" (Augustine). Here is the latent content in the notion of the social contract:

> The social contract establishes corporate virtue as an asylum for individual sin, making a moral society out of immoral men; men whose natural inclination, according to Hobbes and Freud, is murder (p. 16).

The foundation of the state is itself a crime, the primal crime, for the state is formed by the fraternity (here, Brown sides with Plato and Sparta as against Aristotle and Athens), and it is the common crime that creates common solidarity — political, national solidarity. And after the primal crime, the endless struggle among the brothers — the "quarrel over the paternal inheritance": the original unity of the body politic now is divided into a multitude of segments, "moieties"; each acquiring private property, a self, group or individual self, fighting. Law only organizes this fight: "the Rule of Law is the Rule of Force"; and, as the classical myths tell us, right and wrong can be decided only "by an appeal to heaven, that is, by war and violence" (p. 18). The division stays with us: history is fratricide after the parricide. "Political parties are conspiracies to usurp the power of the father" (p. 29); behind politics is the ritual of murder and sacrifice:

> The comic wearing of the Indian mask, in the Boston Tea Party, or Tammany's Wigwam, is the lighter side of a game, a ritual, the darker side of which is fraternal genocide (p. 30).

Brown then traces the development of the latent content in the historical step from absolute monarchy to representative government, from Hobbes to Locke. A step within the same continuum of fraud. The illusion in liberty and equality:

> Locke allows no man the status of father, and makes all men sons of the Heavenly Father. . . . Sonship and brotherhood are espoused against fatherhood: but without a father there can be no sons or brothers. Locke's sons, like Freud's cannot free themselves from father psychology . . . (pp. 4–5).

The father survives in the superego, and in the many new political leaders, now freely elected. The autonomous individual, the "person" — this cherished achievement of bourgeois society is a fraud, Hobbes's "artificial Person." In reality, a person is never himself but always another: he wears a mask, he is possessed by another, represented by another, and representing another. And in all disguises, the other is always the father (p. 98). In theory and in practice, it is always the Oedipus Complex: as in the Apocalypse, "pump, power, and politics is discovered to be sex" (p. 75) — perverted sex, sado-masochistic sex, striving for impossible satisfaction. For the desired object is the "combined object": frozen image of the primal scene — a "male female (vaginal father) or a female male (phallic mother)," "stuck together in eternal coitus, eternal lust, and eternal punishment" (pp. 70, 71). And this "could go on forever; there is eternal recurrence."

It must go on until we have overcome the Fall, which is the division of the original and total unity. The solution, the end of the drama of history is the restoration of original and total unity: unity of male and female, father and mother, subject and object, body and soul — abolition of the self, of mine and thine, abolition of the reality principle, of all boundaries. . . .

* * *

Perhaps only the most extreme imagery can elucidate the depth dimension of history, the web of pleasure and terror,

234

truth and deception in eternal recurrence. But the imagery is not enough; it must become saturated with its reality: symbolism must recapture that which it symbolizes. The king must be shown not only as father but as king, that is to say, as master and lord; war and competition and communication must be shown not only as copulation but as war and business and speech. Unless the analysis takes the road of return from the symbolic to the literal, from the illusion to the reality of the illusion, it remains ideological, replacing one mystification by another.

Brown's concept of illusion (sleep, dream) covers, undifferentiated, the latent and the overt content of history, or, it derealizes reality. To him, the political kingdoms are "shadows," political power is a fraud: the emperor has no new clothes, he has no clothes at all. But unfortunately, he does: they are visible and tangible; they make history. In terms of the latent content, the kingdoms of the earth may be shadows; but unfortunately, they move real men and things, they kill, they persist and prevail in the sunlight as well as in the dark of night. The king may be an erected penis, and his relation to the community may be intercourse; but unfortunately, it is also something very different and less pleasant and more real. Brown skips the mediations which transform the latent into the overt content, sex into politics, the subrational into the rational. Thus he is stuck with the time-honored quandary of psychoanalysis: the airplane is a penis symbol, but it also gets you in a couple of hours from Berlin to Vienna.

The "lower depths," the "underworld" of the Unconscious moves the history of mankind without dissolving its reality, its rationality. The roots of repression are and remain real roots; consequently, their eradication remains a real and rational job. What is to be abolished is not the reality principle; not everything, but such particular things as business, politics, exploitation, poverty. Short of this recapture of reality and reason, Brown's purpose is defeated, and the critical destruction of history, the discovery of its latent and real content, turns into the mystification of the latent and real content. True, in the language which reveals the stuff out of which history is made, the established history of the Establishment, from Romulus and Remus to the Founding Fathers and their representative government, today appears as crime, deception, lie, illusion; we are asleep, we are dreaming, we are dead if we experience this as reality, as life, freedom, fulfillment. But this illusion is itself a historical fact and factor, and its negation, if any, is a historical, definitive negation: historical goal of historical practice. Outside and beyond the historical continuum, the solution is nothing (as Brown's last chapter indicates), and that means: it is not. And within the historical universe (the only one that, in any meaningful sense, can ever be the universe of freedom and fulfillment), there are divisions and boundaries that are real and will continue to exist even in the advent of freedom and fulfillment, because all pleasure and all happiness and all humanity originate and live in and with these divisions and boundaries. Such are the division into the sexes, the difference between male and female, between the penis and the vagina, between you and me, even between mine and thine, and they are, or can be, most enjoyable and most gratifying divisions; their abolition would be not only illusion but nightmare — the acme of repression. To be sure, this gratification is transitory, momentary, and partial, but this does not make it "vicarious" — on the contrary! To be sure, *alle Lust will Ewigkeit,* but this eternity can only be that of the ever returning *moments* of joy, of the ever-returning solution of tension. Tension can be made nonaggressive, nondestructive, but it can never be eliminated, because (Freud knew it well) its elimination would be death — not in any symbolic but in a very real sense. And we still want to live, *within* our boundaries and divisions, which we want to make our own instead of leaving their determination to our fathers and leaders and representatives. For there is such a thing as the Self, the Person — it does not yet exist but it must be attained, fought for against all those who are preventing its emergence and who substitute for it an illusory self, namely, the subject of voluntary servitude in production and consumption, the subject of free enterprise and free election of masters. There is even such a thing as property which is a factor and ingredient of true freedom (Marx knew it well): that which is properly mine because I am different from you and can be with and for you only in this difference — boundaries to be enjoyed by you and by me. And there are "others," strangers who must remain strangers, must not enter my domain or yours because there is no pre-established harmony, and their otherness is not based on any economic position, social status, racial or national heritage but on their own self and own body with its own drives, pleasures, sorrows.

Here is the central fallacy, the mystification in Brown's vision. He obliterates the decisive difference between real and artificial, natural and political, fulfilling and repressive boundaries and divisions. Does the well-trained classicist not recognize the liberating truth in the concepts of *telos* and *mesotes?* Fulfillment becomes meaningless if everything is one, and one is everything. The sinister images of "burning" and "sacrifice" recur in Brown's vision: "The true sacrifice is total, a making holy of the whole" (p. 174); "Love is all fire; and so heaven and hell are the same place. As in Augustine . . ." (p. 179); "The true body is the body burnt up, the spiritual body" (p. 183); "The reality adumbrated in all sacrifice, in animal sacrifice, is human sacrifice, the sacrifice of the human body, as an eternal truth" (p. 228). No symbolism can repulse the repressive connotation: one cannot love in fire — unless one is a Christian or Buddhist martyr. Acme of sublimation: the unsublimated realizations of Eros are burnt up, sacrificed — they evaporate. For Eros lives in the division and boundary between subject and object, man and nature; and precisely in its polymorphous-perverse manifestations, in its liberation from the "despotism of genital organization," the sexual instincts transform the object and the environment — without ever annihilating the object and the environment together with the subject.

*   *   *

Brown's logic is consistent: if the Fall was the division of the original unity which was total unity, then the redemption can only be the restoration of total unity:

> Fusion: the distinction between inner self and outside world, between subject and object, overcome (p. 253).

But such fusion would be the end of human life, in its instinctual as well as rational, unsublimated as well as sublimated, expressions. The unity of subject and object is a hallmark of absolute idealism; however, even Hegel retained the tension between the two, the distinction. Brown goes beyond the Absolute Idea: "Fusion, mystical, participation" (p. 254). But mystical participation is not made less mystical if it is "freely" consummated, and magic does not become less magical if it is "conscious magic."

The last sentence of the last chapter: "Everything is only a metaphor; there is only poetry." To understand the reality of politics is to believe in the myth. We still don't believe in it; we don't understand; we are prisoners in the cave. "Turning and turning in the animal belly, the mineral belly, the belly of time. To find the way out: the poem" (p. 56). This is one of Brown's most advanced formulations: a vision of the truth. But poetry is made in history and makes history; and the poem which is "the way out" will be (if ever) written and sung and heard here on our earth. Brown had such a poem in mind, and he started to write it, but it became adumbrated by the ancient ghosts, by the symbols of sacrifice, death, transubstantiation. The concluding reference in his book contains the sentence:

> Then the body of the Enlightened One becomes luminous in appearance, convincing and inspiring by its mere presence, while every word and every gesture, and even his silence, communicate the overwhelming reality of the Dharma.

This does not work, and no new symbolic interpretation can remove the impact of the many centuries of deception and exploitation which has defined the connotation of these words. To be sure, the sinister spell can be broken: by the power of the poet and singer, even before the historical, the real break with deception and exploitation has occurred. But the poet and singer can give to such words a new and revolutionary connotation only if his speech and song subvert the established meaning not merely symbolically but also literally, that is to say, if he cancels this meaning by translating the impossible into the possible, the mystical absurd into the real absurd, the metaphysical utopia into the historical utopia, the second into the first coming, redemption into liberation. Brown moves in the opposite direction. He begins with tearing the ideological veil; the "history of mankind goes from the natural cave to the artificial cave, from the underground cave to the aboveground underground" (p. 39). In such sentences, the symbolism names the reality as that which it is and thereby invokes revolution:

> The revolution is from below, the lower classes, the underworld, the damned, the disreputable, the despised and rejected. Freud's revolutionary motto in *The Interpretation of Dreams: Flectere si nequeo Superos, Acherunta movebo.* If I cannot bend the higher powers, I will stir up the lower depths. Freud's discovery: the universal underworld (p. 241).

But then, the very next paragraph opens with the statement: "Darkness at noon. A progressive darkening of the everyday world of common sense." Of common sense only? Or has the darkness also descended on the "way out" which Brown has opened? The equating sequence: revolution = revelation = redemption = resurrection strikes not only at common sense but at sense. True, it is not merely common sense that is false; thus it may be an indispensable, rational task to reduce words to non-sense, "to transcend the antinomy of sense and non-sense, silence and speech" (p. 258). However, this task, if it should help us to find "the way out," is a political task: the silence is not that of the Tibetan or any other monastery, nor of Zen, nor of mystical communion — it is the silence which precedes action, the liberating action, and it is broken by action. The rest is not silence but complacency, or despair, or escape. And when and where such action is barred, the task of reducing words to non-sense is the critique of the established language as the language of the Establishment which makes sense out of non-sense: the non-sense of its preservation and reproduction as its sole *raison d'être.*

Brown's "way out" leaves the Establishment behind — that is, the way out is indeed mystical, mystification. The symbolic interpretation works both ways: it reveals the latent, the real content of reality, and it symbolizes the real content: it mystifies the possibilities of liberation. Revolution, freedom, fulfillment become in turn symbolic — symbolic goals and events. Symbolic of what? The answer remains, must remain, shrouded in mystery, because Brown envisions an Absolute, a Totality, a Whole which swallows up all parts and divisions, all tensions and all needs, that is to say, all life. For such a totality does not exist in any sense or non-sense, and should not even be the vision of the free imagination because it is the negation of all freedom, and of all happiness (at least human happiness). To be sure, in dialectical logic, the whole is the truth, but a whole in which all parts and divisions have their place and stage. The relations between them, their specific function, the different levels and modes of reality, its inner development must be demonstrated and defined — only then, in the unending and subverting stream of mediations, appears the true as the bacchanalian whirl: sober drunkenness of the whole: Reason as Freedom. Critical, not absolute vision; a new rationality, not the simple negation of rationality.

*　　*　　*

In the beginning may have been the Uroboros: male and female, father and mother, mother and child, ego-id and outside world in one. But the Uroboros has busted a long time ago; the distinctions and divisions are our reality — real with all its symbols. In the light of its own possibilities, it may well be called a cave, and our life in it dream or death. Its horror has come to penetrate every part of it, every word and every vision. The way out may well be the subversion of this entire reality, but this subversion, in order to be real, must itself be real, look in the face of this reality, and not turn the head. Brown affirms the proposition on the need for changing the world instead of interpreting it. If there is one proposition which should not be understood symbolically, it is this one. And yet, in the development of Brown's argument, both the latent and the overt content of this proposition are being sublimated and mystified, and his vision of total change, of the final union at the end of history remains under the spell of the primordial Uroboros, the unity that is prior to all history.

The way out is also a way back: regression at a higher level, regression sanctified, liberated. Is it again a case of The God That Failed: from politics to a new Communion, from Liberty to Nothing? (When will we realize that there was no god that failed because there was no god, and that the failure was ours, and theirs?) Anyhow, his song of fulfillment ends in silence, not in the sensuous, audible, living silence at the end of the *Lied von der Erde,* but the silence under the cross, after the crucifixion; not the eternity of *Alle Lust will Ewigkeit* (the *"ewig"* which is the last word in the *Lied von der Erde*), but the eternity which is not of this world, the eternity of Nirvana in which all joy and all sorrow are fulfilled — annihilated.

We like to have a different idea of Love's Body, and we like to believe that Brown himself has a different idea:

> To pass from the temple to the body is to perceive the body as the new temple, the true temple. The house is a woman, and the woman is a house, or palace. . . . The land is a woman, the virgin land; and the woman is a land, my America, my Newfoundland (p. 225).

This is it. The woman, the land is here on earth, to be found here on earth, living and dying, female for male, distinguished, particular, tension to be renewed, Romeo's and Don Juan's, self and another, yours or mine, fulfillment in alienation. No Eucharist, no crucifixion, no resurrection, no mysticism. To find this woman, to free this land: *hic Rhodus, hic salta!* And don't jump into Nothing. Waking up from sleep, finding the way out of the cave is work within the cave; slow, painful work with and *against* the prisoners in the cave. Everywhere, even in your own land which is not yet found, not yet free, there are those who do this work, who risk their lives for it — they fight the real fight, the political fight. You have revealed the latent, the true content of politics — you know that the political fight is the fight for the whole: not the mystical whole, but the very unmystical, antagonistic whole of our life and that of our children — the only life that is.

* * *

Among the many sentences in Brown's book which I like best is the opening of the Preface: "At least in the life of the mind, ventures should be carried through to the end." He has not done so; this is not the end. He has reached a point of return; on a new way, return to the earth. *Bon voyage!*

A REPLY TO HERBERT MARCUSE
BY NORMAN O. BROWN

My friend Marcuse and I: Romulus and Remus quarreling; which of them is the *real* "revolutionary."

He will not see the recurrence in revolution. Revolution is not a slate wiped clean, but a revolving cycle (*Love's Body*, p. 204). Even newness is renewal. As it was in the beginning. The idea of progress is in question; the reality of Marx cannot hide the reality of Nietzsche. The thing is to change the world; but it is also true that everything remains always the same. The assignment then is (to put it simply) the simultaneous affirmation and rejection of what is; not in a system, as in Hegel, but in an instant, as in poetry.

There is eternal recurrence; there are "eternal objects" (Whitehead); archetypes. This is a hard lesson. There is a sense in which war cannot be abolished (*Love's Body*, p. 182). Or, there is an eternal object of which literal war is a false image, or inadequate idea. The thing to be abolished is literalism; the worship of false images; idolatry. Allen Ginsberg saw it just the way it is: Moloch. A false idol fed with real victims. This is no joke. (Nor is fire; Heraclitean fire.)

Idolatry is fetishism, mystification; demystification would be an end to idolatry. But an end to idolatry is not so easy (*Love's Body*, p. 114). It is not the abolition of the temple, but the discovery of the true temple: Love's body. Karl Barth saw religion as idolatry; Karl Marx saw religion as the heart of a heartless world. The Sacred Heart. The thing is not to excise the heart but to put it where it belongs. The real atheism is to become divine. In a dialectical view, atheism becomes theurgy, god-making; demystification becomes the discovery of a new mystery; and everything remains the same.

There is another sense in which mystification must be affirmed. We have to surpass the Enlightenment notion that in the life of the species or of the individual there is a definitive change-over from darkness to light. Light is always light in darkness; that is what the unconscious is all about (*Love's Body*, p. 216). Nor can the light become a current, always turned on, in ordinary prosaic language. Truth is always in poetic form; not literal but symbolic; hiding, or veiled; light in darkness. Yes, mysterious. Literalism is idolatry of words; the alternative to idolatry is mystery. And literalism reifies, makes out of everything *things,* these tables and chairs, commodities. The alternative to reification is mystification (*Love's*

Body, p. 234). The world is actually not a collection of commodities;

> *When silence*
> *Blooms in the house, all the paraphernalia of our existence*
> *Shed the twitterings of value and reappear as heraldic devices.*
> — Robert Duncan

Heraldic devices: airplanes as penis symbols rather than "modern conveniences." One of the eternal verities is the human body as the measure of all things, including technology. The businessman does not have the last word; the real meaning of technology is its hidden relation to the human body; a symbolical or mystical relation.

*　*　*

With the whole world still in the bourgeois stage of competitive development and war, the thing to remember about Marx is that he was able to look beyond this world to another possible world, of union, communion, communism. What needs to be reiterated is not reassurance to the bourgeois that he will be able to carry his little old Self, Person, and Property into that world, but that the kingdom of heaven on earth is possible; and that other world, the negation of this jungle, cannot possibly be anything except Communitas. A higher form of chaos; instead of confusion, fusion (*Love's Body*, pp. 248, 253).

And, after Freud, we have to add that there is also a sexual revolution; which is not to be found in the bourgeois cycle of repression and promiscuity, but in a transformation of the human body, an abolition of genital organization. Indeed, *Love's Body* shows that genital organization is the same thing as Self, Person, Property; and, therefore, the abolition of

245

genital organization, foretold by Marcuse in *Eros and Civilization,* turns out to mean what Marcuse calls the impossible unity and union of everything.

Yes, indeed, there was a God that failed; that mortal God, the great Leviathan; or Moloch; discovered to be not only mortal but also dead, an idol. From literalism to symbolism; the lesson of my life. The next generation needs to be told that the real fight is not the political fight, but to put an end to politics. From politics to metapolitics.

From politics to poetry. Legislation is not politics, nor philosophy, but poetry. Poetry, art, is not an epiphenomenal reflection of some other (political, economic) realm which is the "real thing"; nor a still contemplation of something else which is the "real action"; nor a sublimation of something else which is the "real," carnal "act." Poetry, art, imagination, the creator spirit is life itself; the real revolutionary power to change the world; and to change the human body. To change the human body: here is the crisis, *hic Rhodus, hic salta;* which, as Hegel said, is to be translated "here is the Rose, here begin to dance." To begin to dance; who can tell the dancer from the dance; it is the impossible unity and union of everything.

From politics to life. And therefore revolution as creation; resurrection; renaissance instead of progress. To perceive in all human culture the hidden reality of the human body. This is to discover as Freud did, the Holy Communion as the basis of community; the Eucharist; the cannibalism, the hidden *eating;* one of the forms of which is war — making children pass through the fire unto Moloch. Go to the end of the road and that is what you will find. And so the God is not Freud's God Logos, abstract or disembodied Reason, but the Human Form Divine. And the language is the language not of reason but of love. Reason is power; powerful arguments; power-politics; *Realpolitik;* reality-principle. Love comes empty-handed (*Love's Body,* p. 237); the eternal proletariat; like Cordelia, bringing Nothing.

Love Mystified *was first published in* Commentary, *February 1967. Norman O. Brown's response was published in* Commentary *in March 1967.*

I propose to consider here the strains and stresses in the so-called "affluent society," a phrase which has (rightly or wrongly) been coined to describe contemporary American society. Its main characteristics are: (1) an abundant industrial and technical capacity which is to a great extent spent in the production and distribution of luxury goods, gadgets, waste, planned obsolescence, military or semimilitary equipment — in short, in what economists and sociologists used to call "unproductive" goods and services; (2) a rising standard of living, which also extends to previously underprivileged parts of the population; (3) a high degree of concentration of economic and political power, combined with a high degree of organization and government intervention in the economy; (4) scientific and pseudoscientific investigation, control, and manipulation of private and group behavior, both at work and at leisure (including the behavior of the psyche, the soul, the unconscious, and the subconscious) for commercial and political purposes. All these tendencies are interrelated: they make up the syndrome which expresses the normal functioning of the "affluent society." To demonstrate this interrelation is not my task here; I take its existence as the sociological

248

basis for the thesis which I want to submit, namely, that the strains and stresses suffered by the individual in the affluent society are grounded in the normal functioning of this society (and of the individual!) rather than in its disturbances and diseases.

"Normal functioning": I think the definition presents no difficulties for the doctor. The organism functions normally if it functions, without disturbance, in accord with the biological and physiological makeup of the human body. The human faculties and capabilities are certainly very different among the members of the species, and the species itself has changed greatly in the course of its history but these changes have occurred on a biological and physiological basis which has remained largely constant. To be sure, the physician, in making his diagnosis and in proposing treatment, will take into account the patient's environment, upbringing, and occupation; these factors may limit the extent to which normal functioning can be defined and achieved, or they may even make this achievement impossible, but as criterion and goal, normality remains a clear and meaningful concept. As such, it is identical with "health," and the various deviations from it are to various degrees of "disease."

The situation of the psychiatrist seems to be quite different. At first glance, normality seems to be defined along the same lines the physician uses. The normal functioning of the mind (psyche, psyche-soma) is that which enables the individual to perform, to function in accord with his position as child, adolescent, parent, as a single person or married, in accord with his job, profession, status. But this definition contains factors of an entirely new dimension, namely, that of society, and society is a factor of normality in a far more essential sense than that of external influence, so much so that "normal" seems to be a social and institutional rather than individual condition. It is probably easy to agree on what is the normal functioning of the digestive tract, the lungs, and the heart, but what is the normal functioning of the mind in love-making, in other interpersonal relations, at work and at leisure, at a meeting of a board of directors, on the golf course, in the slums, in prison, in the army? While the normal functioning of the digestive tract or the lung is likely to be the same in the case of a healthy corporation executive and of a healthy laborer, this does not hold true of their minds. In fact, the one would be very abnormal if he regularly thought, felt, and operated like the other. And what is "normal" lovemaking, a "normal" family, a "normal" occupation?

The psychiatrist might proceed like the general physician and direct therapy to making the patient function within his family, in his job or environment, while trying to influence and even change the environmental factors as much as this is in his power. The limits will soon make themselves felt, for example, if the mental strains and stresses of the patient are caused, not merely by certain bad conditions in his job, in his neighborhood, in his social status, but by the very *nature* of the job, the neighborhood, the status itself — in their normal condition. Then making him normal for this condition would mean normalizing the strains and stresses, or to put it more brutally: making him capable of being sick, of living his sickness as health, without his noticing that he is sick precisely when he sees himself and is seen as healthy and normal. This would be the case if his work is, by its very nature, "deadening," stupefying, wasteful (even though the job pays well and is "socially" necessary), or if the person belongs to a minority group which is underprivileged in the established society, traditionally poor and occupied mainly in menial and "dirty" physical labor. But this would also be the case (in very different forms) on the other side of the fence among the tycoons of business and politics, where efficient and profitable performance requires (and reproduces) the qualities of smart ruthlessness, moral indifference, and persistent aggressiveness. In such cases, "normal" functioning would be tantamount to a distortion and mutilation of a human being — no matter how modestly one may define the human qualities of a human being. Erich Fromm wrote *The Sane Society;* it deals, not with the established, but with a future, society, the implication being that the established society is *not* sane but insane. Is not the individual who functions normally, adequately, and healthily as a citizen of a sick society — is not such an individual himself sick? And would not a sick society require an antagonistic concept of mental health, a meta-concept designating (and preserving) mental qualities which are tabooed, arrested, or distorted by the "sanity" prevalent in the sick society? (For example, mental health equals the ability to live as a dissenter, to live a nonadjusted life.)

As a tentative definition of "sick society" we can say that a society is sick when its basic institutions and relations, its structure, are such that they do not permit the use of the available material and intellectual resources for the optimal development and satisfaction of individual needs. The larger the discrepancy between the potential and the actual human conditions, the greater the social need for what I term "surplus-repression," that is, repression necessitated not by the growth and preservation of civilization but by the vested interest in maintaining an established society. Such surplus-repression introduces (over and above, or rather underneath, the social conflicts) new strains and stresses in the individuals. Usually handled by the normal working of the social process, which assures adjustment and submission (fear of loss of job or status, ostracism, and so forth, no special enforcement policies with respect to the mind are required. But in the contemporary affluent society, the discrepancy between the established modes of existence and the real possibilities of human freedom is so great that, in order to prevent an explosion, society has to insure a more effective mental coordination of individuals: in its unconscious as well as conscious dimensions, the psyche is opened up and subjected to systematic manipulation and control.

When I speak of the surplus-repression "required" for the maintenance of a society, or of the need for systematic manipulation and control, I do not refer to individually experienced social needs and consciously inaugurated policies: they may be thus experienced and inaugurated or they may not. I rather speak of *tendencies,* forces which can be identified by an analysis of the existing society and which assert themselves even if the policy makers are not aware of them. They express the requirements of the established apparatus of production, distribution, and consumption — economic, technical, political, mental requirements which have to be fulfilled in order to assure the continued functioning of the apparatus on which the population depends, and the continuing function of the social relationships derived from the organization of the apparatus. These objective tendencies become manifest in the trend of the economy, in technological change, in the domestic and foreign policy of a nation or group of nations, and they generate common, supraindividual needs and goals in the different social classes, pressure groups, and parties. Under the normal conditions of social cohesion, the objective tendencies override or absorb individual interests and goals without exploding the society; however, the particular interest is not simply determined by the universal: the former has its own range of freedom, and contributes, in accordance with its social position, to the shaping of the general interest — but short of a revolution, the particular needs and goals will remain defined by the predominant objective tendencies. Marx believed that they assert themselves "behind the back" of the individuals; in the advanced societies of today, this is true only with strong qualifications. Social engineering, scientific management of enterprise and human relations, and manipulation of instinctual needs are practiced on the policy-making level and testify to the degree of awareness within the general blindness.

As for the systematic manipulation and control of the psyche in the advanced industrial society, manipulation and control for what, and by whom? Over and above all particular manipulation in the interest of certain businesses, policies, lobbies — the general objective purpose is to reconcile the individual with the mode of existence which his society imposes on him. Because of the high degree of surplus-repression involved in such reconciliation, it is necessary to achieve a libidinal cathexis of the merchandise the individual has to buy (or sell), the services he has to use (or perform), the fun he has to enjoy, the status symbols he has to carry — necessary, because the existence of the society depends on their uninterrupted production and consumption. In other words, social needs must become individual needs, instinctual needs. And to the degree to which the productivity of this society requires mass production and mass consumption, these needs must be standardized, coordinated, generalized. Certainly, these controls are not a conspiracy, they are not centralized in any agency or group of agencies (although the trend toward centralization is gaining momentum); they are rather diffused throughout the society, exercised by the neighbors, the community, the peer groups, mass media, corporations, and (perhaps least) by the government. But they are exercised with the help of, in fact rendered possible by, science, by the social and behavioral sciences, and especially by sociology and psychology. As industrial sociology and psychology, or, more euphemistically, as "science of human relations," these scientific efforts have become an indispensable tool in the hands of the powers that be.

These brief remarks are suggestive of the depth of society's ingression into the psyche, the extent to which mental health, normality, is not that of the individual but of his society. Such a harmony between the individual and society would be highly desirable if the society offered the individual the conditions for his development as a human being in accord with the available possibilities of freedom, peace, and happiness (that is in accord with the possible liberation of his life instincts), but it is highly destructive to the individual if these conditions do not prevail. Where they do not prevail, the healthy and normal individual is a human being equipped with all the qualities which enable him to get along with others in his society, and these very same qualities are the marks of repression, the marks of a mutilated human being, who collaborates in his own repression, in the containment of potential individual and social freedom, in the release of aggression. And this situation cannot be solved within the framework of individual psychology and therapy, nor within the framework of any psychology — a solution can be envisaged only on the political level: in the struggle against society. To be sure, therapy could demonstrate this situation and prepare the mental ground for such a struggle — but then psychiatry would be a subversive undertaking.

The question now is whether the strains in contemporary American society, in the affluent society, suggest the prevalence of conditions essentially negative to individual development in the sense just discussed. Or, to formulate the question in terms more indicative of the approach I propose to take: Do these strains vitiate the very possibility of "healthy" individual development — healthy defined in terms of optimal development of one's intellectual and emotional faculties? The question calls for an affirmative answer, that is, this society vitiates individual developments, if the prevailing strains are related to the very structure of this society and if they activate in its members instinctual needs and satisfactions which set the individuals against themselves so that they reproduce and intensify their own repression.

At first glance, the strains in our society seem to be those characteristic of any society which develops under the impact of great technological changes: they initiate new modes of work and of leisure and thereby affect all social relationships, and bring about a thorough transvaluation of values. Since physical labor tends to become increasingly unnecessary and even wasteful, since the work of salaried employees too becomes increasingly "automatic" and that of the politicians and administrators increasingly questionable, the traditional content of the struggle for existence appears more meaningless and without substance the more it appears as unnecessary necessity. But the future alternative, namely, the possible abolition of (alienated) labor seems equally meaningless, nay, frightening. And indeed, if one envisages this alternative as the progress and development of the *established* system, then the dislocation of the content of life to free time suggests the shape of a nightmare: massive self-realization, fun, sport in a steadily shrinking space.

But the threat of the "bogey of automation" is itself ideology. On the one hand it serves the perpetuation and reproduction of technically obsolete and unnecessary jobs and occupations (unemployment as normal condition, even if comfortable, seems worse than stupefying routine work); on the other hand it justifies and promotes the education and training of the managers and organization men of leisure time, that is to say, it serves to prolong and enlarge control and manipulation.

The real danger for the established system is not the abolition of labor but the possibility of nonalienated labor as the basis of the reproduction of society. Not that people are no longer compelled to work, but that they might be compelled to work for a very different life and in very different relations, that they might be given very different goals and values, that they might have to live with a very different morality — this is the "definite negation" of the established system, the liberating alternative. For example, socially necessary labor might be organized for such efforts as the rebuilding of cities and towns, the relocation of the places of work (so that people learn again how to walk), the construction of industries which produce goods without built-in obsolescence, without profitable waste and poor quality, and the subjection of the environment to the vital aesthetic needs of the organism. To be sure, to translate this possibility into reality would mean to eliminate the power of the dominant interests which, by their very function in the society, are opposed to a development that would reduce private enterprise to a minor role, that would do away with the market economy, and with the policy of military preparedness, expansion, and intervention — in other words: a development that would reverse the entire prevailing trend. There is little evidence for such a development. In the meantime, and with the new and terribly effective and total means provided by technical progress, the population is physically and mentally mobilized against this eventuality: they must continue the struggle for existence in painful, costly, and obsolete forms.

This is the real contradiction which translates itself from the social structure into the mental structure of the individuals. There, it activates and aggravates destructive tendencies which, in a hardly sublimated mode, are made socially useful in the behavior of the individuals, on the private as well as political level — in the behavior of the nation as a whole. Destructive energy becomes socially useful aggressive energy, and the aggressive behavior impels growth — growth of economic, political, and technical power. Just as in the contemporary scientific enterprise, so in the economic enterprise and in that of the nation as a whole, constructive and destructive achievements, work for life and work for death, procreating and killing are inextricably united. To restrict the exploitation of nuclear energy would mean to restrict its peaceful as well as military potential; the amelioration and protection of life appear as by-products of the scientific work on the annihilation of life; to restrict procreation would also mean to restrict potential manpower and the number of potential customers and clients. Now the (more or less sublimated) transformation of destructive into socially useful aggressive (and thereby constructive) energy is, according to Freud (on whose instinct-theory I base my interpretation) a normal and indispensable process. It is part of the same dynamic by which libido, erotic energy, is sublimated and made socially useful; the two opposite impulses are forced together and, united in this twofold transformation, they become the mental and organic vehicles of civilization. But no matter how close and effective their union, their respective quality remains unchanged and contrary: aggression activates destruction which "aims" at death, while libido seeks the preservation, protection, and amelioration of life. Therefore, it is only as long as destruction works in the service of Eros that it serves civilization and the individual; if aggression becomes stronger than its erotic counterpart, the trend is reversed. Moreover, in the Freudian conception, destructive energy cannot become stronger without reducing erotic energy: the balance between the two primary impulses is a quantitative one; the instinctual dynamic is mechanistic, distributing an available quantum of energy between the two antagonists.

I have briefly restated Freud's conception inasmuch as I shall use it to discuss the depth and character of the strains prevalent in American society. I suggest that the strains derive from the basic contradiction between the capabilities of this society, which could produce essentially new forms of freedom amounting to a subversion of the established institutions on the one hand, and the repressive use of these capabilities on the other. The contradiction explodes — and is at the same time "resolved," "contained" — in the ubiquitous aggression prevalent in this society. Its most conspicuous (but by no means isolated) manifestation is the military mobilization and its effect on the mental behavior of the individuals, but within the context of the basic contradiction, aggressiveness is fed by many sources. The following seem to be foremost:

(1) *The dehumanization of the process of production and consumption.* Technical progress is identical with the increasing elimination of personal initiative, inclination, taste, and need from the provision of goods and services. This tendency is liberating if the available resources and techniques are used for freeing the individual from labor and recreation which are required for the reproduction of the established institutions but are parasitic, wasteful, and dehumanizing in terms of the existing technical and intellectual capabilities. The same tendency often gratifies hostility.

(2) *The conditions of crowding, noise, and overtness characteristic of mass society.* As René Dubos has said, the need for "quiet, privacy, independence, initiative, and some open space" are not "frills or luxuries but constitute real biological necessities." Their lack injures the instinctual structure itself. Freud has emphasized the "asocial" character of Eros — the

258

mass society achieves an "oversocialization" to which the individual reacts "with all sorts of frustrations, repressions, aggressions, and fears which soon develop into genuine neuroses."

I mentioned, as the most conspicuous social mobilization of aggressiveness, the militarization of the affluent society. This mobilization goes far beyond the actual draft of manpower and the buildup of the armament industry: its truly totalitarian aspects show forth in the daily mass media which feed "public opinion." The brutalization of language and image, the presentation of killing, burning, and poisoning and torture inflicted upon the victims of neocolonial slaughter is made in a common-sensible, factual, sometimes humorous style which integrates these horrors with the pranks of juvenile delinquents, football contests, accidents, stock market reports, and the weatherman. This is no longer the "classical" heroizing of killing in the national interest, but rather its reduction to the level of natural events and contingencies of daily life.

The consequence is a "psychological habituation of war" which is administered to a people protected from the actuality of war, a people who, by virtue of this habituation, easily familiarizes itself with the "kill rate" as it is already familiar with other "rates" (such as those of business or traffic or unemployment). The people are conditioned to live "with the hazards, the brutalities, and the mounting casualties of the war in Vietnam, just as one learns gradually to live with the everyday hazards and casualties of smoking, of smog, or of traffic."[1] The photos which appear in the daily newspapers and in magazines with mass circulation, often in nice and glossy color, show rows of prisoners laid out or stood up for "interrogation," little children dragged through the dust behind armored cars, mutilated women. They are nothing new ("such things happen in a war"), but it is the setting that makes the difference: their appearance in the regular program, in togetherness with the commercials, sports, local politics, and reports on the social set. And the brutality of power is further normalized by its extension to the beloved automobile: the manufacturers sell a Thunderbird, Fury, Tempest, and the oil industry puts "a tiger in your tank."

However, the administered language is rigidly discriminating: a specific vocabulary of hate, resentment, and defamation is reserved for opposition to the aggressive policies and for the enemy. The pattern constantly repeats itself. Thus, when students demonstrate against the war, it is a "mob" swelled by "bearded advocates of sexual freedom," by unwashed juveniles, and by "hoodlums and street urchins" who "tramp" the streets, while the counterdemonstrations consist of citizens who gather. In Vietnam, "typical criminal communist violence" is perpetrated against American "strategic operations." The Reds have the impertinence to launch "a sneak attack" (presumably they are supposed to announce it beforehand and to deploy in the open); they are "evading a death trap" (presumably they should have stayed in). The Vietcong attack American barracks "in the dead of night" and kill American boys (presumably, Americans only attack in broad daylight, don't disturb the sleep of the enemy, and don't kill Vietnamese boys). The massacre of hundred thousands of communists (in Indonesia) is called "impressive" — a comparable "killing rate" suffered by the other side would hardly have been honored with such an adjective. To the Chinese, the presence of American troops in East Asia is a threat to their "ideology," while presumably the presence of Chinese troops in Central or South America would be a real, and not only ideological, threat to the United States.

The loaded language proceeds according to the Orwellian

recipe of the identity of opposites: in the mouth of the enemy, peace means war, and defense is attack, while on the righteous side, escalation is restraint, and saturation bombing prepares for peace. Organized in this discriminatory fashion, language designates a priori the enemy as evil in his entirety and in all his actions and intentions.

Such mobilization of aggressiveness cannot be explained by the magnitude of the communist threat: the image of the ostensible enemy is inflated out of all proportion to reality. What is at stake is rather the continued stability and growth of a system which is threatened by its own irrationality — by the narrow base on which its prosperity rests, by the dehumanization which its wasteful and parasitic affluence demands. The senseless war is itself part of this irrationality and thus of the essence of the system. What may have been a minor involvement at the beginning, almost an accident, a contingency of foreign policy, has become a test case for the productivity, competitiveness, and prestige of the whole. The billions of dollars spent for the war effort are a political as well as economic stimulus (or cure): a big way of absorbing part of the economic surplus, and of keeping the people in line. Defeat in Vietnam may well be the signal for other wars of liberation closer to home — and perhaps even for rebellion at home.

To be sure, the social utilization of aggressiveness belongs to the historical structure of civilization and has been a powerful vehicle of progress. However, here too, there is a stage where quantity may turn into quality and subvert the normal balance between the two primary instincts in favor of destruction. I mentioned the "bogey man" of automation. In fact the real spectre for the affluent society is the possible reduction of labor to a level where the human organism need no longer function as an instrument of labor. The mere quantitative decline in needed human labor power militates against the maintenance of the capitalist mode of production (as of all other exploitative modes of production). The system reacts by stepping up the production of goods and services which either do not enlarge individual consumption at all, or enlarge it with luxuries — luxuries in the face of persistent poverty, but luxuries which are necessities for occupying a labor force sufficient to reproduce the established economic and political institutions. To the degree to which this sort of work appears as superfluous, senseless, and unnecessary while necessary for earning a living, frustration is built into the very productivity of this society, and aggressiveness is activated. And to the degree to which the society in its very structure becomes aggressive, the mental structure of its citizens adjusts itself: the individual becomes at one and the same time more aggressive and more pliable and submissive, for he submits to a society which, by virtue of its affluence and power, satisfies his deepest (and otherwise greatly repressed) instinctual needs. And these instinctual needs apparently find their libidinal reflection in the representatives of the people. The chairman of the Armed Services Committee of the United States Senate, Senator Russell of Georgia, was struck by this fact. He is quoted as saying:

> There is something about preparing for destruction that causes men to be more careless in spending money than they would be if they were building for constructive purposes. Why that is, I do not know; but I have observed, over a period of almost thirty years in the Senate, that there is something about buying arms with which to kill, to destroy, to wipe out cities, and to obliterate great transportation systems which causes men not to reckon the dollar cost as closely as they do when they think about proper housing and the care of the health of human beings.[2]

262

I have argued elsewhere the question of how one can possibly gauge and historically compare the aggression prevalent in a specific society; instead of restating the case, I want now to focus on different aspects, on the specific forms in which aggression today is released and satisfied.

The most telling one, and the one which distinguishes the new from the traditional forms, is what I call *technological aggression and satisfaction.* The phenomenon is quickly described: the act of aggression is physically carried out by a mechanism with a high degree of automatism, of far greater power than the individual human being who sets it in motion, keeps it in motion, and determines its end or target. The most extreme case is the rocket or missile; the most ordinary example the automobile. This means that the energy, the power activated and consummated is the mechanical, electrical, or nuclear energy of "things" rather than the instinctual energy of a human being. Aggression is, as it were, transferred from a subject to an object, or is at least "mediated" by an object, and the target is destroyed by a thing rather than by a person. This change in the relation between human and material energy, and between the physical and mental part of aggression (man becomes the subject and agent of aggression by virtue of his mental rather than physical faculties) must also affect the mental dynamic. I submit a hypothesis which is suggested by the inner logic of the process: with the "delegation" of destruction to a more or less automated thing or group and system of things, the instinctual satisfaction of the human person is "interrupted," reduced, frustrated, "supersublimated." And such frustration makes for repetition and escalation: increasing violence, speed, enlarged scope. At the same time, personal responsibility, conscience, and the sense of guilt is weakened, or rather diffused, displaced from the actual context in which the aggression was committed (i.e.

bombing raids), and relocated in a more or less innocuous context (impoliteness, sexual inadequacy, etc.). In this reaction too, the effect is a considerable weakening of the sense of guilt, and the defense (hatred, resentment) is also redirected from the real responsible subject (the commanding officer, the government) to a substitute person: not I as a (morally and physically) acting person did it, but the thing, the machine. The machine: the word suggests that an apparatus consisting of human beings may be substituted for the mechanical apparatus: the bureaucracy, the administration, the party, or organization is the responsible agent; I, the individual person, was only the instrumentality. And an instrument cannot, in any moral sense, be responsible or be in a state of guilt. In this way, another barrier against aggression, which civilization had erected in a long and violent process of discipline is removed. And the expansion of advanced capitalism becomes involved in a fateful psychical dialectic which enters into and propels its economic and political dynamic: the more powerful and "technological" aggression becomes, the less is it apt to satisfy and pacify the primary impulse, and the more it tends toward repetition and escalation.

To be sure, the use of instruments of aggression is as old as civilization itself, but there is a decisive difference between technological aggression and the more primitive forms. The latter were not only quantitatively different (weaker): they required activation and *engagement* of the body to a much higher degree than the automated or semiautomated instruments of aggression. The knife, the "blunt instrument," even the revolver are far more "part" of the individual who uses them and they associate him more closely with his target. Moreover, and most important, their use, unless effectively sublimated and in the service of the life instincts (as in the case of the surgeon, household, etc.), is criminal — individual

264

crime — and as such subject to severe punishment. In contrast, technological aggression is not a crime. The speeding driver of an automobile or motor boat is not called a murderer even if he is one; and certainly the missile-firing engineers are not.

Technological aggression releases a mental dynamic which aggravates the destructive, antierotic tendencies of the puritan complex. The new modes of aggression destroy without getting one's hands dirty, one's body soiled, one's mind incriminated. The killer remains clean, physically as well as mentally. The purity of his deadly work obtains added sanction if it is directed against the national enemy in the national interest.

The (anonymous) lead article in *Les Temps Modernes* (January 1966) links the war in Vietnam with the puritan tradition in the United States. The image of the enemy is that of dirt in its most repulsive forms; the unclean jungle is his natural habitat, disembowelment and beheading are his natural ways of action. Consequently, the burning of his refuge, defoliation, and the poisoning of his foodstuff are not only strategic but also moral operations: removing of contagious dirt, clearing the way for the order of political hygiene and righteousness. And the mass purging of the good conscience from all rational inhibitions leads to the atrophy of the last rebellion of sanity against the madhouse: no satire, no ridicule attends the moralists who organize and defend the crime. Thus one of them can, without becoming a laughingstock, publicly praise as the "greatest performance in our nation's history," the indeed historical achievement of the richest, most powerful, and most advanced country of the world unleashing the destructive force of its technical superiority on one of the poorest, weakest, and most helpless countries of the world.

The decline of responsibility and guilt, their absorption by the omnipotent technical and political apparatus also tends to invalidate other values which were to restrain and sublimate aggression. While the militarization of society remains the most conspicuous and destructive manifestation of this tendency, its less ostensible effects in the cultural dimension should not be minimized. One of these effects is the disintegration of the value of *truth*. The media enjoy a large dispensation from the commitment to truth, and in a very special way. The point is not that the media lie ("lie" presupposes commitment to truth), they rather mingle truth and half-truth with omission, factual reporting with commentary and evaluation, information with publicity and propaganda — all this made into an overwhelming whole through editorializing. The editorially unpleasant truths (and how many of the most decisive truths are not unpleasant?) retreat between the lines, or hide, or mingle harmoniously with nonsense, fun, and so-called human interest stories. And the consumer is readily inclined to take all this for granted — he buys it even if he knows better. Now the commitment to the truth has always been precarious, hedged with strong qualifications, suspended, or suppressed — it is only in the context of the general and democratic activation of aggressiveness that the devaluation of truth assumes special significance. For truth is a value in the strict sense inasmuch as it serves the protection and amelioration of life, as a guide in man's struggle with nature and with himself, with his own weakness and his own destructiveness. In this function, truth is indeed a matter of the sublimated life instincts, Eros, of intelligence becoming responsible and autonomous, striving to liberate life from dependence on unmastered and repressive forces. And with respect to this protective and liberating function of truth, its devaluation removes another effective barrier against destruction.

The encroachment of aggression on the domain of the life instincts also devalues the aesthetic dimension. In *Eros and Civilization* I have tried to show the erotic component in this dimension. Nonfunctional, that is to say, not committed to the functioning of a repressive society, the aesthetic values have been strong protectors of Eros in civilization. Nature is part of this dimension. Eros seeks, in polymorphous forms, its own sensuous world of fulfillment, its own "natural" environment. But only in a protected world — protected from daily business, from noise, crowds, waste, only thus can it satisfy the biological need for happiness. The aggressive business practices which turn ever more spaces of protective nature into a medium of commercial fulfillment and fun thus do not merely offend beauty — they repress biological necessities.

Once we agree to discuss the hypothesis that, in advanced industrial society surplus-aggression is released in quite unsuspected and "normal" behavior, we may see it even in areas which are far removed from the more familiar manifestations of aggression, for instance the style of publicity and information practiced by the mass media. Characteristic is the permanent repetition: the same commercial with the same text or picture broadcast or televised again and again; the same phrases and clichés poured out by the purveyors and makers of information again and again; the same programs and platforms professed by the politicians again and again. Freud arrived at his concept of the death instinct in the context of his analysis of the "repetition compulsion": he associated with it the striving for a state of complete inertia, absence of tension, return to the womb, annihilation. Hitler knew well the extreme function of repetition: the biggest lie, often enough repeated, will be acted upon and accepted as truth. Even in its less extreme use, constant repetition, imposed upon more or less captive audiences, may be destructive: destroying mental autonomy, freedom of thought, responsibility and conducive to inertia, submission, rejection of change. The established society, the master of repetition, becomes the great womb for its citizens. To be sure, this road to inertia and this reduction of tension is one of high and not very satisfactory sublimation: it does not lead to an instinctual nirvana of satisfaction. However, it may well reduce the stress of intelligence, the pain and tension which accompany autonomous mental activity — thus it may be an effective aggression against the mind in its socially disturbing, critical functions.

These are highly speculative hypotheses on the socially and mentally fateful character of aggression in our society. Aggression is (in most cases) socially useful destructiveness — and yet fateful because of its self-propelling character and scope. In this respect too, it is badly sublimated and not very satisfying. If Freud's theory is correct, and the destructive impulse strives for the annihilation of the individual's own life no matter how long the "detour" via other lives and targets, then we may indeed speak of a suicidal tendency on a truly social scale, and the national and international play with total destruction may well have found a firm basis in the instinctual structure of individuals.

This is the first publication of this essay in English.

Foreword

1. *Translator's note: "Bedürfnis"* means "need" or "want." I have often rendered it by "want," which, while denoting an objective condition of lack, has taken on the connotation, derived from recent usage of "to want," of subjective and conscious desire.

2. The last time in Europe. Today the historical heritage of this struggle is to be found in those nations which defend their freedom in uncompromising struggle against the neo-colonial powers.

3. *Translator's note: "Herrschaft,"* from *"Herr"* (lord), means "lordship," i.e. generally "domination," from *"dominus"* (lord), and thus by extension "authority," "control," even, *mirabile dictu,* "imperative coordination." I have used "domination" except where English usage seemed to make "authority" or "control" advisable.

4. *Translator's note: "Möglichkeit"* means both potentiality and possibility (both derived from *"posse"* [to be able]). I have usually used "potentiality" except in the contexts "real possibility" and "formal possibility."

5. Karl Marx, *Grundrisse der Kritik der politischen Ökonomie* (Berlin, 1953), p. 593.

6. *Ibid.,* pp. 599–600.

The Struggle Against Liberalism
in the Totalitarian View of the State

1. *Translator's note:* In common parlance, *"Volk"* means "people" or "nation," and in such contexts I have so translated it. In National Socialist ideology and its precursors, it means an organic, racial community. In this

usage I have in principle rendered it as "folk," and the derived adjective "*völkish*" as "folkish." To the extent, however, that the meaning attached to the English words "nation" and "people" by chauvinists does not differ as much from that of "*Volk*" as one would imagine on seeing "folk," I have used "nation" or "people" when the German text seemed to be of chauvinistic, rather than explicitly racist or natural-organic, import.

2. Ernst Krieck, *Nationalpolitische Erziehung*, 14th–16th impression (1933), p. 68.

3. In the following we shall use the expression "heroic-folkish realism" to designate the entirety of the view of history and society adopted by the total-authoritarian state. Also, in speaking of the "totalitarian view of the state," we do not mean the doctrine of the state taken in its strictest sense, but the "weltanschauung" appropriated by this state. Recent developments reflect attempts being made to split up the concept of the total state and differentiate it according to distinct modes of totalization. So, to mention only the most characteristic terms, Germany is spoken of as a total "folkish," "authoritarian," or "leadership" state. See Köllreutter, *Allgemeine Staatslehre* (1933), p. 64; Freisler in *Deutsche Justiz* (1934), No. 2; E. R. Huber in *Tat*, XXVI (1934), No. 1. But these differences do not affect the foundations of the total state, which are the object of our interpretation. To the extent that they fall within these foundations, our interpretation applies to them even when they are not mentioned explicitly.

4. *Translator's note:* "*Führer*" means "leader." I have so translated it except when its identification with the person of Adolf Hitler makes it no more than a proper noun.

5. Krieck, *op. cit.*, p. 37.

6. See the discussion of Spengler's *Jahre der Entscheidung* in *Zeitschrift für Sozialforschung*, II, No. 3.

7. Othmar Spann, *Gesellschaftslehre* (3d ed., 1930), p. 98.

8. Möller van den Bruck, *Das dritte Reich*, Special edition (Hamburg: Hanseatische Verlagsanstalt, 1933), p. 69. The political theory of antiliberalism was created by Carl Schmitt, who was followed by Köllreutter, Hans J. Wolff, *et al.*

9. Köllreutter, *op. cit.*, p. 21: "Marxism is a spiritual fruit of liberalism. . . ."

10. A good collection of all antiliberalist slogans may be found in Krieck, *op. cit.*, p. 9. The best portrayal of liberalism from the standpoint of totalitarian political theory is to be found in Carl Schmitt's introduction and appendix to the second edition of his *Begriff des Politischen*, as well as in his *Die geistesgeschichtliche Lage des heutigen Parlamentarismus*, 2d ed. (1926).

11. As in Möller van den Bruck's "definition": "Liberalism is the freedom to have no convictions and yet to believe that precisely this is a conviction"

(*op. cit.*, p. 70). The height of confusion is reached when Krieck brings liberalism, capitalism, and Marxism together as "forms of counter-movement" (*op. cit.*, p. 32).

12. Leopold von Wiese in *Festgabe für Lujo Brentano*, I (1925), p. 16: "I repeat my assertion that there practically has not yet been any [liberalism] to any adequate degree. . . ." Richard Behrendt in *Schmollers Jahrbuch*, LX, No. 3, p. 14: "In no period of world history has economic rationality operated in a decisive manner for a long period of time. One can and must deny that liberalism, even in the nineteenth century, was ever in this sense the ruling power." On German liberalism, see H. Schroth, *Welt- und Staatsideen des deutschen Liberalismus* . . . (1931), especially pp. 69 and 95ff.

13. "In private initiative in the area of production, the corporate state sees the most valuable and effective instrument for protecting the nation's interests." "The state intervenes in the economy only where private initiative is lacking or insufficient or where the state's political interests are at stake." *Carta del Lavoro*, Articles VII and IX, in Niederer, *Der Ständestaat des Faschismus* (1932), p. 179. "Fascism affirms fundamentally the private entrepreneur's role as director of production and as instrument for the augmentation of wealth." W. Koch, "Politik und Wirtschaft im Denken der faschistischen Führer," *Schmollers Jahrbuch* (1933) No. 5, p. 44. For Germany, see especially the quotation given by Köllreutter, *op. cit.*, pp. 179–180.

14. Quoted in the periodical *Aufbau*, F. Karsen, ed., IV (1931), p. 233.

15. *Ibid.*, p. 258.

16. Gide and Rist, *Geschichte der volkswirtschaftlichen Lehrmeinungen* (1913), p. 402. Wilhelm von Humboldt's statement is characteristic: "The best human operations are those which most faithfully imitate the operations of nature." "Über die Grenzen der Wirksamkeit des Staates," *Klassiker der Politik*, VI (1922), p. 12.

17. Classical statements are to be found in Adam Smith's *The Wealth of Nations*, Book III, Chap. I, "Of the Natural Progress of Opulence." On Bastiat, see Gide and Rist, *op. cit.*, p. 373. For liberalism nothing "stands on such shaky ground as the assertion of the equality of all that bears a human visage" (Mises, *op. cit.*, p. 25). Liberalism proceeds from the essential inequality of men, which is considered the presupposition of the harmony of the whole. See R. Thoma in *Erinnerungsgabe für Max Weber*, II (1923), p. 40.

18. On this function of the liberalist concept of nature, see Myrdal, *Das politische Element in der nationalökonomischen Doktrinbildung* (1932), p. 177. The concept of nature, he writes, is a "cliché that functions just like every other political recommendation." It is used "when anyone, in some political question, wants to assert something without adducing proof of it."

19. Möller van den Bruck, *op. cit.*, pp. 200 and 210.

20. Mussolini in *Der Faschismus*, trans. by Wagenführ (1933), p. 38.

21. Hans J. Wolff in *Recht und Staat in Geschichte und Gegenwart* (1933), No. 104, pp. 8–9.

22. See *Zeitschrift für Sozialforschung*, III, No. 1, pp. 1ff.

23. *Translator's note:* "*Grund*" means "ground," "principle," "reason," or one of the four "causes."

24. This "coincidence" of ground, reason, and cause comes strikingly to expression in Leibniz's formulation of the rationalist principle of "ground": "This principle is that of the need for a sufficient reason for a thing to exist, for an event to occur, for a truth to take place." *Letters to Clarke*, Fifth Paper, to paragraph 46, No. 125.

25. Within a rationalist theory of society, therefore, the "autonomy of reason" definitely does not mean setting reason as the absolute ground or essence of what is. To the extent, rather, that reason is comprehended as the reason of concrete individuals in their specific social situation, the "material" conditions of this situation enter into the conditions of the rational practice that is required. But these conditions as well are to be comprehended rationally and, on the basis of this comprehension, to be transformed.

26. H. Forsthoff, *Das Ende der humanistischen Illusion* (1933), p. 25.

27. Carl Schmitt gives a brilliant portrayal of liberalist rationalism in his *Geistesgeschichtliche Lage des heutigen Parlamentarismus*, especially pp. 45ff.

28. To be sure, in the legal sphere rationalization is, in principle, "general"; but this generality is bought at the price of complete formality in civil law and complete abstractness in constitutional law.

29. We can readily do so, since Friedrich Pollock has explained them in *Zeitschrift für Sozialforschung*, II, No. 3.

30. Sombart, *Das Wirtschaftsleben im Zeitalter des Hochkapitalismus*, I (1927), Part I, p. 69.

31. Krieck, *op. cit.*, p. 23.

32. Nicolai, *Grundlagen der kommenden Verfassung* (1933), p. 9.

33. Sombart in *Verhandlungen des Vereins für Sozialpolitik* (1928), p. 30.

34. Köllreutter, *op. cit.*, pp. 184–185.

35. Bernhard Köhler, *Das dritte Reich und der Kapitalismus* (1933), p. 10.

36. G. Ipsen, *Programm einer Soziologie des deutschen Volkstums* (1933), p. 11. See also Köllreutter, *op. cit.*, pp. 34ff.

37. H. Forsthoff, *Der totale Staat*, pp. 40ff.

38. G. Ipsen, *Das Landvolk* (1933), especially p. 17.

39. Following are some characteristic passages taken from Möller van den Bruck's *Das dritte Reich*, pp. 180–182: "Conservative thought . . . can be understood only from the spatial viewpoint. Space is sovereign, and time presupposes it." "Things grow in and emerge from this space. In time, they rot." "In the history of a folk, with time, things may change as they will: the immutable, which remains, is more powerful and important than the mutable, which consists only in something being added or subtracted. The im-

mutable is the presupposition of all changes, and whatever may change returns, when its time has come, to the immutable." "All revolution is background noise, a sign of disturbance; it is neither the walk of the creator through his workshop, nor the fulfillment of his commands, nor agreement with his will. The world is conceived as something to be preserved, and when it has fallen into confusion, it immediately, through its own force, falls back into place: it returns to its equilibrium."

We cite only one characteristic example of the employment of "Gestalt theory" for the depravation of history: "A Gestalt simply is, and no development augments or diminishes it. Hence developmental history is not the history of a Gestalt, but at most a dynamic commentary on it. Development knows both beginning and end, birth and death; the Gestalt knows them not." "A historical Gestalt is most profoundly independent of the time and circumstances from which it appears to originate." Ernst Jünger, *Der Arbeiter: Herrschaft und Gestalt*, 2d ed. (Hamburg, 1932), p. 79.

40. Karl Marx, *Der achtzehnte Brumaire des Louis Bonaparte* (Berlin, 1927), pp. 122–123.

41. Karl Marx, *Das Kapital (Volksausgabe:* Berlin, 1928), I, p. 43.

42. Ernst Krieck in *Volk im Werden* (1933), No. 3, p. 4.

43. *Ibid.*, p. 1. An even clearer statement can be found in *Volk im Werden*, No. 5, pp. 69 and 71: "Radical critique teaches us to see that so-called culture has become totally inessential and that in any case it is not one of the highest values." "Finally, let us take care here, too, to be straightforward, truthful, and genuine, lest the growing force and health of the folk be corrupted by the swindle of culture. Let them call us barbarians, if they will!"

44. Eugen Diesel in *Deutsche Rundschau* (January, 1934), p. 2.

45. Krieck, No. 3, p. 1.

46. *Der deutsche Student* (August, 1933), p. 1.

47. H. Kutzleb, "Ethos der Armut als Aufgabe," in *Volk im Werden* (1933), No. 1, pp. 24ff.

48. On this function of heroic realism see *Zeitschrift für Sozialforschung*, III, No. 1, pp. 42ff.

49. Carl Schmitt, *Der Begriff des Politischen*, p. 37.

50. *Ibid.*, p. 15.

51. Although the formula for the political relationship is "friend-enemy grouping," the friend relationship is always spoken of only incidentally and in the shadow of the enemy grouping.

52. Alfred Bäumler, *Männerbund und Wissenschaft* (1934), p. 94.

53. *Ibid.*, p. 109.

54. Ernst Krieck, "Zehn Grundsätze einer ganzheitlichen Wissenschaftslehre," *Volk im Werden*, No. 6, pp. 6ff.

55. Bäumler, *op. cit.*, p. 108.

56. Aristotle *Politics* 1253 a 14f., trans. by Benjamin Jowett in *The Basic*

Works of Aristotle, Richard McKeon, ed. (New York: Random House, 1941), p. 1129.

57. E. Rothacker, *Geschichtsphilosophie* (1934), p. 96.

58. Martin Heidegger, *Die Selbstbehauptung der deutschen Universität* (1933), p. 13.

59. Carl Schmitt, *Politische Theologie* (1922), p. 1. We present the fundamental theses of the theory of the total state in accordance with Carl Schmitt's *Begriff des Politischen.* The superabundant literature succeeding this work contains nothing but the dregs of Schmitt's thought.

60. H. Forsthoff, *Der totale Staat,* p. 29.

61. Köllreutter, *Vom Sinn und Wesen der nationalen Revolution* (1933), p. 30. See also his *Allgemeine Staatslehre,* p. 58.

62. Forsthoff, p. 31.

63. *Ibid.,* p. 30.

64. *Ibid.* Forsthoff's justification of authority is undercut by the flatly zoological one given by Carl Schmitt in his latest work: "Both the continuing unerring contact between leader *(Führer)* and following as well as their reciprocal loyalty are based on identity of species. Only species identity can prevent the leader's power from becoming tyranny and arbitrariness. . . ." *Staat, Bewegung, Volk* (1933), p. 42.

65. Forsthoff, p. 42.

66. *Ibid.,* p. 41.

67. *Translator's note:* "Person" means, in Kantian ethics, the individual considered as end in himself, as worthy of reverence owing to his self-determined obedience to the moral law.

68. The possible reproach that we are playing off philosophical against political existentialism has been refuted by philosophical existentialism itself, which, as Heidegger's most recent publications show, has politicized itself. The original opposition is thus canceled.

69. *Volk im Werden* (1933), No. 2, p. 13.

70. Köllreutter, *Der deutsche Führerstaat,* p. 31. See also *Allgemeine Staatslehre,* p. 101.

71. *Translator's note:* The word *"allgemein"* (literally "common to all") means "general" or "universal." In philosophy it means "universal" in contrast with "particular," especially in the form *"(das) Allgemeine,"* "(the) universal." As *"(die) Allgemeinheit"* it means both the quality of "universality" or "generality" *and* "community," "society," "collectivity," and "general will," as well as "general public." For Hegel *"Allgemeinheit* means at one and the same time, first, a society in which all particular and individual interests are integrated into the whole, so that the actual social organism that results accords with the common interest (community), and, second, a totality in which all the different isolated concepts of knowledge are fused and integrated so that they receive their significance in their rela-

tion to the whole (universality). The second meaning is obviously the counterpart of the first." Herbert Marcuse, *Reason and Revolution* (Boston: Beacon Press, 1960), p. 52.

72. Hegel, *Vorlesungen zur Philosophie der Weltgeschichte*, Lasson, ed., p. 1.

73. Kant in *Werke*, Ernst Cassirer, ed., VI, p. 468.

74. Heidegger in the *Freiburger Studentenzeitung*, November 10, 1933.

75. From Hegel's address to his students at the opening of his lectures in Berlin in 1818. *Werke*, 2d ed., VI (1843), p. xl.

76. Heidegger in the *Freiburger Studentenzeitung*, November 3, 1933.

77. Kant, *op. cit.*, IV, p. 284.

78. *Der deutsche Student, op. cit.*, p. 14.

79. Carl Schmitt expresses profound comprehension (which he intended quite differently, of course), when he writes: "Accordingly one can say that on this day (January 30, 1933) 'Hegel died.'" *Staat, Bewegung, Volk*, p. 32.

The Concept of Essence

1. *Translator's note:* "*(Das) Sein*" (*esse*) I have rendered as "Being." "*(Das) Seiende*" (*ens*) I have rendered as "beings" or "the world of beings" or, when there was no escaping it, "being."

2. The relevant passages for the dynamic form of Plato's theory of Ideas are *Sophistes* 247 e ff. and *Philebos* 23 b-27 b.

3. "Accidens dicitur large omne, quod non est pars essentiae, et sic est esse in rebus creatis" (Thomas Aquinas, *Quaestiones quodlibetales* 12, 5). — "Oportet ergo, quod illud, cuius esse est aliud ab essentia sua, habeat esse causatum ab alio" (Thomas Aquinas, *Summa Theologica*, Ia, 3, 4).

4. The change wrought by the mitigation of the critical tensions in the theory of essence is evident in the altered meaning of the classical ontological concepts incorporated into Aquinas' philosophy. Essence as such is no longer "authentic" Being but pure possibility. Compared with reality, possibility is inferior, a privation. Aristotle, too, had characterized the relationship of *dynamis* and *energeia* in this way, but for him the relationship of possibility to reality was one of movement; the *on dynamei* was conceived as an existing "power" or "potentiality" which in itself strives for actuality (Aristotle *Metaphysics* 1045 b 33ff.). Essence as *potentia transcendentalis*, in contrast, is no longer the "real possibility" of "power," and its relation to reality is no longer the dynamic one of movement.

5. Descartes, *Discours de la Méthode*, in *Oeuvres Choisies* (Paris: Garnier, 1930), I, pp. 24ff.

6. *Ibid.*, p. 54.

7. *Ibid.*, p. 22.

8. Descartes, *Méditations Métaphysiques*, in *Oeuvres Choisies* I, p. 150.

9. Hegel, *Vorlesungen über die Geschichte der Philosophie*, in *Werke*, original edition, XVI, p. 338.

10. *Ibid.*, p. 336.

11. Kant, *Kritik der reinen Vernunft*, in *Werke*, Cassirer, ed. (Berlin, 1913), III, p. 264.

12. *Ibid.*, p. 250.

13. *Ibid.*, p. 262.

14. *Ibid.*, p. 265.

15. *Ibid.*, p. 334.

16. *Ibid.*, p. 303.

17. *Ibid.*, pp. 503 and 509.

18. Schelling, *Vom Wesen der menschlichen Freiheit*, in *Werke* (Stuttgart, 1856–57), Section I, VII, p. 383.

19. Edmund Husserl, *Formale und transzendentale Logik*, in *Jahrbuch für Philosophie*, X (Halle, 1929), p. 227.

20. Edmund Husserl, *Ideen zu einer reinen Phänomenologie und phänomenologischen Philosophie*, in *Jahrbuch für Philosophie und phänomenologische Forschung*, I (Halle, 1913), p. 9.

21. Husserl, *Formale und transzendentale Logik*, pp. 237 and 241.

22. Husserl, *Ideen*, p. 13.

23. Husserl, *Formale und transzendentale Logik*, p. 201.

24. *Ibid.*, p. 202.

25. *Ibid.*, p. 225.

26. Fink, *Die phänomenologische Philosophie Edmund Husserls in der gegenwärtigen Kritik* (Berlin-Charlottenburg, 1934), p. 20.

27. *Translator's note:* "Gleichgültig" literally means "equivalent" and, as equi-valent, "indifferent."

28. Husserl, *Ideen*, p. 93.

29. *Translator's note: "Erfassung"* literally means "grasping."

30. *Ibid.*, p. 130.

31. Husserl, *Formale und transzendentale Logik*, p. 219.

32. Husserl, *Méditations Cartésiennes* (Paris, 1931), p. 49.

33. Husserl, *Formale und transzendentale Logik*, p. 244.

34. *Ibid.*, p. 243.

35. Husserl, "Philosophie als strenge Wissenschaft," *Logos*, I (1910–11), p. 337.

36. *Ibid.*, p. 315.

37. Scheler, *Zur Ethik und Erkenntnislehre*, in *Schriften aus dem Nachlass* (Berlin, 1933), I, p. 288.

38. Scheler, *Der Formalismus in der Ethik und die materiale Wertethik*, in *Jahrbuch für Philosophie*, Husserl, ed., II (Halle, 1916), p. 465.

39. Scheler, "Vorbilder und Führer," in *Zur Ethik und Erkenntnislehre*, *op. cit.*, pp. 163–164.

40. A characteristic utterance from a representative source makes the connection obvious: "Recent philosophy says that intuitive 'seeing of essences' (*Wesensschau*) is the immediate intuition of what is lawlike. This quality finds its strongest expression in the personality of Adolf Hitler . . . . The Führer possesses not only the infinitely valuable capacity of seeing what is essential in things, but also, to a great extent, the instinct for bold and accurately timed action." — Otto Dietrich, *Die philosophischen Grundlagen des Nationalsozialismus* (Breslau, 1935), pp. 36–37.

41. M. Schlick, "Erscheinung und Wesen," *Kant-Studien*, XXIII, No. 2–3 (Berlin, 1918), p. 206.

42. M. Schlick, *Allgemeine Erkenntnislehre* (Berlin, 1918), p. 205.

43. M. Schlick, "Erscheinung und Wesen," *op. cit.*, p. 194.

44. Hegel, *Wissenschaft der Logik*, in *Werke*, original edition, IV, pp. 119–120.

45. Hegel, *Enzyklopädie*, I, VI, p. 260 (§131).

46. *Ibid.*, pp. 224 and 242 (gloss to §112 and gloss 2 to §119).

47. *Ibid.*, p. 292 (gloss to §146).

48. *Translator's note: "Sich erinnern,"* the word for "to remember" or "to recollect," literally means "to go into oneself." That is, in remembering, one is re-membered or re-collected by returning to oneself from a state of externality, dispersion, or alienation.

49. Hegel, *Wissenschaft der Logik*, p. 79.

50. *Ibid.*, pp. 5 and 14.

51. Karl Marx, *Das Kapital* (Hamburg: Meissner, 1921–22), III, 2, p. 352.

52. On the concept of truth in dialectical logic see *Zeitschrift für Sozialforschung* (1935), pp. 321ff.

53. On the distinction between confirmation and efficacy and the differentiation from pragmatism that it permits, see *ibid.*, pp. 342–343.

54. Hegel, *Enzyklopädie*, p. 225 (§112).

55. Aristotle *Met.* 1030 a and Hegel, *Wissenschaft der Logik*, p. 3.

56. O. Neurath, *Empirische Soziologie* (Wien, 1931), pp. 128 and 132.

57. Wilhelm Dilthey, *Einleitung in die Geisteswissenschaften*, in *Gesammelte Schriften* (Leipzig, 1923), I, p. xviii.

58. Kant, *Logik*, VIII, p. 374.

59. Aristotle *Politics* 1254 b 20ff.

60. Hegel, *Wissenschaft der Logik*, p. 208.

61. *Ibid.*, p. 209.

62. *Ibid.*, p. 210.

The Affirmative Character of Culture

1. This essay was prompted by Max Horkheimer's remarks about "affirmative culture" and the "false idealism" of modern culture. Cf. *Zeitschrift für Sozialforschung*, V (1936), p. 219.

2. Aristotle *Politics* 1333 a 30ff., trans. by Benjamin Jowett in *The Basic Works of Aristotle*, Richard McKeon, ed. (New York: Random House, 1941), p. 1298 (with change in translation).

3. *Translator's note:* While *"Seele"* has an adjectival form, *"seelisch,"* its English counterpart "soul" does not. I have used "psychic" or "spiritual," depending on the context. Accordingly, although the word *"geistig"* means both "spiritual" and "mental," in the present essay I have rendered it as "mental," and "spiritual" refers to a quality of "soul," not of "mind."

4. *Translator's note: "Sinnlich"* means simultaneously "sensual," which stresses its appetitive aspect, and "sensuous," which stresses its aesthetic aspect. I have translated it in each case according to the emphasis of the context, but both meanings are always implied. For further discussion, see Herbert Marcuse, *Eros and Civilization* (Boston: Beacon Press, 1955), pp. 166–167.

5. Plato *Republ.* 553 in *The Republic of Plato*, trans. by Francis M. Cornford (New York: Oxford, 1945), p. 277. Cf. *Republ.* 525.

6. *Ibid.*, pp. 306–307.

7. Plato *Leges* 831, trans. by A. E. Taylor in *The Collected Dialogues of Plato*, Edith Hamilton and Huntington Cairns, eds. (New York: Bollingen Foundation-Pantheon Books, 1964), p. 1397. Cf. J. Brake, *Wirtschaften und Charakter in der antiken Bildung* (Frankfurt am Main, 1935), pp. 124ff.

8. See *Studien über Autorität und Familie* ("Schriften des Instituts für Sozialforschung," V [Paris, 1936]), pp. 7ff.

9. Spengler interprets the relationship of culture and civilization not as simultaneity, but as "necessary organic succession." Civilization is the inevitable fate and end of every culture. See *Der Untergang des Abendlandes*, 23d to 32d editions (Munich, 1920), I, pp. 43–44. Such reformulation does not modify the abovementioned traditional evaluation of culture and civilization.

10. La Mettrie, "Discours sur le Bonheur," *Oeuvres Philosophiques* (Berlin, 1775), II, p. 102.

11. *Ibid.*, pp. 86–87.

12. Herder, *Ideen zur Philosophie der Geschichte der Menschheit* in *Werke*, Bernhard Suphan, ed. (Berlin, 1877–1913), XIV, p. 208.

13. *Ibid.*, XIII, p. 154.

14. *Ibid.*, XIV, p. 209.

15. Kant, *Idee zu einer allgemeinen Geschichte in weltbürgerlicher Absicht* in *Werke*, Ernst Cassirer, ed. (Berlin, 1912ff.), IV, p. 153.

16. Alfred Weber, "Prinzipielles zur Kultursoziologie," *Archiv für Sozialwissenschaft*, XLVII (1920–21), pp. 29ff. See also Georg Simmel, "Der Begriff und die Tragödie der Kultur," where "the soul's way to itself" is described as the fundamental fact of culture [in *Philosophische Kultur* (Leipzig, 1919), p.

222]. Spengler characterizes culture as "the realization of the spiritually possible"; *op. cit.*, p. 418.

17. Descartes, *Traité des Passions*, François Mizrachi, ed. (Paris: Union Générale d'Editions, 1965), p. 39.

18. See Descartes' reply to Gassendi's objections to the second Meditation, *Meditationen über die Grundlagen der Philosophie,* trans. by A. Buchenau (Leipzig, 1915), pp. 327–328.

19. Kant, *Critique of Pure Reason*, trans. by Norman Kemp Smith (London: Macmillan, 1958), p. 664 (with changes in translation).

20. *Die Philosophischen Hauptvorlesungen Immanuel Kants*, A. Kowalewski, ed. (Munich and Leipzig, 1924), p. 602.

21. Marx, *Das Kapital*, Meissner, ed. (Hamburg, n.d.), I, p. 326.

22. Hegel, *Enzyklopädie der philosophischen Wissenschaften*, II, par. 388.

23. *Ibid.*, par. 387, addendum.

24. Spengler, *op. cit.*, p. 406.

25. Characteristic is the introduction of the concept of the soul in Herbart's psychology: The soul is "not anywhere or anytime" and has "absolutely no predispositions and faculties either to receive or produce anything." "The simple nature of the soul is fully unknown and forever remains so; it is as little an object of speculative as of empirical psychology." Herbart, *Lehrbuch zur Psychologie* in *Sämtliche Werke*, Hartenstein, ed. (Leipzig, 1850), V, pp. 108–109.

26. Wilhelm Dilthey on Petrarca in "Weltanschauung und Analyse des Menschen seit Renaissance und Reformation," *Gesammelte Schriften* (Leipzig, 1914), II, p. 20. See also Dilthey's analysis of the transition from metaphysical to "descriptive and analytical" psychology in the thought of L. Vives, *ibid.*, pp. 423ff.

27. *Ibid.*, p. 18.

28. Spengler, *op. cit.*, p. 407.

29. Herder, *Abhandlung über den Ursprung der Sprache, op. cit.*, V, p. 135.

30. Herder, *Auch eine Philosophie der Geschichte zur Bildung der Menschheit, ibid.*, p. 503.

31. Ranke, *Über die Epochen der neueren Geschichte*, in *Das politische Gespräch und andere Schriften zur Wissenschaftslehre*, Erich Rothacker, ed. (Halle, 1925), pp. 61–62.

32. On the quietist character of spiritual demands in Dostoevski see L. Löwenthal, "Die Auffassung Dostojewskis im Vorkriegsdeutschland," *Zeitschrift für Sozialforschung*, III (1934), p. 363.

33. David Hume, *A Treatise of Human Nature*, L. A. Selby-Bigge, ed. (Oxford, 1928), p. 301.

34. Nietzsche, *Werke* (large 8vo ed., 1917), XVI, p. 233, and VII, p. 408.

35. Goethe, *Faust II*, Phorkias: "Old is the saying, yet noble and true its

meaning still, that shame and beauty never hand in hand traverse earth's green path." *Werke* (Cotta Jubiläumsausgabe), XIII, p. 159.

36. "The Moralists, a Philosophical Rhapsody" in *Characteristics of Men, Manners, Opinions, Times, etc.* by the Right Honourable Anthony Earl of Shaftesbury, John M. Robertson, ed. (in two volumes; New York: E. P. Dutton & Co., 1900), II, p. 143.

37. Schiller, *Über die ästhetische Erziehung des Menschen*, end of the second letter.

38. Nietzsche, *op. cit.*, X, p. 245.

39. Goethe, *Der Sammler und die Seinigen*, toward the end of the sixth letter.

40. Nietzsche, *op. cit.*, XIV, p. 366.

41. *Ibid.*, VIII, p. 41.

42. *Die Kultur der Renaissance in Italien*, 11th. ed., L. Geiger, ed. (Leipzig, 1913), especially I, pp. 150ff.

43. Kant, *Kritik der praktischen Vernunft, op. cit.*, V, p. 95.

44. Goethe once expressed as follows the quality "only" that is present in the idea of personality: "People are always carping at the personality, reasonably and boldly. But what do you have that gladdens you aside from your beloved personality, of whatever sort it be?" "Zahme Xenien," *Werke*, IV, p. 54.

45. See *Zeitschrift für Sozialforschung*, V (1936), pp. 219ff.

46. Walter Stang, *Grundlagen nationalsozialistischer Kulturpflege* (Berlin, 1935), pp. 13 and 43.

47. Ernst Jünger, *Der Arbeiter: Herrschaft und Gestalt*, 2d ed. (Hamburg, 1932), p. 198.

48. *Ibid.*, p. 199.

49. *Ibid.*, p. 200.

50. *Ibid.*, p. 203.

51. *Ibid.*, p. 204.

52. *Ibid.*, p. 210.

53. *Ibid.*, p. 201.

54. Heinrich Rickert, "Lebenswerte und Kulturwerte," *Logos*, II (1911–12), p. 154.

55. Nietzsche, *op. cit.*, VIII, p. 50.

56. Program of the *Sozialdemokratische Partei Deutschlands* (German Social Democratic Party) of 1921 and of the *Sächsische Volkspartei* (Saxon Popular Party) of 1866.

57. Karl Kautsky, *Die materialistische Geschichtsauffassung* (Berlin, 1927), II, pp. 819 and 837.

58. *Ibid.*, p. 824.

59. Nietzsche, *op. cit.*, XI, p. 241.

Philosophy and Critical Theory

1. Hegel, *Vorlesungen über die Philosophie der Geschichte* in *Werke*, 2d ed. (Berlin, 1840–47), IX, p. 22.

2. Hegel, *Vorlesungen über die Geschichte der Philosophie* in *Werke*, XIII, p. 34.

3. Hegel, *Enzyclopädie der philosophischen Wissenschaften*, par. 158, *op. cit.*, VI, p. 310.

4. Hegel, *Vorlesungen über die Geschichte der Philosophie, op. cit.*, p. 41.

5. See Max Horkheimer, "Ein neuer Ideologiebegriff?", *Grünbergs Archiv*, XV (1930), pp 38–39.

6. Kant, *Nachlass Nr. 4728* in *Gesammelte Schriften*, Preussische Akademie der Wissenschaften, ed. (Berlin, 1900–1955), XVIII.

7. Hegel, *Vorlesungen über die Geschichte der Philosophie, op. cit.*, p. 67.

8. See Max Horkheimer, "Traditionelle und kritische Theorie," *Zeitschrift für Sozialforschung*, VI (1937), p. 245.

9. Kant, *Werke*, Ernst Cassirer, ed. (Berlin, 1911ff.), III, p. 540.

10. *Ibid.*, VIII, p. 344.

11. Hegel, *Enzyclopädie*, par. 166, *op. cit.*, p. 328.

12. See *Zeitschrift für Sozialforschung*, VI (1937), pp. 257ff.

13. Kant, *Kritik der reinen Vernunft, op. cit.*, p. 625.

14. Edmund Husserl, *Formale und transzendentale Logik* in *Jahrbuch für Philosophie*, X (Halle, 1929), p. 219.

On Hedonism

1. Kant, *Critique of Practical Reason*, 6th ed., trans. by T. H. Abbott (London: Longmans, 1909), pp. 112–113.

2. Hegel, *Vorlesungen über die Philosophie der Geschichte* in *Werke*, 2d ed., E. Gans, K. Hegel, *et al.*, eds. (Berlin, 1840–47), IX, p. 34.

3. Hegel, *Glauben und Wissen* in *Werke*, I, pp. 8ff.

4. Aristotle *Politics*, 1323 b 27ff., *Magna Moralia*, 1206 b 30ff., *Politics*, 1332 a 30.

5. Diogenes Laertius, *Lives of Eminent Philosophers*, trans. by R. D. Hicks (2 vols.; New York: Putnam, 1925), I, p. 217.

6. *Ibid.*, p. 221.

7. *Ibid.*, p. 217.

8. *Ibid.*, p. 219.

9. *Ibid.*, p. 227.

10. *Ibid.*, II, p. 655.

11. *Ibid.*, p. 657.

12. *Gorgias* 497–498.

13. Cf. *Zeitschrift für Sozialforschung*, II (1933), pp. 169ff.

14. Cf. *Zeitschrift für Sozialforschung*, V (1936), pp. 190–191, 201–202.

15. Kant, *Kritik of Judgement*, trans. by J. H. Bernard (New York: Macmillan, 1892), p. 52 (with changes in translation).

16. Kant, *Kritik der praktischen Vernunft* in *Werke*, Ernst Cassirer, ed. (Berlin, 1912ff.), V, pp. 125 and 129.

17. Fichte, *System der Sittenlehre* in *Werke*, Fritz Medicus, ed. (Leipzig, n.d.), II, p. 540.

18. By critical theory we mean here social theory as presented in the fundamental essays of the *Zeitschrift für Sozialforschung* on the basis of dialectical philosophy and the critique of political economy. See the essay "Philosophy and Critical Theory" in this volume.

19. Hermann Cohen, *Ethik des reinen Willens*, 3d ed. (Berlin, 1931), p. 163.

20. Spinoza, *On the Improvement of the Understanding*, trans. by R. H. M. Elwes, in *Selections*, J. Wild, ed. (New York: Scribner, 1930), pp. 4 and 6.

21. Leibniz, *Von der Glückseligkeit* in *Opera Philosophica*, J. E. Erdmann, ed. (Berlin, 1840), p. 672.

22. Fichte, *Die Staatslehre* (1813) in *Werke*, VI, pp. 523–524.

23. Hermann Cohen, *op. cit.*, p. 584.

24. Bruno Bauch, *Grundzüge der Ethik* (Stuttgart, 1933), pp. 240–241.

25. A. Görland, *Ethik als Kritik der Weltgeschichte* (Leipzig, 1914), pp. 119–120.

26. Cf. *Zeitschrift für Sozialforschung*, V (1936), pp. 229ff.

27. Even in the case of the firmest advocates of bourgeois sexual reform, the taboo of pleasure still appears, concealed in ethical or psychological rationalizations.

28. Hegel, *Enzyclopädie* in *Werke*, VII, p. 372 (§478).

29. Hegel, *Vorlesungen über die Philosophie der Geschichte*, *op. cit.*, p. 41.

30. *Ibid.*, p. 39.

31. *Translator's note:* That is, they pursue in practice what they have rationally come to know as the tendencies immanent in the status quo — tendencies that can be realized only by transforming the status quo. For this Hegelian use of "Idea" as substance developing both subjectively and objectively through a dialectical process, see Herbert Marcuse, *Reason and Revolution* (Boston: Beacon Press, 1960), pp. 164ff., and "The Concept of Essence," in this volume, pp. 67ff. and 82ff.

32. Cf. Hegel, *Vorlesungen über die Geschichte der Philosophie* in *Werke*, XIV, p. 101.

33. Hegel, *Enzyclopädie*, *op. cit.* (§478, 480).

34. Hegel, *Vorlesungen über die Philosophie der Geschichte*, *op. cit.*, p. 22.

35. Hegel, *Vorlesungen über die Ästhetik* in *Werke*, X, Part 1, pp. 227–228.

Industrialization and Capitalism

1. Max Weber, *Gesammelte Aufsätze zur Soziologie und Sozialpolitik* (Tübingen: Mohr, 1924), p. 419.

2. *Ibid.,* p. 402.

3. Max Weber, Foreword to the first volume of *Gesammelte Aufsätze zur Religionssoziologie* (Tübingen: Mohr, 1920), pp. 1ff.

4. *Ibid.,* pp. 4–5.

5. For documentation, see Wolfgang J. Mommsen, *Max Weber und die deutsche Politik* (Tübingen: Mohr, 1959), where the documentation is collected and analyzed in an exemplary manner.

6. Max Weber, *Gesammelte politischen Schriften* (München: Drei Masken Verlag, 1921), pp. 20–21.

7. *Ibid.,* p. 27.

8. *Ibid.,* p. 29.

9. *Wirtschaft und Gesellschaft* (Tübingen: Mohr, 1922), p. 48. Cf. *The Theory of Social and Economic Organization,* translated by A. M. Henderson and Talcott Parsons (New York: Oxford University Press, 1947), pp. 191–192.

10. Weber, *Wirtschaft und Gesellschaft,* p. 49 (original italics). Henderson-Parsons translate the passage as follows (*Theory,* p. 193): "Thus the highest degree of rational capital accounting presupposes the existence of competition on a large scale."

11. Weber, *Theory,* pp. 213–214 (translation modified); *Wirtschaft und Gesellschaft,* p. 60 (italics added).

12. Weber, *Wirtschaft und Gesellschaft,* p. 44 (cf. *Theory,* p. 185). *Translator's note:* Weber's "materiale rationalität" is rendered by Henderson-Parsons as "substantive rationality." Here, both "material" and "substantive" are used.

13. Weber, *Wirtschaft und Gesellschaft,* p. 167 (cf. *Theory,* pp. 406–407).

14. Weber, *Theory,* pp. 184–185; *Wirtschaft und Gesellschaft,* pp. 44–45.

15. Weber, *Gesammelte Aufsätze zur Soziologie und Sozial politik,* p. 501 ("Der Sozialismus").

16. *Ibid.,* p. 502.

17. *Ibid.,* p. 511.

18. Weber, *Wirtschaft und Gesellschaft,* pp. 19–23 (cf. *Theory,* pp. 130–139).

19. *Ibid.,* p. 128 (cf. *Theory,* p. 337).

20. Weber, *Theory,* p. 338 (translation modified); (cf. *Wirtschaft und Gesellschaft,* pp. 128–129).

21. Weber, *Wirtschaft und Gesellschaft,* p. 762.

22. *Ibid.,* pp. 156–157, 174, 763ff.

23. *Ibid.*, p. 667.
24. *Ibid.*, p. 669.
25. *Ibid.*, p. 607.
26. *Ibid.*, p. 127.
27. *Ibid.*, p. 96.
28. *Ibid.*, p. 240.
29. Weber, *Gesammelte politische Schriften*, p. 151.
30. *Ibid.*, p. 151.

Love Mystified: A Critique of Norman O. Brown

1. Norman O. Brown, *Love's Body* (New York: Random House, 1966).
2. "Nothing but the beginning of terror we can just barely endure . . . ."
— Rilke, *Duino Elegies* (the translation is by C. F. MacIntyre) [*pub.*].
3. Preface to the *Phenomenology of the Spirit,* trans. by Walter Kaufmann, in *Hegel* (Doubleday), p. 424.

Aggressiveness in Advanced Industrial Society

1. I. Ziferstein, in the UCLA *Daily Bruin,* Los Angeles, May 24, 1966. See also: M. Grotjahn, "Some Dynamics of Unconscious and Symbolic Communication in Present-Day Television," *The Psychoanalytic Study of Society,* III, pp. 356ff., and *Psychiatric Aspects of the Prevention of Nuclear War,* Group for the Advancement of Psychiatry (New York, 1964), passim.
2. Quoted in *The Nation,* August 25, 1962, pp. 65–66, in an article by Senator William Proxmire.

INDEX